ALEXANDER HAMILTON

Books by David Loth

LORENZO THE MAGNIFICENT

THE BROWNINGS

CHARLES II, RULER AND RAKE

PHILIP II, MASTER OF THE ARMADA

PUBLIC PLUNDER, A HISTORY OF GRAFT IN AMERICA

ALEXANDER HAMILTON, PORTRAIT OF A PRODIGY

ALEXANDER HAMILTON, AFTER A MINIATURE BY
ARCHIBALD ROBERTSON

ALEXANDER HAMILTON

PORTRAIT OF A PRODIGY

DAVID LOTH

CARRICK & EVANS, INC.

NEW YORK

PRINTED IN THE UNITED STATES OF AMERICA
BY QUINN & BODEN COMPANY, INC., RAHWAY, N. J.

CONTENTS

5

CONTENTS

ILLUSTRATIONS

ALEXANDER HAMILTON

I

CHRISTMAS PARTY

CHRISTMAS HAD NEVER BEEN A PARTICULARLY JOYOUS DAY for Captain Alexander Hamilton, but December 25, 1776, was distinguished above all the others by profound discomforts, discouragements and a complete lack of holiday cheer. It was not only that the Captain was cold, hungry and tired. He was used to that. More galling to a proud spirit was the consciousness that he was one of a thoroughly beaten, almost disheartened mob that only occasionally remembered to call itself an army.

The fact that they had been routed out of comparatively warm quarters to stand about in the snow for twelve hours did not seem at the time to be the first gallant step in one of the greatest feats of arms in modern history. This was an opinion for posterity (and an older Alexander Hamilton).

Today, as he stamped his feet on the frozen ground, felt gingerly of his ears to see if they were still there and pulled his cocked hat lower to keep the wind out of his eyes, the uncomfortable Captain was aware that he and his 2,500 fellows gathered in the fields of Bucks County, Pa., near a place the local lads called McKonkey's Ferry, were a forlorn hope. The fate of forlorn hopes in general was familiar to him. It was his industrious custom to write into the pay book of his company choice bits from his reading and random reflections inspired by the wisdom of the printed page. He had learned from this source that forlorn hopes are usually cut to pieces, achieving only brief, admiring, anonymous mention as a macabre minor in the shining, successful symphony of the great.

11

The start of his Christmas adventure gave the observant Hamilton little reason to suspect it might meet a different fate. At two in the afternoon, the little army had been summoned from its stuffy, highly odorous huts, supplied with what an optimistic commissariat said was three days' cooked rations and led into the fields to embark for an unknown destination. Eight hours later the 2,500 heroes were still at McKonkey's Ferry, grumbling and cursing with soldierly directness at the delays which even well-organized high commands usually inflict upon their long-suffering troops.

Useless for anyone on this Christmas night to pretend that things were going smoothly. Occasional glimpses of the General, his big nose turned crimson by cold as it never was by wine, might have given an illusion of security. Unfortunately his men had seen too much of George Washington's serenity in disaster to derive appreciable comfort from his calm fortitude.

Of other comfort there was none. The snow of a bitter blizzard on the twenty-third was stained a gruesome holiday red by the unshod feet of marching men, the pitiful track of all American armies in winter. (It was much better when there was no snow and the blood could soak unnoticed into the earth.) However, the gory traces would soon be wiped out, for it was beginning to rain in the darkness, a cold, stinging rain whipped by a cruel wind which mocked the inadequate rags that the army vainly attempted to draw around itself. Large, flat pancakes of ice swirled past like menacing ghosts, dancing clumsily in the swift current of the Delaware.

Bad as it was on the Pennsylvania side, there was little consolation in contemplating the hazards that waited on the New Jersey shore. By this time the whole army, through that busy military grapevine by which the thoughts of leaders are filtered to their followers, had a fair idea of what was in the General's mind—a dash across the river to surprise a strong post of Hessians stationed at Trenton, one of a line of such detachments stretching from Bordentown to Princeton. These dreaded, well-equipped troops were part of the force which had driven the Americans across the Jerseys from New York so easily that General Earl Cornwallis was even now sending his baggage aboard ship, homeward bound to inform the King that the impudent rebellion in His Majesty's ungrateful colonies had been crushed.

A quick, successful blow at the Hessians, celebrating their pagan festival with German thoroughness and awesome potations, might give a new twist to his Lordship's report. But the time for surprise attacks is dawn, and to reach Trenton by then the Americans should have been crossing the Delaware in the early winter dusk, for they would have seven miles of execrable road to negotiate on the other side of the river. Yet it was eleven o'clock before the vanguard began to board the clumsy flat Durham boats in which Colonel Glover's regiment of Marblehead fishermen had undertaken to ferry the army.

Captain Hamilton, for one, knew that this meant no surprise of Trenton at dawn. He saw the first of the infantry struggle aboard and disappear in the darkness. He saw the General himself step into one of the long, pointed barges so unlike the future pictures of the scene, and he turned away to give his men a little of the confidence he himself was far from feeling.

After all, he was responsible only for his two cannon, his thirty-two men—there had been sixty-three of them when the campaign started—and his lean, bony horses. Captain Hamilton was proud of his New York Provincial Artillery Company. He liked to hear men say it was one of the best disciplined in the army, and he did not mind when some added that he took a more paternal care of his guns than of his men. The Captain had taught his little band the lesson he had learned from books, that an artilleryman's first concern is for the machinery with which he fights. So his two fine brass pieces were in excellent condition, even if the cannoneers were ragged and his own regimentals somewhat shabby for a former New York beau to be wearing.

The rain turned to snow, but Glover's amphibious warriors were still pushing the boats through the ice-filled river. Soon it would be the turn of the rear guard and the guns, and now the loudest voice in the army, a noble bellow belonging to Colonel Harry Knox, commander of all the Continental artillery, was reverberating between the banks of the Delaware. It rose above the dull mutter of struggling men, the squealing of frightened horses, the rattle of wheels and the bump of cannon being hauled aboard. In the faint light, Colonel Knox's gigantic figure—the campaign had reduced him to a mere two hundred and eighty pounds, but he looked more—was grotesquely active while he roared out choice profanities culled from between the covers of his beloved wares when he had been a bookseller in Boston only a couple of years ago. He almost blew the reluctant horses aboard by sheer lung power. Then the last boat pulled away from the shore, maneuvering amid the floating ice.

It was nearly three in the morning. Christmas was over. The Hessians slept in drunken security. The crisis of the Revolution (one of them) was at hand. And Captain Hamilton, huddled in an inadequate coat cut to afford the stomach no protection, a slight figure almost lost in the overcrowded craft, had leisure to think.

He could reflect, if his thoughts ran that way, that in spite of cold and damp and defeat and the dread of an irretrievable disaster that might well be lurking in the snow-spangled New Jersey night, in spite of an extremely miserable Christmas, one of his earliest desires was being fulfilled. For there was a war, an indubitable, bitter, bloody, brutal war, and he was part of it. No doubt that was what he had meant when seven years before, already wearying of a promising career in the world of business, he had confided his most exalted ambitions to a friend whose discretion he could trust, concluding:

"I'm no philosopher, you see, and may justly be said to build castles in the air; my folly makes me ashamed, and beg you'll conceal it; yet, Neddy, we have seen such schemes successful when the projector is constant. I shall conclude by saying, I wish there was a war."

Martial longings had been well suppressed, for he had continued in trade for three more years. Perhaps in that scow on the Delaware he remembered those days with regret, for at least he had been warm, the chief and confidential assistant of a leading West Indies merchant. But he had left the beautiful, peaceful islands to pursue his dreams, in which tropical scenery had no part. Of course those dreams had been rather boyish imaginings, for Captain Hamilton had been young then, with an all too youthful enthusiasm for war. But, although he had since become a veteran artilleryman of a year's hard and often perilous service, he knew that his career was bound yet to the Revolution, feeble as that cause's prospects seemed on the river crossing of 1776. It was now no matter for visions or confidential outpourings to Neddy Stevens. It was harsh reality, and a harshly realistic alternative of victory or ruin.

So Captain Alexander Hamilton, who would be twenty years old in a few weeks, scrambled ashore with numb limbs, cocked his hat with a characteristic gesture low over his eyes, saw the horses put to the guns and stepped out as smartly as the rough ground and sore feet would permit toward Trenton and the Hessians. Thankful for small mercies, he observed that the storm, in which sleet had come to mingle with the snow and rain, now beat upon his back.

II

BASTARD BRAT

THE BOY WHO HAD WISHED THERE WAS A WAR INDULGED IN few other typically childish fantasies. He had no time; he was too busy mushrooming into maturity with a rapidity of growth that was genuinely tropical. There was more than the climate of his native West Indies to explain his haste. There had been born in him an urge to make a career, and it was a more compelling impulse than most adult ambitions. But if ever he happened to need a spur, it was supplied in a reminder of the circumstances of his birth.

These were what the world called shameful, although Alexander Hamilton never admitted he was ashamed of them. That he was an illegitimate child was one of the hurdles to be vaulted in the race to success, and not, perhaps, as difficult an obstacle as poverty or lack of influence. When, in the days of his own greatness, learned, well-born gentlemen taunted him with his illegitimacy—usually for lack of better arguments—it could only have the effect of stimulating him to new demonstrations that the bar sinister need not be a bar to estimable achievement. John Adams's ponderous denunciation of "the bastard brat of a Scots pedlar," the journalistic Callender's sneer at "the son of a camp girl," Jefferson's philosophic jibe at "a foreign bastard" were directed at a man who had long ago armored himself in conscious intellectual pride against the similar vulgarities of lesser men.

The romance that Adams and Jefferson reduced to such coarse terms, and of which Alexander and his little brother, James, were the tangible results, was not unique in the West

16

Indies. (It was not as unknown elsewhere as Hamilton's later enemies by their outcries seemed to hint.) The sacred bonds of matrimony had been evaded lightly in the islands on occasion even before chance threw a sprig of the powerful Scottish family of Hamilton across the path of a young St. Croix matron who was living apart from her husband.

The attractive stranger was a wandering, ineffectual, incapable younger son of the Hamiltons of the Grange in Ayrshire. He had a careless charm that matched his inability to do anything that might be remunerative. The lady was a French Huguenot, born Rachel Fawcett, who after three or four years of a miserable marriage with a much older Danish merchant, John Levine or Lawein, had fled back to her mother's home, leaving a small son to keep alive his father's resentment at being abandoned. Legend credited her with great beauty of an exotic type, and she was not yet twenty when James Hamilton drifted along in search of the fortune that was not to be wrung by such mediocrity as his from the grim competition of Scotland.

Instead of attending to his ostensible trading business, he spent his time making love to Rachel Levine, a more profitable enterprise than any commercial venture he ever undertook. For Rachel had a small competence, and it enabled them to set up their own pleasant little establishment at Nevis in the nearby Leeward Islands. Levine, busy with his own mercantile affairs in Christianstadt, St. Croix, made no trouble at the time, and the easy conventions of the place and period were not disturbed by the irregular household, into which, on January 11, 1757, a son was born.

If any of Rachel's kinfolk were shocked by the menage, they did not broadcast the sentiment sufficiently to win immortality for their disapproval. More practical difficulties beset the early boyhood of Alexander. His father succeeded in dissipating Rachel's money in a very few years, and, after the birth of the second James, moved on in search of that elusive fortune, leaving his little family to return to St.

Croix and the charity of tolerant relatives. He left with the certainty that his sons would never be legitimized. When Alexander was two years old, Levine obtained a divorce on grounds of abandonment and his wife's "profligacy." Under the then state of Danish law, he as the injured husband was free to marry again, but Rachel, the "guilty party," was debarred from such legal sanction for her life with the handsome young Scot.

What damage Alexander may have suffered from this confirmation of his illegitimacy he more than recovered in the loss of a father. For, from the growing poverty of the paternal home, he was translated to the comfortable, expansive life of the Mitchell and Lytton plantations, owned by well-to-do connections of his mother. He grew up to an easy familiarity with the beauties of palm trees against an early morning sky, the lavish, improbable colors of lush vegetation, the soft splendors of tropical moonlight on dark waters, the rhythmic grace of black bodies swaying at their work in the cane.

He took, too, his place as a member of that Creole aristocracy which had developed the most gracious society in the New World. Life for these masters of the plantations was easy, friendly, secure. The virtues innate in a superior caste were tempered by fewer than usual of the harsher qualities which make most aristocracies obnoxious to all who cannot enter the charmed circle. Exquisite manners, a fine tenderness for the pride of equals and an almost noble sense of responsibility for inferiors who admitted inferiority distinguished the Creole above many with loftier pretensions. Privileged children of the plantations, such as little Alexander, absorbed the delicate courtesy, the charm and the unobtrusive consideration for others as readily as they learned to speak French and English and the strange patois of the blacks.

The gentleness, the familiarity without condescension, were shared by a whole class in the West Indies, down to

little girl children such as the infant Marie Rose Josephine
Tascher de la Pagerie, who was being formed a few miles to
the south, on the island of Martinique, by the same social
standards that forged for young Hamilton a charm that he
could use as a weapon and a shield. The girl developed those
truly royal manners (notably absent in most royal personages)
that made her one of the few figures who fitted the imperial
court of her rather boorish Corsican husband. Remarkable
for their amiable urbanity in the circles where they were to
make their careers, the Empress Josephine and Alexander
Hamilton were simply average specimens of Creole politeness.

The boy's introduction to learning seemed as natural as
his breathing or his easily cultivated manners. Before he
was any bigger than a sugar cutter's knife, he had startled
an admiring young Presbyterian minister with his capacity
for educational absorption. The Rev. Hugh Knox was better
qualified than most Virgin Island preachers to express an
opinion. He had enjoyed the best schooling available in the
mainland colonies, and had sat under no less a paragon of
scholarship than the Rev. Aaron Burr at the College of New
Jersey in Princeton. Furthermore, Mr. Knox was a man of
keen perceptions, devoted to books and unable to conceive
of greater felicity than the perusal and production of literary
masterpieces.

To such a teacher, a child like Alexander Hamilton was
a godsend. The little boy had the pale face of a student—or
of a Creole whose skin remains forever immune to its native
sun—his reddish, sandy hair was drawn back from a forehead
which Mr. Knox believed was the façade of genius; his big
violet eyes looked once at a printed page and imprinted on
the brain a photographic impression of whatever of value
that page contained. Where other boys sweated and groaned
over their Latin or history or mathematics, Alexander lapped
up knowledge like milk and with greater relish. In short,
Mr. Knox had a child prodigy on his hands and was glad.

Two days a week the boy spent at the Stevens plantation, sharing lessons with Ned, who was destined for medicine. Here Alexander, ever conscious of his dependent position in the world, basked in Neddy's admiration and Mr. Knox's praise, of which he was always greedy, more so than most boys, for it fed that strong desire for achievement which the clergyman had noted almost at their first meeting.

Intense as it was, Alexander's childhood was short. In February, 1768, Rachel died, and her son, always a little morbidly fearful of seeming to seek favors, insisted that it was time he began to make his own way.

He was spurred to the decision by one of the earliest unpleasant experiences which his illegitimacy entailed. The expenses of the establishment at Nevis had used up all of his mother's estate except half a dozen slaves, and these she wished to leave to her two boys. But once again the malice of her former husband intervened when he brought a successful suit to claim all of Rachel's little property for "her lawfully begotten heir, Peter Levine."

Penniless as he was, it did not occur to Alexander to turn to his father, for James Hamilton, although he spent the rest of a moderately long life in the West Indies, never got any closer to the receding mirage of a fortune than he had been when he arrived. His eldest son had seen him for the last time.

The world which the boy proposed to conquer was giving to its gullible inhabitants one of those rare illusions of stability which history produces to soothe the nerves of mankind between eras of upheaval. The nations had grouped themselves into a pattern which seemed fairly well fixed. The hot hatreds of Reformation and Counter-Reformation had cooled to mere prejudices. Imitators of Columbus and Cortez and Drake had perished or turned pirates or become prosaic merchants in accepted marts. Political and social theory were sunk in a complacent decadence which most men mistook for finality. The daring originality of Renais-

sance thinkers had provided, it was thought, all the ideas
mankind could use. The rulers of European nations were
concerned more with holding what they had than with extending their dominions. Actually the whole Western World
was at peace.

Only three of its potentates were of much immediate concern to a West Indian. Spain, long since fallen from her
high estate as the mistress of Europe, still mismanaged with
languid jealousy the greater part of the New World—Mexico,
Louisiana, the Floridas, the Californias, assorted islands of
the sea and almost all of South America except Brazil. More
astute traders than the Castilians reaped the profit of these
rich possessions. In time of peace legitimate commerce was
hampered by the pirates, in time of war by the privateers—
often the same fellows. But always colonials of every nation
were mindful of the fact that the gold and silver came from
Spanish territory.

France, ousted from Canada and the Mississippi at the end
of the Seven Years' War in 1763, remained five years later a
factor of greater political importance than Spain. She had
lost a continental empire but cherished imperial ambitions.
There were French islands in the West Indies. French merchants were busy in many others, for their home market was
the destination of much West Indian produce. The armed
power of France by sea and land was believed to be even
more formidable than it was. Although Louis XV had been
on the throne for fifty-three years, the memory of Louis
XIV's magnificence lingered. The prodigal court of Ver-
sailles was supposed to prove by the very extravagance of its
display the power of the nation. The few travelers who saw
that millions lived in squalor failed to establish any connection between the fabulous luxury of the nobility and the
bitter misery of the people. France was still a great nation.

Perhaps not so great as England. However contemptuously
the Parisian might regard the German simplicity of George
III's court, a West Indian could see that the British Empire

represented a more vital political principle than the simple Franco-Spanish belief that colonies existed for the sole purpose of having their natural resources looted by royal favorites. London had quite recently discovered that possessions overseas might be converted into useful markets for manufactures. Imperialism was entering a new phase.

In the Western Hemisphere this had led to the acquisition of Canada after the Seven Years' War, which a few farsighted Englishmen realized was something more than the personal triumph of the elder Pitt and their twenty-five-year-old monarch. The vast wilderness added to the thirteen Atlantic colonies and the British share of the islands made a well-balanced empire. The only check to complete success was the difficulty of political administration, and in 1768 this did not seem insuperable. However, the eighteenth century's blight, which was seen in Spain as incompetent languor and in France as ostentatious extravagance, was quite as strong in England, where it took the form of a lordly corruption, an ignoble scramble for the fruits of office which reached an all-time high during these days of faction run riot, in the clash of personalities without regard to policies.

The British did enjoy the advantage of a young, still popular King who was trying to restore the Crown as an active factor in government. But His Majesty was almost alone in having any genuine political principles, and his were so old-fashioned as to be valueless. In London the great world applied itself with zeal only to the formal pleasures of society—gambling, dancing, flirting, drinking, fighting—all governed by meticulous codes which took almost as much learning as the intricacies of a man of fashion's elaborate costumes.

Beneath the powdered and beribboned pomp of the best families lay the real strength of the nation. This was to be found in the terrible slums from which Hogarth had recently drawn his inspiration and where the masses who made up the British people lived out their squalid lives knowing no better pleasures than the aristocracy. They were, of course, a more virile lot; their fighting was without code; their drink the new raw tipple, gin; their women ragged, battered harridans; their dances wild, rude, primitive stampings; their gambling the chance of keeping alive another day in a world of epidemics and vermin.

Strength lay, too, in the merchants and bankers of the City. Sober, severe men garbed in drab blacks and browns, they were gathering power quietly into their own hands while the descendants of Dukes and Earls who had won or confirmed their titles in the "Glorious Revolution" of eighty years before bickered and postured in the political limelight.

A little colonial on a tropical island could hardly aspire to make a distinguished place for himself in that cold and empty society. But, nearer at hand, was another British society in which it seemed possible to escape the binding rigidity of caste. This was developing in the North American colonies where the problems of exploiting a new land led the exploiters to relax some of the close class distinctions of England. All the world had heard of Benjamin Franklin, whose literary and scientific achievements enabled him to attain to familiar converse with men of rank in London itself. All the world knew, too, that the learned man, active in politics and land speculation and trade as well as research and letters, had begun life as a printer's apprentice.

To a youth without family influence or wealth, this seemed the field in which to try one's talents. Furthermore, it was a field which the stories of Hugh Knox rendered somewhat more attractive than the reality. The clerical pedagogue naturally enough remembered only the best features of the land of his education. He recalled, for example, the fine frenzy of independent righteousness, the generous spirit of co-operation with which the colonies had resisted George Grenville's stamp tax in '64. He did not mention and had probably forgotten the mean desire to enjoy the spoil

of war without paying for it which had inspired much of
that resistance.

To little Hamilton, the contrast between the busy cities
of the mainland, as described in the rosy phrases of Knox,
and the sleepy beauty of St. Croix was all to the advantage
of the unknown. Of course he had to admit that an orphan
of eleven, no matter how precocious, was hardly qualified
to tackle a new world unaided. Alexander reconciled himself to delay, but meanwhile he would gratify his already
strong distaste for a state of dependence. The round-faced,
under-sized, sandy-haired boy was sufficiently mature to copy
letters, add columns of figures and carry messages. St. Croix
was small enough for everyone to know his needs and abilities; it was advanced enough to approve his spirit; it was
sufficiently of the eighteenth century to accept calmly the
imprisonment of a child within the walls of a counting
house.

So, at eleven, Alexander Hamilton put childish things
behind him and entered the man's world of work and strife.

III

MERCHANT PRINCELING

One small boy's entry into trade made far less stir among the good folk of St. Croix than among the future purveyors of campaign literature to the American people. To these latter, the fact itself was unique and wonderful and beyond all superlatives. To the lad's neighbors and friends in 1768, it presented a more usual aspect. The eighteenth century did not believe in wasting higher education on poor youths destined for business; it approved of idleness only in the peerage, and eleven was not far from the normal age for beginning an apprenticeship.

Of course it was a heartless system, but in the West Indies its victims escaped much that made their London contemporaries objects of horror to the humane. Shut up in hovels above or below his place of employment, underfed and used for a wide variety of menial tasks, the average apprentice to an English merchant served out his time in unwholesome drudgery. No white in the color-conscious West Indies could be allowed to suffer such treatment, which was reserved for Negroes and mixed bloods. Alexander's skin was pale enough to win him immunity from the work of a slave. He who had so narrowly missed being a slave-owner himself was still of the caste that eschewed manual labor and took its ease in the heat of the day.

There was, then, congratulation rather than sympathy when Nicholas Cruger made a place for the boy in one of the most considerable trading companies of the islands. In the cool warehouses of St. Croix, in the airy offices where, behind arched colonnades, ship captains and supercargoes came to drink and bargain and report, Alexander was in touch with the commerce of two continents. Cruger's interests ranged from South America to New York and Boston. He was, like most merchants of his time, his own banker to a great extent. Timber and sugar, rum and cloth were carried about the world for his account in his own ships.

The intricacies of his business were no more puzzling to the new clerk than had been the works of Plutarch and Tacitus. The boy learned to understand markets, prices and cargoes as quickly as, under the direction of Hugh Knox, he had grasped the meaning of Milton and Pope—and even more accurately. His mental processes were of that intuitively rapid kind by which the occasional prodigy seems to arrive by instinct at a mastery of chess as soon as he has learned how to move the pieces.

Similarly, Alexander substituted for experience an ability to divine the knowledge that the experience would have brought him and without which older men were helpless. Apart from any rational or logical workings of his mind, it turned out that he also had the successful speculator's feeling for likely trends which, while it may be based subconsciously on facts and an analysis of them, seems to the speculator himself to be no more than a guess, a hunch, a lucky inspiration.

However astonishing this may have been to the men with whom he came into contact, it did not satisfy the boy. Trade, as he observed it from the vantage point of Cruger's counting house, was perhaps too simple. Its most immediate value to Hamilton lay in a corrective which it applied to an unfortunate literary quality fostered by Knox and the masters they had read together. Between the clergyman and the classics, the prodigy's prose style had assumed a pomposity that was more than typical of his time. All his life Alexander remained just a little too fond of the lofty phrase, the too carefully rounded sentence that shows how much care has been lavished on it, the stilted tone of conscious superiority. But never, after he was twelve years old, did he carry these literary vices to the extent that he did before he was confronted with the necessity for writing business letters in a language the recipients could comprehend without the help of an interpreter.

Of course it was the fashion where Hugh Knox and many better men learned their literary manners to distinguish between utilitarian and decorative prose. The former was base, unworthy, and therefore could be simple and natural. The other demanded what in that day was taken for the creative impulse but was in reality a stylistic sterility akin to the useless frills and furbelows that made a gentleman's toilet a thing of complete futility in a workaday world. At twelve, Hamilton was sufficiently master of this sort of bombast to assure Neddy Stevens, who had gone to New York to complete his education:

"I wish for the accomplishment of your hopes, provided they are concomitant with your welfare."

Drawing his pen with great care across the paper, he said he supposed Ned was enjoying a meeting with his father and sister. This simple, friendly thought was embellished with verbiage, emerging as a prayer "that they may convey that satisfaction to your soul that must naturally flow from the sight of absent friends in health."

In this exalted strain, he found it difficult to be satisfied with the prosaic delights of commerce. Trade furnished very little food for his own soul, as far as he could then see. He had hardly embarked upon his business career than he was ready to leave it, writing:

"To confess my weakness, Ned, my ambition is prevalent, so that I contemn the groveling condition of a clerk or the like, to which my fortune condemns me, and would willingly risk my life, though not my character, to exalt my station. I am confident, Ned, that my youth [he was still twelve] excludes me from any hopes of immediate preferment, nor do I desire it; but I mean to prepare the way for futurity."

These were the earnest words that led him to wish there

was a war. But the world remained profoundly at peace, and in Cruger's office Hamilton mustered his patience and refrained from allowing disgust with his "groveling condition" (in which, of course, he never actually groveled) to interfere with his duties. So well did he perform them that by the time he was fourteen he had become Cruger's right hand man and confidential aide. When the master was away on his frequent trips, the boy was in complete charge of the business. That meant a full measure of responsibility, for communications were as slow as freight. Once Cruger had bestowed his parting injunctions, the details of management, the handling of emergencies, the decisions of when and what to sell were Hamilton's.

He was no longer quite so conscious of his youth, and his letters took on a note of calm authority. This may have been only a reflection of Cruger, but in that case showed a very shrewd talent for presenting the views of others as his own. In any event, the substance was his, and the improvement in style may be laid to the fact that Hamilton did not think commercial correspondence was worth the trouble of being adorned. He kept his sentences short, expressed himself plainly and vigorously, and was as ready with his own opinions as he was sure of their value. This was very ready and very sure, for Hamilton possessed the prodigy's unhesitating confidence, which, like his quick perceptions, transcends mere reason and logic.

Already his judgment of men was both keen and uncharitable. He had little patience for talents inferior to his own, and of one of Cruger's skippers, evidently about to undertake a cruise that would combine trading with filibustering in Spanish waters, he wrote bluntly:

"You cannot be too particular in your instructions to him. I think he seems to want experience in such voyages."

Hamilton's own experience in these matters was nonexistent, but that did not prevent him from being very particular in issuing instructions, and this in a day when mer-

chant skippers were supposed to be at least as good at business as at navigation. However, the boy's orders were as wise
as if he had made hundreds of piratical cruises, and at the
end of his very minute and detailed commands to Captain
Newton he had the grace to say:

"I place an entire reliance upon the prudence of your
conduct."

No doubt the Captain was grateful for that much trust,
and if he was not, Cruger expressed himself as extravagantly
pleased with his young helper's manipulations of the complicated West Indian exchanges, where a couple of dozen
coinages of varying degrees of worth and stability confused
every transaction; with his skill in divining the very top of
the market; with his prudent use of credit; even with his
handling of such men as Captain Newton.

Much as Alexander may have enjoyed exercising authority, basked in Cruger's satisfaction with his work and relished
the modest financial independence of a superior clerk, he
never lost sight of the fact that no merchant could reach
such a goal as he had set for himself. Wealth alone was not
the means to appease his craving for success, and of other
rewards the life of a business man in that day was barren.
Giving orders to elderly captains and selling timber at a
profit were just marking time.

His release came on the wings of the wind, the biggest
wind anyone in St. Croix could remember. The hurricane of
August 31, 1772, cut a broad swath of ruins through the
island, but was destined to leave its mark in history, not for
its majestic fury or the amount of wreckage in its wake but
because it gave Alexander Hamilton an opportunity.

That young man acted promptly, as if nature had put
forth her full force solely for his benefit. Within a week he
had composed an account of the hurricane in the then popular form of a letter to an imaginary correspondent, and on
October 3 *The Royal Danish-American Gazette* of Christianstadt offered the unsigned effusion to its rather limited pub-

lic. Far from being the finest product of its author's pen, the hurricane story nevertheless affected his life more profoundly than anything else he ever wrote, and at the same time revealed more than mere skill with words. So far as the letter was really an account of the storm, it showed the salutary effect of business on the boy's style.

"It began," according to his description, "about dusk, at North, and raged very violently till ten o'clock. Then ensued a sudden and unexpected interval, which lasted about an hour. Meanwhile the wind was shifting around to the South West point, from whence it returned with redoubled fury and continued so till near three o'clock in the morning. Good God! what horror and destruction—it's impossible for me to describe—or you to form any idea of it. It seemed as if a total dissolution of nature was taking place. The roaring of sea and wind—fiery meteors flying about in the air—the prodigious glare of almost perpetual lightning—the crash of falling houses—and the ear-piercing shrieks of the distressed, were sufficient to strike astonishment into Angels. A great part of the buildings throughout the Island are leveled to the ground—almost all the rest very much shattered—several persons killed and numbers utterly ruined—whole families running about the streets unknowing where to find a place of shelter—the sick exposed to the keenness of water and air—without a bed to lie upon—or a dry covering to their bodies—our harbor is entirely bare. In a word, misery in all its most hideous shapes spread over the whole face of the country.—A strong smell of gunpowder added somewhat to the terrors of the night; and it was observed that the rain was surprisingly salt. Indeed, the water is so brackish and full of sulphur that there is hardly any drinking it."

So far Hamilton had been writing about facts, which were the only things that really interested him. But he knew that this was not the way to interest others, and with keen insight into the tastes of his prospective readers, he devoted the remaining three-quarters of his letter to "my reflections and feelings on this frightful and melancholy occasion." The least introspective of mortals, professing only so much religion as was necessary to avoid scandal, Hamilton suddenly betook himself to what he called "self-discourse" and a very creditable imitation of ultra-pious breast-beating.

"Where now, Oh! vile worm," he says he asked himself, "is all thy boasted fortitude and resolution?"

Gone, was the answer in formally stilted phrases, with the hurricane. For about three times the length of his actual description he elaborated eloquently on the spiritual therapeutics of suffering, exhorted himself to "see the gulf of eternal mystery open" and commanded himself abjectly to "despise thyself and adore thy God." The tone of high-minded sincerity in which all this was uttered would have done credit to a young Saint John, and may even have represented one of the genuine moods of Alexander Hamilton at fifteen. Fortunately it was a mood that neither friends nor enemies ever caught him in again, and it must have passed even before the article was finished, for the composition ends on a practical, tactful note far more characteristic of the Hamilton the world came to know.

"Our General," he concluded with an eye to that gentleman's influence in high places, "has several salutary and humane regulations, and both in his public and private measures has shown himself *the man*."

The effect of the whole was naturally far greater than any of its parts. The thing was destined to edify as wide a public as a writer could possibly reach in the West Indies, and was well suited to the taste of that public. Practical men were pleased with the terse, vivid account of the storm itself; ladies and gentlemen who prided themselves on taste and piety admired the young man's rarefied morality; the Governor General was gratified to see his manhood italicized. The standard by which the article should be judged today is the run of current periodical literature rather than the youthful productions of a Keats or a Shelley. According to such a test,

Hamilton had written a masterpiece, and this was recognized even before publication.

His relatives, Mrs. Ann Mitchell and Peter Lytton, as well as strangers who saw the piece in manuscript, agreed, some of them after a bit of urging by Hugh Knox, that so much genius could not be permitted to dissipate itself in a vulgar counting house. The boy was worthy of a better education than trade and all West Indian culture could afford, and there was a brisk subscription, headed by the Governor General, to a scholarship. Hamilton himself possessed the nucleus for such a fund in the form of a tiny legacy from a kinsman of his mother which Levine either did not know about or had been unable to attach for his own son.

Only Cruger struck a dissenting note. However brilliant a writer might be concealed within his best clerk, the merchant knew that the lad's talents for business and finance were even more important. He objected to having his unique business prodigy turned into an aesthete, and his objection took the very practical form of temptation. Cruger proposed immediate escape from "the groveling condition of a clerk" by offering Hamilton an interest in all his enterprises. It meant a speedy road to wealth, but the boy was not seriously tempted. He could then and later, without hypocrisy, affect to despise money, and he was looking for an even more complete escape—escape from the West Indies into a wider, freer society. Study in the north opened up a broad field. Knox said it was the door to literary fame. Mrs. Mitchell could see it leading to some glamorous if vague professional future. Even Cruger had to admit that the scope of commercial opportunities on the mainland would be larger.

Hamilton rejected the junior partnership without hesitation. He would not even wait for the publication of the article which had won him his chance. Within a week or two of the first suggestion that his education be resumed, he had packed his few belongings, including a box of books donated by Knox, and was settling himself on board of one of Cruger's ships for the six weeks' voyage to Boston.

Behind him St. Croix was painfully digging itself out of the debris of the hurricane, and the boy's last glimpse of the islands of his birth showed a scene of desolation in the midst of which the friends and neighbors he was never to see again were trying to rebuild their homes. Just ahead of him loomed those bright and shining "castles in the air" whose lofty pinnacles he had reared so lightly for Ned Stevens's edification three years before.

IV

IMMIGRANT

Boston, whatever its good opinion of itself, had small reputation for culture anywhere else, least of all in the West Indies, where it was known only as a city of canting Puritan smugglers famous for their rum. Hamilton did not linger long enough to learn that there might be something else to the place. The friends of his friends were all located in New York or New Jersey, and he was off to join them by the first stagecoach.

The journey, more than two hundred miles of incredibly rough road, over much of which the passengers had to walk in order to spare the horses, was his first practical experience of the size of his new country. It was impressive, but much too uncomfortable to be appreciated, and the young traveler was very glad indeed to reach New York.

His first shelter was in the home of Hercules Mulligan, a name suggestive of a soldier of fortune but actually belonging to one of Cruger's correspondents, a highly respectable merchant, through whom Hamilton was to receive his funds from the West Indies. Mulligan was his host for no more than a week; the boy had no desire to remain in the atmosphere of trade. Advisers recommended by Knox suggested that he enroll in Dr. Francis Barber's grammar school in Elizabethtown. So, after a brief reunion with Ned Stevens and a glimpse of New York, he hurried to the little New Jersey village to prepare himself for college as speedily as might be.

Of the city, he had seen only that its narrow streets were dirtier than anything he had known outside the slave quar-

ters of St. Croix, and that the possibly 20,000 inhabitants
lived in a huddle of houses and gardens at the tip of Manhattan. The built-up part of the place shredded out above
Reade Street into fields and woods and isolated dwellings.
Filing away in his mind first impressions of the town for
later confirmation, Hamilton settled himself at Barber's
school. Readily he adapted himself to a new land, new customs and a new climate. He saw his first snow, sampled the
heavy, numerous meat dishes of northern dinners, discovered the cozy friendliness of log fires, developed a habit of
solitary walks among the bare trees.

He learned more than lessons. Among his letters was one
to Elias Boudinot, another of Cruger's acquaintances, and
one who had a circle of friends that transcended trade.
Through Boudinot he was introduced to William Livingston of Liberty Hall, and in that new, cheerfully hospitable
mansion found the society of which he had dreamed in St.
Croix.

For a century the Livingstons had been rich and powerful,
stemming from a remarkably shrewd, unscrupulous Scots
trader and land speculator who was one of the first Britishers
to attempt competition with the Dutch on their own ground
and had been the patron of a certain Captain William Kidd.
The Livingstons no longer needed any of old Robert's pushing qualities. They had wealth; they took social position for
granted; they could devote an ample leisure to the cultivation of a gentleman's role on a larger stage. True colonial
aristocrats, they found the conservatism inherent in their
large holdings undermined by resentment against the calm
British refusal to recognize their claims to aristocracy. When
this was deepened by blundering British interference with
Livingston profits and contemptuous hints that colonials
were by nature an inferior race existing for the benefit of
the mother country, the master of Liberty Hall began to use
language of a sort that was soon to be labeled as "patriotic."

To Hamilton, brought up under the mild colonial administration of Denmark, the British attitude seemed unduly harsh, and he sympathized with the sentiments expressed by Livingston, Boudinot and their friends. But political discussion was not what drew him to Liberty Hall almost every hour he could spare from his self-imposed heavy schedule of study. Nor was it affection for Brockholst Livingston, his fellow-student at Dr. Barber's. Polite society attracted him more powerfully than politics or boyish comradeship, and the houseful of handsome Livingston girls was more attractive still.

These young women had been reared to the rather free and easy manners of the place and time. They talked and flirted and danced with men, were allowed to read books and hold opinions, and in general indulged in natural, wholesome lives which would have shocked their grandchildren. The colonies had not yet attained to a degree of sophistication that would permit doubts as to whether women were people, and at sixteen Hamilton discovered with pleasure the humanness of the opposite sex.

For their part, the Livingston sisters and cousins, abetted by such of their friends as Lady Kitty and Lady Mary Alexander, petted the young stranger outrageously. He looked very much like a small boy with his rosy face and slight figure, yet he behaved with mature gallantry. The soft Creole courtesy lent a singular sweetness to his youthful vivacity. Starting with that almost intuitive equipment for social success, he learned from precept and example to say the right kind of amiable nothings, to plan his conversation for laughs, to devote some of his little leisure to seeking out trifling gifts that might amuse feminine recipients. He learned to dance, and discovered that his small feet and slender frame lent themselves well to the graceful, stately measures of eighteenth century gambolings. These displayed none of the intimacy which men of his generation deplored in that "indecorous exhibition," the waltz, when they first saw it many years later.

It was not enough, however, to be a beau; the complete
young gentleman must also be a dandy, and not all of Hamilton's shopping was on behalf of the Livingston girls. His
own wardrobe made serious inroads on the West Indian
legacy, but the aspiring youth of fashion was pleased with
the result. He became very meticulous as to the set of coat
shoulders, the unwrinkled fit of those difficult tight breeches,
the exact length of cuff that should fall over the back of the
hand. He had, it seemed, the true flair for keeping lace ruffles carefully disarranged on the bosom. With the same in-
tensity that he gave to the study of Locke's philosophy, he
prepared his person for the inspection of the world.

It was, he argued, no more than the respect he owed to his
friends and his new position in life, a position which was
emphasized by the existence of titles in the Livingston circle. Lady Kitty and Lady Mary were perhaps not strictly
entitled to the courteous prefixes, but it would have been a
legalistic quibble to address them as plebeians. Their father,
William Alexander, was Earl of Stirling according to the old
Scottish law under which the earldom had been created, and
if the churlish English refused to admit the claim, it was
only one more instance of British oppression of legitimate
colonial aspirations.

His Lordship's rights were disputed on a purely legalistic
interpretation of the Act of Union. The general phraseology
of patents for Scottish peerages before that event provided
for transmission to "heirs male" of the original holder. In
England the usual wording was "heirs male of his body."
William Alexander was a descendant of the first Earl's
brother and heir male to the fifth Earl. He contended that
the Scottish custom prevailing at the time his remote kinsman was ennobled governed the case and a Scottish court
agreed with him. The House of Lords held otherwise—there
were some land grants that went with the title—but no
honest American ever denied him his claim and as Lord
Stirling he was known to his generation.

The Alexanders in Scotland had never been of as much consequence as the Hamiltons, and the least of the greater family's descendants did not allow himself to stand in awe of anyone. Fortunately no one expected him to, and other than the ladies began to take an interest in a student whose progress was being extolled by Dr. Barber. Hamilton met and won the notice of such rising figures as Gouverneur Morris, a young fellow of ample means recently admitted to the bar, and John Jay, a Huguenot lawyer who was somewhat neglecting a thriving practice to court Sarah Livingston.

With these men he played the difficult part of a man, and they accepted him as such. He gained their friendship by that instinctive charm that was one day to terrify good democrats who saw it as a species of devilish seduction, but which in 1773 was only admirable. He put himself out to be agreeable, shopping for the ladies, composing parts of a play for amateur theatricals, sitting up with Boudinot's sick child. When the infant died, he was inspired to one of his rare flights of verse, declaiming with a sensibility which the unhappy father long cherished and really found soothing:

> On the sweet babe, my doating heart
> Did All a Mother's fondness feel;
> Careful to act each tender part
> And guard from every threatening ill.

> But what alas availed my care?
> The unrelenting hand of death,
> Regardless of a parent's prayr
> Has stopped my lovely Infant's breath.

There was more of the same, and the general level of American poetry of the period was not lowered by it. Aside, however, from its purpose of proving friendship for a man who had been kind to him, the verses are significant only as showing that the exaggerated piety noticeable in the account of the hurricane no longer infected the boy's style, even on

an occasion which the most profane versifiers of his time
were wont to adorn with extremely elaborate, tearful ejacu-
lations in the name of the Almighty. Beside the general run
of late eighteenth century dirges, Hamilton's is restrained
dignity, concluding:

> Thou'r gone, forever gone—yet where;
> Oh! pleasing thought, to endless bliss.
> Then why Indulge the rising tear
> Canst thou, fond heart, lament for this?

Despite this melancholy incident, Hamilton's stay in
Elizabethtown was a happy, busy interlude, but it did not
last long. In less than a year—working often from dawn to
far past midnight—he absorbed all the knowledge that Dr.
Barber's establishment could boast, and was ready for college.

Naturally he proposed to follow in Knox's footsteps, for
the institution at Princeton had been often and lovingly in
the teacher's conversation. However, Hamilton did not wish
to restrict himself to the plodding pace of ordinary students.
In the autumn of 1773, therefore, he applied to the trustees
for permission to move ahead as fast as his mastery of scho-
lastic subjects would permit. There was some debate, for the
President was favorably inclined, but the precedents were all
against it. Princeton had refused to break its rules even for
little Aaron Burr, who at eleven, although qualified for the
freshman class in all but age, could not get in. It was true
that in the case of the son of the real organizer of the college
and grandson of that Puritan saint, Jonathan Edwards, the
trustees had relented two years later. Burr had been admitted as a sophomore at thirteen and graduated at sixteen, in
the very month that Hamilton was watching the hurricane
devastate St. Croix.

After some deliberation, it was decided that in spite of the
President's impression of Hamilton's ability, no rules should
be relaxed. The young student was just as stubborn as the

board of trustees, and King's College in New York was more obliging than Princeton. It was willing to take the boy on his own terms. So, while the tone of transatlantic conversations about duties on tea and the general right of England to exploit the colonies deepened and sharpened to an ominous thunder, Hamilton was once again a boarder in the home of Hercules Mulligan.

New England, its Puritan fervor aroused by the twin forces of outraged ideals and threatened profits, seethed with disaffection. To the south, Virginia's more deliberate opposition to British policies was hardening. New York, heavily conservative, more cosmopolitan than any other city in the New World, hesitated, wavered and split. A collegian could be forgiven for devoting as much time to study as to politics. In the college building, on the outskirts of the city near the Hudson, almost a mile above the Battery, the faculty leaned towards the side of royal or at least Parliamentary authority, established order and obedience to law. Most institutions of higher learning were still inclined in the same direction, although President Witherspoon of Princeton was scornful of British yokes and an indignant loyal alumnus of Yale was bewailing the degeneration of his alma mater into a "nursery of sedition, of faction and republicanism."

No such pernicious doctrines permeated King's. In the coffee houses and taverns of the city, however, every shade of opinion was sure to be defended by some among the extremely mixed population of New York. Dutch, English, German, French, Scandinavian and mixtures of all of them— not to mention the sizable population of Negro slaves— mingled in the narrow streets. But trade, agriculture and land speculation dwarfed political argument in New York long after most of the other colonies were concerned with nothing so much as a decision on what constituted the rights of a free-born British subject.

On closer acquaintance, the city revealed charms that had not been apparent at Hamilton's first, brief visit. Beside the

muddy streets, where pigs rooted amid refuse or fled squealing from the savage dogs, there were trim, comfortable
homes, many of them the high old Dutch houses with peaked
roofs and gabled ends. Others, more modern, were in the
English style with brick fronts lending distinction to the
wooden structure behind. Almost all of them boasted well-
kept gardens, and the uneven ground offered advantages
more practical than simple pleasure to the eye. Because the
town was hilly, said Dr. John Bard, the leader of its medical
profession, "most of the impurities left by the scavengers are
washed by the rains into the rivers." This, he thought,
helped make New York a remarkably healthy city, and so it
was, despite the epidemics which swept it periodically to the
mystification of the learned and the terror of all. (Nature's
street cleaning system was supplemented by more than the
pigs and dogs, for late revelers homeward bound would meet
silent, grotesque figures in the dimly lighted paths—stately
Negroes each bearing on his head a large tub of sewage to
be dumped into the Hudson.)

To satisfy the varying social tastes of its inhabitants, New
York offered churches of thirteen denominations, a couple
of hundred taverns, theaters, coffee houses, formal assemblies. Cock fights enlivened evenings not devoted to cards or
dancing or drinking. This last pastime was the most popular
of all, and in higher society was conducted in accordance
with elaborate conventions. The pleasant custom of toasts at
dinner or testimonial celebrations was complemented by
regularly organized drinking clubs, and years later Alexander Graydon recalled his youthful delight when, "without
the slightest addiction to liquor," he found himself "a member of a large bottle association sat in for serious drinking;
the table officers appointed, the demi-johns filled, the bottles
arranged, with the other necessary dispositions for such engagements; and I put no inconsiderable value upon myself
for my supposed 'potency in potting,' or, in modern phrase,
my being able to carry off a respectable quantity of wine.

Although a grievous headach was the usual penalty of my debauch, the admonition vanished with the indisposition."

Young Hamilton, however, needed no such admonitions. He could not spare the time for hangovers, nor did his taste incline that way, and in an age when it was quite the mark of a gentleman to be found helpless under a table, the small quantity of wine he took, even on convivial occasions, excited remark, so that Gouverneur Morris once wrote to him:

"You, who are temperate in drinking, have, perhaps, noticed the awkward situation of a man who continues sober after the company are drunk."

Turning from these pleasures of the table, Hamilton in winter could join the other young folk in excursions to the country where, nestling amid wooded hills interspersed with a few houses and fields, the Collect Pond, a site on which a greater city would one day build the Tombs, offered a fine expanse of ice for skating. Beyond that, except for the country estates at Greenwich Village and the rural settlement of Harlem, there was nothing of much value or interest. When a pious parishioner offered to give his church six acres at Canal Street and Broadway, the donation was rejected because land in that remote wilderness was not worth the expense of fencing.

While New York had attained neither the size nor the importance of Boston and Philadelphia, its trade was almost world wide. The produce of the rich hinterland, freighted down the Hudson, was piled on its wharfs. What Dr. Franklin called the "Fashions & Fineries & Fopperies" of England were eagerly purchased in exchange. All this activity, however, failed to make business men the dominant faction in the colony, for New York had a landed aristocracy second to none.

Few Southern planters, masters of vast estates and docile slaves, could count as many acres or as extensive London credits as the barons of the Hudson valley, who indeed measured their holdings in miles. Dr. Franklin's Grand

WALL STREET IN HAMILTON'S DAY, AFTER A WATER COLOR
BY ROBERTSON

Ohio Company, the Mississippi Company of Washingtons and Lees, the land grabbers of New England might bid for principalities of millions of acres in the uninhabited wilderness beyond the Alleghenies. But the Van Rensselaers and Schuylers, Philipses and Delanceys had their broad grants well stocked with tenants who were really serfs. They did not need to speculate on future westward expansion. They dwelt in lordly mansions, ruling in feudal splendor, sitting on the Governor's Council, taking to themselves such lucrative offices as British placemen left and offering to ambitious young professional men their chief opportunities for practice.

Hamilton studied the motives and structure of New York society as assiduously as his books. He read avidly whatever he could lay hands on—history and politics, poetry and pamphlets, even sermons and plays. But he also explored the ale houses and coffee houses and drawing rooms, usually with Ned Stevens and Robert Troup, a classmate at King's. He talked trade with Mulligan, law with Jay, philosophy with anyone who would listen, and when there was no audience available, he talked to himself. His fellow students— among them this year was Jacky Custis, son of Mrs. George Washington—accustomed themselves to the sight of "the West Indian" rehearsing his studies alone but aloud. Residents along Batteau Street just south of the college, a thoroughfare noted for its venerable trees, remembered years later the slender youth who had stalked up and down by the hour, moving as briskly as if he were going somewhere and muttering to himself all the while.

He seemed to be always in a hurry, and perhaps he was, for he had so little time to achieve an education. Scholarship must be acquired rapidly or put off to another day. The pressure of history in the making would not wait upon history in the learning. For, as the spring of 1774 wafted to the stroller in Batteau Street the "fragrant odors from the apple orchards and buckwheat fields in blossom on the pleasant banks of the Jersey shore"—the poetic Dr. Bard's description —the opportunity for study and reflection was slipping fast. Soon even a college lad would have to plump for action one way or the other. The war of words, increasingly widespread and bitter, would be succeeded by the sharper debate of bayonet and bullet.

V

GENESIS OF A REBEL

FUTURE GENERATIONS OF AMERICANS FOUND IT HARD TO understand that in 1774 there could have been any choice for an honest man. England was blackly wrong; the colonists held aloft the pure white banner of the Right. But to the men who had to make the decision, it was by no means as simple as that. Hamilton himself admitted to "strong prejudices on the ministerial side." His belief that constituted authority ought to be obeyed outweighed his sympathy for Livingston's anger against those British measures that threatened the prosperity of Liberty Hall. The lad from the West Indies was converted finally by "the superior force of the arguments in favor of the colonial claims"—so he himself reported—but he did not mean by this the same arguments that appeared so forcible, say, to Samuel Adams or Thomas Paine, Patrick Henry or Charles Carroll.

As an Englishman brought up under foreign rule, as he then regarded himself, he combined an unthinking loyalty to his King with a complete inexperience of British administration at first hand. He had read widely in constitutional history. More to the point, he understood what he had read. The theory of the great Whig aristocrats who made the "Glorious Revolution" of 1688 was familiar to him and congenial to his tastes, but the corruption of that theory had not been as widely publicized as its virtues. In principle, therefore, Hamilton believed a system of co-operation between King and an enlightened oligarchy, supported by docile masses, was the ideal form of government. He also

45

believed it to be the system the British people actually enjoyed.

To retain this view, it would have been necessary for him to continue to live outside the Empire. After a year and a half in New York, he could not fail to see how lamentably short of the theory the practice fell. But his prejudices remained. One of them was a genuine horror of disorder in any form, a repulsion that was beyond logic, although it was easy to frame a logical basis for the feeling. Another was a profound distrust of the virtue, intelligence and good will of the masses. Nor were these to be overcome in him by sentimental attachments to the colonies as home.

All in all, such a youth was hardly the most promising material from which to mold a rebel. The fact that it was done was attributed by the subject himself to reason, but one reason, which he did not parade, was the consideration that ambition can be served better in time of change than under any status quo, however admirable in principle. He was still the boy who wanted a war.

In 1774 war was far from most men's thoughts. The conflict was one of economic and political interests, and reasonable men balked at an appeal to force, since that is a senseless arbiter in practical affairs. Words, economic pressure and influence were tried first. They succeeded only in intensifying the bitterness of irreconcilable differences, which had been growing ever since England acquired her new imperialism along with the spoil of the Seven Years' War.

In the beginning, the issue was fairly simple. The war ended with the colonists enjoying an immediate, substantial profit from the enlarged empire, while England complained about the burden of debt left by victory on the battlefield. Englishmen thought it only fair that the colonies should share this burden. That was the purpose of George Grenville's stamp tax. It ignored the fact that the colonies had troubles other than taxes. Gnawed by land hunger, they were told to stay on their own side of the mountains to avoid costly Indians wars. Driven by the need to develop their untouched natural resources, they were blocked by the greediest set of grafters the world ever saw, the British politicians. Forbidden freedom of trade, they were compelled to rely on English merchants on unfavorable terms or resort to smuggling, with the result that the cost of living was higher in Boston than in London.

Actually the taxes they did not pay would have been less than the heavy tribute exacted whenever a colonial dealt with any department of government, whether he wanted to form a land company, license a trading corporation or seek justice in the courts. Of course these bribes did not enrich the British treasury, but they drained money out of the colonies just the same.

The stamp tax, withdrawn after a demonstration of resistance had taught the scattered settlers from New Hampshire to Georgia that violence can get results, was therefore regarded as another attempted extortion. Imperial policy, bowing momentarily to unwelcome force, did not change, probably could not change, for spokesmen of every shade of opinion in London agreed that colonies existed for the benefit of the mother country. In pursuit of this fallacy, Grenville had imposed the stamp tax. Charles Townshend, Chancellor of the Exchequer in the Pitt-Grafton ministry, inaugurated obnoxious duties on paper, tea and a few other articles. Lord North, mouthpiece for George's personal government, by which the King hoped to restore royal authority, attempted to collect them.

Taxes, writs of assistance, graft, navigation acts, restrictions on westward expansion were all essential ingredients in imperial policy, and most of them not only legal but entirely justifiable and proper in British eyes. They were becoming intolerable tyranny to Americans, although there was no unanimity of aim behind the opposition. Frontiersmen, impatient of any restraint other than that imposed by the harshness of nature, resisted all kinds of control. Traders

chafed at the handicaps to commerce. Speculators, immigrants and planters were aroused by artificial limitations on
land grants. Men who considered themselves of consequence
in their provinces felt threatened in position and property
by English assertions of superiority.

From them the infection spread. Former bond servants,
artisans and small farmers began to apply to themselves the
arguments of aristocratic liberals. They thought, and soon
put the thought into words, that they were as much entitled
to a voice in their own affairs as their so-called betters. Out
of this confusion of motives emerged a strong radical movement of a leveling, egalitarian nature. It was vociferous in
New England, and frightened many of the more moderate
leaders of the patriot party.

"God forbid that we should ever be so miserable as to
sink into a Republick!" exclaimed James Duane just six
years before he took the lead in drafting a thoroughly republican constitution for New York.

Some conservatives of his type who would have remained
aloof from the fray—as a great many actually did—joined
the newly organized colonial resistance only to temper the
excessive zeal of the "wild men," the radical agitators like
Sam Adams, who was preaching raw democracy, and the
Sons of Liberty, who were perilously indistinguishable from
riotous mobs. Of course the conservatives were swept along
in the swift current of events. Before some of them quite
realized what they were doing, they found themselves one
brisk December night, decked out in Indian disguises,
dumping a cargo of the East India Company's tea into
Boston harbor. The provocation was extreme, for by that
time the port had been closed, the existing political rights
of colonists contemptuously abrogated, the policy of forcing
recalcitrant Boston into line by economic pressure backed
by military menaces openly adopted. Even so, the outrage
to property in that famous tea party of 1773 cooled a good
many hotter heads than that of little Hamilton.

At this time he still clung to his "strong prejudices." But Dr. Franklin, who was so far from sharing them that his letters teemed with scurrilities on the incompetence and even thievery of ministry and Parliament, thought at first that the incident was a piece of vandalism much to be deplored. The venerable sage changed his opinion no faster than the young ministerialist.

Undecided on the merits of many disputed points, Hamilton paid a visit to Boston in the spring of 1774 and saw for the first time the magnitude of the problem and the opportunity before him. New York was still mostly on the side of established authority, sluggish and contented. In Boston, Hamilton saw a people really aroused and at the same time maintaining a degree of self-discipline that was more truly admirable to the lover of order than the arrogant sword-rattling of the King's emissaries.

The smugglers, land grabbers and idealists, the farmers, artisans and professional men were united in a course of action, no matter by what diverse paths they had arrived at the same end. The effective force of town meeting, fallen long since into the hands of astute tavern keepers who understood political machinery, was being put to work behind the eloquence of more distinguished leaders. In the expression of their views they were exercising a greater freedom of speech than radicals at home enjoyed, but they were contending for property rights as well as for personal rights.

Hamilton's stay in Boston was well timed. It was long enough to give him a glimpse of an orderly change as beneficent and well regulated as that of 1688. It was not so long as to permit him to see the dissensions below the surface, the weaknesses, the difficulties which a few weeks later led John Adams to confide mournfully to his diary:

"We have not men fit for the times. We are deficient in genius, in education, in travel, in fortune, in every thing."

But Adams had been chosen a delegate to the new Continental Congress, which was to meet in Philadelphia to devise methods of co-operation against British oppression, and he was afflicted with a sense of responsibility. As he wandered through the fields on a bright Saturday afternoon, noting mechanically that grain was well along for the time of year, he caught glimmerings of the fundamental confusion that confronts all revolutionaries. Although he was the least modest of men, given to an absurd vanity that alarmed his friends and mortified himself, he was appalled by his visions and confessed:

"The objects before me are too grand and multifarious for my comprehension."

Hamilton, returning to New York, had none of this humility or prescience, for he had simplified the issue quite satisfactorily. The revolutionary goal he envisaged now was a sort of autonomy that would be worked out in another hundred years of experience into Dominion home rule. Disregarding the agitation for a genuinely popular form of government as the empty mouthings of demagogues perverted by the fallacies of Rousseau, he was content to reform the British constitutional system to fit colonial needs and aspirations. It had not escaped his notice that the revolution which brought this system into existence three generations earlier had lifted two indigent young men to commanding positions among the successful aristocratic rebels. The unlucky reign of James II had found Charles Montague and John Somers of little more consequence than a colonial college boy. A plunge into revolution gave a spin to the wheel of their fortunes that whirled them to power and fame. Hamilton's opportunity, he thought, was as great, and he knew his abilities were not inferior to theirs.

He proclaimed his new principles speedily and publicly. The New York Assembly, indifferent if not hostile to Boston's appeals, had done nothing about sending delegates to Congress. An open air mass meeting, called for July 6, was designed to exert pressure upon the legislators, and Hamilton, on the outskirts of the crowd, listened to the oratory.

He was not impressed. Pushing his way forward, he leaped to the platform and offered to explain the issues. Whether the organizers of the meeting had been waiting for just such a revelation or were too dumbfounded to protest, they permitted Hamilton to plunge into a fervent speech that was well enough received, although the only expressions indicative of the audience's reaction remembered later were amazed exclamations:

"It is a collegian!"

If the student had any talent as a rabble rouser—as the legend that he swept the meeting off its feet hints—he never displayed it again. His oratory was to be effective in its place, but his style was too direct, his reasoning too close, his appeal to emotion too negligible to sway large throngs. Few in the crowd that heard him this summer day were susceptible to logic even if many may have been moved by his eager youth, but those few included some who were directing the newspaper and pamphlet propaganda for the cause.

On both sides, the volume of such literature was enormous, taxing to capacity the colonial presses and making printers the busiest men in the provinces. Every man who could read pored over the thin newspapers and thick pamphlets, while the illiterate gathered to hear their side of the case read aloud. The pen that had described a West Indies hurricane was not to be daunted by this fiercer storm. Invited to contribute, Hamilton selected as his target the most able writer in the enemy ranks, a high-flying Church of England clergyman, Dr. Samuel Seabury, whose learning and eloquence were one day to elevate him to the episcopate.

In the autumn of 1774 the reverend critic published, over the signature of "A Westchester Farmer," some severe strictures on the course of the Continental Congress. They were not as severe as those of John Adams, whose ideas for energetic defiance were a little too rich for the solons, "one third whig; another tory; the rest mongrel." Dr. Seabury's

objections were different, and Hamilton dealt with them so
well in "A Full Vindication of the Measures of Congress
from the Calumnies of Their Enemies," that Dr. Seabury
was moved to a reply. Hamilton drew a deep breath and
rattled off a tract of seventy-eight pages under the resound-
ing title:

"The Farmer Refuted; or, a More Comprehensive View
of the Disputes between Great Britain and the Colonies,
Intended as a Further Vindication of the Congress."

Prudently anonymous, as was the custom, Hamilton was
ready to avow his works when their success, no less than
the forceful reasoning, led his efforts to be attributed variously to William Livingston and Jay. The patriot chieftains
were not the men to scorn literary skill and ability to handle
a constitutional argument merely because these useful qualities were lodged in an eighteen-year-old. Hamilton was admitted to the councils of the leaders in very much the way
that the financial genius of the Whig party, Charles Montague, had been taken up early in his career for his clever
writings and nimble wit.

Unfortunately the revolution in which Hamilton was being involved was not following the precedent of 1688. The
oppressor of honest men and his tools declined to abdicate
peacefully. They preferred to ram the tenets of British
imperialism down colonial throats with the bayonet. General Thomas Gage, with an army and a governor's commission, was in Boston to perform the operation. On an April
day in 1775 he sent some soldiers out to arrest John Han-
cock, and if the shots fired on the road to Concord were not
heard round the world, their sharp echoes carried plainly
over thirteen colonies. Advocates of independence rejoiced
sternly. Loyalists were further alienated from impious scoun-
drels who would fire on the troops of their King. Thousands
upon thousands of indifferent neutrals prayed only that
they might keep out of trouble.

New York was full of these last, and many of them were

in high places where they could be embarrassed by the fact that George Washington of Virginia, appointed by the Congress to take command of its new army outside Boston, was passing through on June 25, the same day the royal mouthpiece, Governor Tryon, was expected. In this crisis, Colonel Lasker of the provincial militia received the impartial order to parade his regiment, in spite of the fact that it was Sunday, "to receive either the general or Governor Tryon, whichever should arrive first, and wait on both as circumstances would allow." So Washington was escorted into the city by nine companies and a considerable proportion of the population, who four hours later were doing Tryon the same honor.

This feat of fence-sitting was beyond Hamilton's power. Since he could not get the kind of a revolution he wanted, he was ready to take the kind of a revolution he could get. He was ready to do more than write about it, too. He gave up Newton and Aristotle for books on military strategy. He organized a student corps at King's, and wore proudly a very natty green uniform adorned with the badge of the "Hearts of Oak." At their head he was under fire at the Battery when the British warship *Asia* bombarded the town. He directed a few ineffectual shots at the ship and then bore off the useful cannon which were in danger of being destroyed.

In the heat of battle he did not lose his passion for order. Roused by the damage inflicted by the *Asia's* guns, he yet looked disdainfully on the Sons of Liberty, who were rushing wildly about the streets threatening to take an indemnity out of the hides of local tories, particularly that tool of the court, Dr. Myles Cooper, president of King's College. Scornfully the young militiaman noted that this vengefulness for property destroyed burned brightest in the bosoms of those who had no property. Shrewdly he conjectured that they sought loot and excitement and the sport of inflicting pain rather than justice.

When the mob, having paused to sample goods in the royal storehouse, reached Dr. Cooper's dwelling, they found Hamilton and Troup waiting for them. While his friend ran in to rouse the President, Hamilton attempted to divert the crowd by urging them to consider the true principles for which they were fighting. He spoke as fervently and as logically as on the day in the fields, and he made quite as attractive a picture, slim and flushed and earnest. But lynching mobs are seldom susceptible to logic or even to youthful charm.

The real diversion in this instance was provided by Dr. Cooper himself. Wakened by Troup and hearing angry roars, he poked his night-capped head out of a window. He could see Hamilton's hands moving in gesticulation, but he could not hear any words. With the suspicion born of a dozen years' experience as a college head, he was confident that the student was suggesting tar and feathers at the very least.

"Don't listen to him, gentlemen; he's mad," the Doctor shouted, and before the mob's anger had recovered from its laughter he had escaped by the back door.

A few months later the "Heart of Oak" interrupted his newspaper writing and study of tactics to commit to paper some evidence of his immunity to popular hysteria, aversion to popular excesses, distaste for popular government—and, perhaps, a little generous youthful chivalry toward an enemy. The occasion was the appearance in New York of one Captain Isaac Sears of Connecticut, a friend of Jay, with a party of horsemen bent on destroying the press of James Rivington, publisher of *The New York Gazetteer*. The newspaper and its supplementary pamphlets and the man himself were violently tory. Hamilton characterized them as "dangerous and pernicious." But his revolutionary principles were outraged when property was destroyed by unauthorized bands no better than vandals. He actually believed a revolution might be accomplished without destruc-

tion or injustice, and so on November 26, while less thoughtful patriots were laughing over the plight of the miserable
Rivington, the young apostle of law and order was writing
to Jay in deep disapproval:

"The same state of the passions which fits the multitude,
who have not sufficient stock of reason and knowledge to
guide them, for opposition to tyranny and oppression, very
naturally leads them to a contempt and disregard of all
authority. The due medium is hardly to be found among
the more intelligent, it is almost impossible among the unthinking populace. When the minds of these are loosened
from their attachment to ancient establishments and courses,
they seem to grow giddy and are apt more or less to run
into anarchy. These principles, too true in themselves, and
confirmed to me both by reading and my own experience,
deserve extremely the attention of those who have the direction of public affairs. . . . I am always more or less
alarmed at every thing which is done of mere will and
pleasure without any proper authority. . . . It is not safe
to trust to the virtue of any people."

Whereupon the young rebel put down his pen and resumed the study of those military arts which were to fit
him, he hoped, for a glorious part in a revolution that was
to be based on the theory that the multitude is virtuous,
that the will of the people is the voice of God.

VI

DEFEATS

ONCE COMMITTED TO REBELLION, HAMILTON WAS NOT CON-
tent to play at soldier with the "Hearts of Oak," write pamphlets and harangue mobs. If his dream of an orderly revolution had faded, his desire for a war had been fulfilled.
While he was protesting against popular excesses and
unauthorized raids, there were armies in the field. One
under Washington besieged Boston. Another, marching on
Quebec in a mad throw for conquest so reckless it almost
succeeded out of sheer audacity, was to stagger back, defeated, on the last day of the year in a failure so glorious that
the names of Montgomery, Arnold and Burr were ringing
proudly from patriot lips.

From such glory as this, Hamilton did not propose to be
omitted. For this he had been studying tactics, and as 1776
opened with bright prospects for the rebel cause, he decided
he was as well qualified for a small command as any other
nineteen-year-old. He intimated as much to his influential
friends, and on March 14 Alexander Hamilton was commissioned captain of the New York Provincial Company of
Artillery.

Master of sixty-three men and four officers, all older than
himself, the Captain lost no time in putting his military
education to the test. The last of his West Indian remittances
went into equipment and uniforms for his company. As fast
as they were recruited, his men were put through a course
of discipline unusual in the Continental Army of '76. Few
officers knew their business any better than the rank and file;

56

fewer still thought that strict obedience was of much importance.

Hamilton, lover of order, had the makings of a martinet
and might have developed into a fine specimen of that offen-
sive species if his objects had not been broader than mere
perfection in military minutiae. For thirty days his little
band drilled, marched and practiced the handling of their
clumsy cannon. The main army, having driven the British
from Boston, was on its way to defend New York, and when
Washington arrived on April 16, the sixty-eight effectives
of the Provincial Artillery Company were ready to be
absorbed into the straggling, noisy crowd that followed the
Commander-in-Chief.

Nothing in that gentleman's public manner indicated that
he had any misgivings, any suspicion as to the quality or
bravery or efficiency of his troops, any doubts of victory. At
this time forty-four years old, George Washington presented
to the world a sufficiently imposing picture. Six feet two
inches and more than two hundred pounds of athletic figure,
with a wonderful seat on a horse, a magnificently powerful
pair of hands, a size thirteen boot and a pock-marked face,
he had schooled himself to conceal behind a grave serenity
of manner the violence of his passions. Neat in his blue and
buff, scorning the gold lace and frills of lesser generals, he
inspired more confidence in his army of perhaps 20,000 than
they inspired in him. With a comprehensive education in
the art of war still ahead of him, he already knew enough
to realize the immediate difficulties of his present task.

Most of the citizens of New York did not want to be defended. In addition to the active loyalists, said to outnumber
the patriots, there was a substantial majority whose only
desire was that any fighting should take place out of range
of their homes and fields. Furthermore, if it should be true,
as reported, that the British were coming in real force, New
York was indefensible against an enemy holding command
of the sea. That was as plain to the General's newest captain

as to the General's staff. It was equally plain that the cause would be deserted by thousands if the city should be surrendered without a struggle. The trick, therefore, was to fight without being annihilated, and while His Excellency grappled with that problem, his troops spread out over Manhattan and Long Island, drilling a little, drinking a great deal, eating what they could find and singing that old popular favorite "Sally in Our Alley" and the newer war song, "The Drum."

Hamilton took part only in the drilling. For the other activities he exchanged a course of reading in economics, and the company pay book, handiest blank paper available, soon bristled with figures unrelated to pay and with speculative questions and answers on the finances of governments, the reasons for the commercial greatness of certain peoples, the rise and fall of trading nations. So the spring passed into summer, and on July 2, while the Congress in Philadelphia was adopting Richard Henry Lee's resolution of independence, the Captain was reading Washington's general orders to the troops:

"The time is now near at hand which must probably determine whether Americans are to be Freemen, or Slaves. . . . The fate of unknown millions will now depend, under God, on the Courage and Conduct of this Army."

Then there was the more practical note as the British drew near:

"Evening orders.—'Tis the General's desire that the men lay upon their arms in their tents and quarters, ready to turn out at a moment's warning, as there is the greatest likelihood of it."

Eight days later the army learned that a new nation had been born, and at six o'clock of a fine summer evening, the 20,000 stood at attention on parade in reasonably orderly brigade formation and heard the eloquent phrases of Mr. Jefferson's Declaration read "with an audible voice." Their commander reported temperately that they then testified

"warmest approbation," while in the town itself the patriotic element marred the occasion (so Captain Hamilton
thought) by pulling down King George's statue in the
Bowling Green. Captain Hamilton felt a little better about
it when he learned that the leaden man and horse had been
run into bullets.

The celebration was mild, for the idea of independence
had already been accepted generally in the army, and declarations, however eloquent, could not compete in interest
with the approaching portent of General Sir William Howe's
32,000 well-furnished troops and Admiral Lord Howe's
formidable fleet. The suspense lasted for another month.
Then in mid-August Hamilton was placing his battery in a
not very advantageous position on Long Island where Washington had decided to risk his battle. With thousands of
others, the young Captain kept body and soul together on
an unsatisfactory diet of raw pickled pork, cursed the rain
and dysentery and Britishers, and waited—already more than
half-beaten—for the blow to fall.

It was duly launched with professional, methodical preci-
sion, and Captain Hamilton's first experience of battle was
how to work his guns to cover a rout. Then, as Sir William
obligingly waited for the rain to stop before completing ex-
termination of the rebels, and his brother, the Admiral,
co-operated by keeping his ships out of the East River where
they might have prevented escape, Colonel Glover's invaluable regiment of Marblehead fishermen ferried their dispir-
ited comrades through a chilling drizzle back to New York.

Two weeks later Sir William struck again, but he was not
trying for a knockout blow. This feint only sent the Continental Army scrambling out of the city on September 15. It
was the retreat that first showed his awed followers the full
fury of an aroused Washington temper, and some of them
forgot their terror of the enemy as their General, so blind
with rage that he almost allowed himself to be captured, laid
the flat of his sword with all the power of his mighty arm

across the backs of brigadiers and colonels and privates alike.

Hamilton did not witness the spectacular exhibition. He was in the last brigade to quit the city, and he lost one of his guns and all his baggage that Sunday afternoon before the hurrying fugitives reached a point where one day Grant Street was to cross Mulberry. Here Colonel Harry Knox, the Boston bookseller, who was in command, learned that they had not been quick enough. The British, landing on the east side of the island, were above them. Knox, proposing to sell life and liberty as dearly as might be, led his men into a sod fort erected for unknown reasons on this unlikely spot, called by the inspiring name of Bunker's Hill. The name was the most formidable thing about it, but the brigade was saved from the necessity of putting it to a test by the most improbable emissary Hamilton's guardian angel ever employed.

While Knox was disposing his men to meet an attack, a young major, aide to General Israel Putnam, the wolf killer, rode up, and the boy from the West Indies caught his first glimpse of Aaron Burr. He saw a singularly handsome youth even smaller than himself and only a year older, bearing lightly the burden of a great name, a reputation for precocious brilliance and the laurels of remarkably distinguished conduct at the siege of Quebec.

Impatiently, the natty young officer demanded to know what the brigade was waiting for. Brushing aside the sweating Knox's melodramatic explanation, he offered to guide them along a road that was still open. Knox refused to take the chance, his massive frame towering over the dapper little major as he thunderously proclaimed his intention to fight and die on the spot. There was no time to waste in argument, and Burr never had much use for heroics. With the authority of an aide to Knox's superior he turned from the giant to ask the men if they really wanted to rot in the pestilential British prison hulks. Lacking their Colonel's dash, they did not hesitate and in a few minutes the column was in motion behind the major's debonair figure. Night found them breathless but safe with the rest of the army on Harlem Heights.

The leisurely Howe took another month to maneuver them out of this position into Westchester, which was such unexplored territory that one British plan of action called for the fleet to sail up the Bronx River to turn the American flank. Unfortunately the Admiral refused to try. Sir William adopted other tactics, and on October 28 Hamilton was working his battery on Chatterton's Hill and escaping again from the advancing British as the Battle of White Plains was lost, but with honor.

Fort Washington was stormed; Fort Lee abandoned. Disasters crowded so fast upon the beaten Continentals that hardly anyone except the General knew how many they were. Then, in the cold November rains, the remnants of the army of freedom reeled back across New Jersey. On December 1, when many of the militia enlistments expired, there were only 3,000 left of the 20,000 who had faced Howe so shakily in August. Most of them wore only the clothes they had had then, few had eaten a hearty meal in weeks, but one thinning company stood out from the rabble and caused comment.

"It was," one observer noted, "a model of discipline; its captain a mere boy, with small, slender, and delicate frame, who with cocked hat pulled down over his eyes, and apparently lost in thought, marched beside a cannon, patting it every now and then as if it were a favorite horse or pet plaything."

Sometimes the thoughtful expression vanished, as when at New Brunswick his battery covered the exodus of the army, the guns playing briskly on the advancing British until the retreat was safely launched. Then the horses were hitched to the two remaining brass pieces and New York's Provincial Artillery Company, Captain Alexander Hamilton commanding, ran smartly down the Princeton road.

The weather remained atrocious, but Howe was in one of

his more lethargic moods, and he was only leaving New Brunswick when his quarry reached Trenton, having been driven one hundred miles in three weeks. The village was no refuge, and after collecting every conceivable kind of craft for miles up and down the river to prevent pursuit, Washington led his weary men across into Bucks County, safe at last, anyway until the water froze or the pursuers could build boats of their own.

Sir William preferred to let nature work for him, and from their security on the Pennsylvania side, the Americans watched the warmly-clad red- and blue-coated regiments take post along the stream. Soon they heard that Lord Cornwallis, who had commanded the British advance, had returned with Howe to the civilized comforts of New York, then that the noble Earl had applied for leave, then that he was going home to report the rebellion crushed except for the final mopping up of a few isolated bands. To this lugubrious news, Congress added its mite. Prudently fleeing to Baltimore before the ice should be thick enough to permit the foe to march across the Delaware into Philadelphia, the delegates called for a day "of fasting and humiliation, to implore Almighty God the forgiveness of the many sins prevailing among all ranks."

The army had had quite enough of fasting, and its cup of humiliation was running over without any help from Congress. But Hamilton noted with approval that defeat and flight had not destroyed all semblance of orderliness. There was spirit in the lean scarecrows around him, for there marched with the men that winter a more powerful moral influence than any Congressional proclamations.

Thomas Paine was lugging his long musket through the wet, and scribbling on drum heads beside the camp fires at night when he was too cold and hungry and angry to sleep. The hot-headed English radical—he had been in the country even a shorter time than Hamilton—had struck a mighty blow for independence at the beginning of the year with "Common Sense." Now that 1776, begun so hopefully with the liberation of Boston, was ending in misery and depression in Pennsylvania, the literary soldier had shifted his gun to his left hand to leave his right free for the pen. On December 19, his discouraged comrades were seeing in the first number of "The American Crisis" those words which even 160 years later have the power to quicken the pulse and rouse the pride of men who want to be free.

"These are the times that try men's souls," the ragged, defeated, ill-fed toughs of town and country read in the blurry print on the grayish paper. "The summer soldier and the sunshine patriot will, in this crisis, shrink from the service of their country; but he that stands it *now*, deserves the love and thanks of man and woman."

Next day a snowstorm swept the camp and the hard-bitten objects of Paine's exhortation concealed behind bitter, scoffing words their pride in the new spirit he had infused into them. They would, they jested, exchange the love of man, and woman too, for a blanket and a hot joint of beef. But the summer soldier and the sunshine patriot had been purged from the thin ranks in those horrible three weeks of flight across the Jerseys. Those who remained might be fit for some heroic exploit.

Washington, for one, thought so, and he was no longer the man to overestimate the excellence of the troops under his command. Paine had inspired them, moreover, with words so burning that the soldiers almost got the illusion of being warmed by them. Howe had given them an opportunity. And, heaven knew, it was time for their luck to turn. This combination of circumstances, aided perhaps by a council of despair at General Greene's quarters and some sage strategic suggestions by that officer, brought the army back across the Delaware on Christmas night. It was with keen appreciation of what the next few hours might bring that His Excellency gave his password and heard the premonitory rumblings of history in the low murmur as the phrase was muttered from man to man down the invisible ranks:

"Victory or Death!"

VII

VICTORIES

From mc konkey's ferry two roads led to trenton seven
miles away. Washington, with half his 2,500 men, including
Hamilton's battery, took the slightly longer upper road, and
his desperate anxiety for haste was noticeable only in his
low-voiced urging as he rode his big chestnut sorrel up and
down the ranks:

"Press on, press on, boys."

Hamilton, marching with General Stephen's brigade in
the van, should then if ever have modified his low opinion
of mankind. The road, a mere track of frozen ruts and
bumps, was so slippery the horses slid and slithered and
balked. The sharp ridges of ice cut through the thin shoes
and thick cloths with which the luckier men were shod.
The less fortunate stumbled along on bare feet. Rags that
might have been used to advantage on the backs of the
drenched, freezing soldiers had been bound around the
wheels of the guns to deaden noise. Breakfast, snatched halfway to Trenton from the three-day store of rations each
man carried—the General gulped his without getting off his
horse—was a cold tasteless, unsatisfactory interlude in a
bone-wearying struggle to drag one foot in front of the
other. Nature and man had combined to do their worst to
these plodding scarecrows, and could not even keep them
from cracking jokes.

Daylight, which enabled them to avoid some of the roots
and stumps over which they had been falling, also showed
them the bloody tracks their feet were leaving on the snow.
They groaned and cursed, but these toughened dregs of

the "unthinking populace" grinned, albeit wryly, and repeated a jest that was far more popular that morning than their password.

"These are the times that try men's soles," they whispered to each other.

Grim humor, and perhaps Captain Hamilton was in no mood to appreciate the courage that can chuckle in the face of pain and fear. For they were all afraid. None could be sure that the Hessians had celebrated Christmas so thoroughly that they could be surprised in broad daylight. No one knew that their commander, Colonel Johann Gottlieb Rall, had just turned in after a merry night of wine and cards. No one knew that the first attack would be mistaken for a raid by guerrillas who had been beaten off once before during the night.

All these things, however, came to pass. At eight o'clock the Hessian pickets were driven in without immediately spreading the alarm. The little column came on fast after them, Captain Hamilton pushing men and horses relentlessly until, all out of breath and almost warm from their exertions, they swung their battery into position on the highest ground in town, the top of King Street. They were just in time. Down the road they could see the Hessian guns being unlimbered and the Hessian soldiers, conspicuous through the rain and snow in their blue, cross-belted coats, yellow breeches, black gaiters and high, brass-fronted caps, running into line.

Exultantly Captain Hamilton shouted his orders in his eager young voice. He was busier than a battery commander ought to be, for he had only the two juniors of his four officers with him. Captain Lieutenant James Moore was at that very moment dying on his sickbed back in quarters and First Lieutenant James Gilliland, who was to win a niche in history as the only member of the Society of the Cincinnati to be expelled for "ungentlemanlike conduct," had just been transferred to another corps. So the little

Captain worked for three. His two brass guns roared, erupting smoke and grapeshot; they roared again, and down King Street the colorful Germans were breaking and running, or perhaps dropping and lying still.

In a very few minutes it was all over. About six hundred Hessians were flying faster than any exhausted American could follow toward Bordentown. Nearly a thousand others were holding hands high in token of surrender. Twenty-two of the "brass caps" had been killed, eighty-four wounded; of the attackers only Captain William Washington, Lieutenant James Monroe and two privates had been injured.

Before noon the Americans were on their way back to McKonkey's Ferry, shepherding their prisoners ahead of them, and darkness found them again in their Pennsylvania quarters. They had performed an immortal feat of arms and endurance—nearly half of them were unfit for duty next day. Hungry as he was, Captain William Hull could not stay awake long enough to eat a bowl of soup. He fell out of his chair before he could touch a mouthful and woke in the morning on the floor with the spoon still clutched in his hand.

Out of all proportion to its size, the moral effects of the raid spread over the country with a rapidity usually reserved for bad news. Before it heard of Trenton, Congress had conferred the powers of a dictator upon Washington, the usual recourse of a deliberative assembly faced with military disaster and afflicted with lack of leadership. Now the members took heart and were ready to begin interfering with the army again.

Lord Cornwallis decided to postpone his report on the rebellion and came posting back to his command, which had been concentrating from its various stations and was nearing full strength at Princeton. The Continentals, spirits raised by their first successful battle with the "brass caps," were discovering that the fearsome Hessians with their pigtails plastered with tallow and flour and their long mus-

taches darkened with soot or lampblack, were just home-
sick German lads such as might have come from almost any
farm in western Pennsylvania. Their discipline in fighting,
their thoroughness in looting and their fierce physical appearance had terrified the colonials, who faced the British
redcoats calmly enough. After Trenton, the spell of the
Hessians too was broken.

Their captors, refreshed by three days' rest, were fairly
cheerful when the General, wondering what he ought to
do with his new dictatorial powers, led them back across
the Delaware and took up quarters at Trenton. Here they
were waiting for Cornwallis as December ended and with it
a twelvemonth which has loomed very large and glorious in
historical retrospect, but held only unpleasant memories for
those who lived through it. Robert Morris, who had remained behind his fellow Congressmen in Philadelphia to
carry on what government business there might be, expressed the view of all true patriots when he wrote to Washington:

"The year 1776 is over. I am heartily glad of it, and
hope you nor America will ever be plagued with such another."

To the anxious General in Trenton, 1777 did not seem to
be more promising. Collecting detachments from various
other posts, he had about 5,000 poorly equipped troops to
meet Cornwallis's 8,000, not counting reserves. But he also
had a plan which might prevent the Earl from driving the
Continental Army into the Delaware.

For once the weather helped him. It turned warmer just
long enough to soften the frozen roads, and on January
2 the mud and American skirmishers managed to hold
up the British advance until it was too late to attack that
day. There was only time for Hamilton to get a little target
practice in an artillery duel before dark. Both commanders
watched night fall over Trenton with satisfaction. Corn-

wallis was quietly confident that he had "the old fox in a trap." Washington had his plan.

In broad outline, it was a repetition of his recent coup, a successful raid. At New Brunswick, Sir William Howe had collected his main field stores and the tidy sum of £70,000 in coin. The new American dictator, looking beyond Cornwallis's army and a strong detachment at Princeton, had his eye on that spoil. He proposed to elude the enemy in front of him and make a dash for the treasure.

At one o'clock on January 3, a nippy, frosty morning, the Continentals were roused from their first slumber, which was just as well, for the mud in which they had stretched themselves was beginning to freeze around them. Once again Hamilton's cannoneers gave of their inadequate rags to bind the wheels of the guns to muffle telltale creakings. While a party of four hundred remained to keep the fires burning and make a noise like an army, their fellows pushed off into the night.

There was more confusion than silence, for not even Washington could keep the men from muttering and swearing or the horses from squealing. But the British were sleeping soundly after a difficult march, and heard nothing. Suddenly in the darkness of the woods behind the British lines, someone thought he saw the shadow of a Hessian. It was a false alarm, but it started some thousand of the new militia running, and they never stopped until they pelted into Burlington, far from the action of the day.

The remaining 4,000 met the dawn two miles from Princeton. Unfortunately, they met also two British regiments, up early and on the road to join Cornwallis. A brisk fight of fifteen minutes scattered this small force, and as the Americans rushed on the town, Captain Hamilton fired his last shots as an artillery officer. Some of the retreating British had taken refuge in Nassau Hall. The little Captain, by driving his men and horses to the limit, had caught up with the foremost infantry. He was able to get his guns unlimbered just as the storming party moved forward to the assault. His first shot neatly decapitated a portrait of King George II in the college chapel. His second, bouncing back from the wall, almost performed for his new country a really substantial military service. The ball narrowly missed Major James Wilkinson, another of those nineteen-year-old prodigies of the Revolution. But it did miss, and Hamilton was deprived both of an opportunity to repay his debt to Aaron Burr and of the honor of ridding the army of a demoralizing influence. Wilkinson, uninjured, rode on to pursue to its end a career of intrigue, corruption and outright treason through two wars and many years of peace.

Hamilton did not get another shot, for the defenders of Nassau Hall prudently surrendered. Quickly the victors formed again for the march, but Washington reluctantly gave up ideas of the £70,000 in New Brunswick. In fact, His Excellency was going to be lucky to get away safely, for an enraged nobleman was close upon him.

Cornwallis, awakened to find his trap sprung and the "old fox" escaped, was furious. Since dawn his 8,000 men had been on the go "in a most infernal sweat—running, puffing, and blowing, and swearing at being so outwitted." They made such good time that the first of them were coming into Princeton on one side as the Americans moved out on the other. Fortunately Cornwallis, too, was thinking about the cash at New Brunswick and headed that way, leaving the Continentals to turn off unmolested toward the sanctuary of the Short Hills.

All afternoon men were collapsing by the roadside, falling asleep under their knapsacks and being kicked awake again by more alert comrades. At eleven at night they stumbled into Somerset Court House, where even soldiers who were lucky enough to own blankets were too weary to cover themselves, and were found in the morning frozen to death where they had dropped from exhaustion. Three days later, still staggering from fatigue, the survivors reached the highlands of Morris County and could stop to realize the magnitude of their achievement.

In two weeks of campaigning through weather that was supposed by experts to be impractical for military operations, they had retrieved a year's defeats. With nothing but the wits of Washington and Greene and their own tremendous fortitude in marching and starving, they had drawn a greatly superior army out of almost all of New Jersey. Sir William, no longer daring to leave his army in scattered posts, had drawn all the detachments together near New York for mutual protection. The troops he had so easily beaten had in their turn defeated and taken prisoners their most feared enemies. They had captured military supplies (but, alas, little food). And, above all, they had inspired renewed confidence in armchair patriots who had been despairing of the cause. All this they had done with a minimum of fighting and fewer than one hundred battle casualties.

Their reward was to be kept in the rough New Jersey hills for the rest of the winter on short rations, flogged ceremoniously but vigorously when they misbehaved—the General was a great believer in the disciplinary value of the lash —and drilled unendingly but incompetently in the complicated maneuvers of the troops they had beaten—or, anyway, outrun.

Junior artillery officers were spared only the delicate attentions of the "cat" in this program, and Captain Hamilton, a reflective youth, began to ask himself if this sort of anonymous, all too pedestrian heroism was what he had joined up for. Men who passed through that campaign of '76 could be forgiven such thoughts in the relaxation following sustained effort. Captain Hamilton, although by no means satiated with military glory, was ready for a change. He was also in a mood to agree with Harry Knox, who, in writing his round, merry wife an account of the hardships he had undergone, concluded:

"War, my Lucy, is not a humane trade."

VIII

THE GROVELING CONDITION OF A CLERK

PROMOTION CAME TO CAPTAIN HAMILTON FOR QUALITIES that he admired least in himself. He had imagined it as the reward of brilliant strategy daringly executed. He got it because he wrote easily, clearly and legibly, had a good memory and handled figures readily. Washington needed such talents in a secretary and had been unable to find them. If he had heard of his young artillery officer at all, it was as the college mate of Jacky Custis, as the author of an audaciously impractical plan for recapturing Fort Washington or as one of the tougher young fellows who had lasted through the campaign of '76. But General Nathanael Greene, on whose military judgment His Excellency placed great value, was acquainted with the lad's background and precocity.

A Rhode Islander, son of a Quaker preacher, Greene had inherited from somewhere in his peace-loving ancestry a genius for warfare that many experts considered superior to that of his chief. He was a familiar of some of Hamilton's New York friends, and suggested to Washington that the young Captain would be of more use at a desk than with his battery. The offer of a military secretaryship followed, and on March 1, 1777, the headquarters orderly book recorded its chief item of historical interest for those who delve into the reasons why national development takes the turns it does.

"Alexander Hamilton Esqr is appointed Aide de Camp to the Commander in Chief and is to be respected and obeyed as such," reads the brief notice.

Brevet rank as a lieutenant colonel went with the job, but that was not altogether why Hamilton accepted. Neither

71

were the other immediate advantages, although obvious, decisive. It was true that a staff officer rode a horse, a delightful prospect for a youth who had run his legs off up and down the State of New Jersey. The General's aides also could be sure of fairly comfortable quarters, even in the field, as well as regular meals, wine to drink most of the time and a change of clothing when needed—all tempting to a Captain who had shared most of his men's miseries in a hard campaign.

Hamilton saw all this, and would have sacrificed it for his little chance of immortal glory on a stricken field, but he saw further, too. The work itself was essentially clerical, even if "military secretary" had a loftier sound, and it had been to escape such a "groveling condition" that he had longed for war. But aides de camp to commanders-in-chief meet interesting people. He would be thrown into contact with the molders of a new nation. He could impress on them the potential value of his services, since they would be unable to overlook him, whereas even the bravest fighters sometimes performed their most astounding exploits outside the range of influential notice, thereby losing the good of them. And finally, although Hamilton was apt to plume himself on talents for which he was not especially notable, he knew in his heart that his was genius for the cabinet rather than the camp.

Other twenty-year-olds in the army might have been inspired too by veneration for the man they were to serve, especially after Trenton and Princeton, which Hamilton himself was to describe as "the dawning of that bright day which afterward broke forth with such independent luster." But the new aide was incapable of hero worship. Temperamentally he was more observant of a man's faults than of his virtues, and to the impatient youngster some of Washington's most admirable qualities wore the aspect of blemishes.

The man's very enthusiasms were chilling to the ardor of an adventurer on the make. When Hamilton joined the

General's "family," it was in the midst of the army's subjec-
tion to what grumbling thousands complained was the
gratification of a martinet's whim. For His Excellency was a
zealot for inoculation against the smallpox, and the entire
army had at his order been immunized with a "mild" form
of the disease. The quarters, the temporary hospitals, the
very churches were filled with sick soldiers. They all came
out of it very well in the end, but it seemed to hot-blooded
skeptics that this was just luck.

Nor was Washington's attitude toward his job quite what
an ambitious youngster could understand. He held the dignity of his position and person high, and that was good. But
he seemed hardly to know that Congress had made him a
dictator. Great men in history had schemed and contrived
and intrigued and soiled their reputations to have such
powers thrust upon them. The chance fell unsolicited into
the hands of the supremely fortunate Washington, and he
would not use it to impose his will on the country. Apparently he did not want to be a dictator. A generation whose
ideas of greatness had been formed on Caesar, Charlemagne
and Cromwell thought His Excellency's distaste for personal
power argued a lack of spirit.

If Hamilton had any such ideas when he entered on his
new duties, he soon lost them. The General had spirit
enough and to spare to suit his family. He drove his aides as
hard as he drove himself, and in doing it was as dictatorial
as any admirer of Caesar could wish. As an administrator, he
had a genius for extracting their best work from his assist-
ants, but failed to inspire that fanatical devotion which
characterized the familiars of more colorful, less rigidly just
commanders. Some of his aides and generals stood in awe of
him, the others admired and respected. That was all.

His good sense and a fundamental simplicity of nature
dictated his attitude toward Hamilton. He was soberly delighted with the master clerk's capacity for work and detail.
He was pleased with the easy yet courtly manners of the

young West Indian, understanding that they relieved his own rather stiff dignity. He came to feel a quite genuine, almost paternal affection for the boy, and in a remarkably short time he was relying, perhaps more than he realized, upon the ability, integrity and instinctively brilliant judgment of the army's junior lieutenant colonel.

The huge mass of headquarters correspondence took on a polish and clarity which it owed to the new secretary. Gradually Hamilton was left more and more to draft the details of important papers, for which his chief supplied only a general outline. Soon the aide was familiar with all the manifold aspects of rebellion. Through his hands passed the confidential papers that revealed the verbose impotence of Congress, the intriguing jealousy of some generals and the intriguing incompetence of others, the rascality of supply agents, the reluctance of state governments to act in concert with each other, the course of foreign and domestic negotiations.

He entered at once upon a private correspondence with the leaders of the provisional New York government, ostensibly keeping them informed of the state of affairs in the army, but actually pouring forth a steady stream of propaganda skillfully designed to persuade the provincial legislators to subordinate local jealousies to the needs of the soldiers. Models of discretion and tact, these letters explicitly repudiated any intention of speaking for the General, but Washington could hardly have expressed his own sentiments any more forcibly, and certainly could not have done so as freely.

Not quite all the young aide's life was spent at his desk. While the army slowly recovered from its smallpox inoculations and began to prepare for the next campaign, there was a mild social life at headquarters in the old Freeman tavern. In mid-March the General's wife, usually called with awful politeness "Lady Washington," arrived to lend a gracious air to the tavern and attract respectable female company. There were adequate dinners, and wine for the subsequent toasts. Dances were not unknown. There were a few girls to flirt with, and Hamilton gained his first newspaper notoriety in an ill-natured British account of rebel headquarters. Mocking the enforced simplicity of Morristown, the satirist in New York recorded that the plump and unaffected Martha had conferred the name of Hamilton upon a pet tomcat with thirteen yellow rings around his tail.

His seniors in the family were inclined to make much of him. Colonel Robert Harrison, more devoted to his chief than all the others put together, had a great capacity for friendship, and hovered over Hamilton protectingly. The "old secretary," as he was always called, dubbed his new colleague "the little lion," and it was not his fault the nickname never proved popular. Tench Tilghman and later John Laurens and James McHenry became his close friends. Whatever intrigues might be going on elsewhere in the army, the General had selected for his immediate staff a united, harmonious, efficient group.

All these qualities were sorely needed, for the campaign of 1777 opened much less auspiciously than that of the year before, and independence could hardly survive another such. "Gentleman Johnny" Burgoyne was leading a proud, confident army down from Canada. Washington despaired of being able to stop Howe from joining him somewhere in the neighborhood of Albany and effectively splitting the country in half.

Sir William saved him the trouble of trying. Philadelphia was more to that easy-going knight's taste, and, herding his troops aboard ship, he set sail for the Continental capital. The Morristown army got there ahead of him, and enjoyed for a few days the comforts of America's largest city. Patriots cheered the tattered soldiers, while loyalists remained glumly indoors. Early in August there was a quite magnificent ball at which Colonel Hamilton somewhat neglected the ladies

to talk with a Frenchman of his own age who had just received a major general's commission from Congress.

The Marquis de Lafayette, tall and plain and enthusiastic,
was the lion of the hour. Symbolizing the French aristocracy's ardor for democracy (when there could be an ocean
between them and it) and French enmity for England, the
young nobleman had accompanied supplies sent by his country to assist the rebels. Hamilton, who had spoken French
in the West Indies almost as much as English, spent a good
deal of his time with the Marquis. They were together when
Washington risked the Battle of Brandywine in September,
and lost both it and Philadelphia. They had parts at Ger-
mantown three weeks later when fog and the British beat
off one of His Excellency's best planned raids. Hamilton was
still helping to bring order out of the resulting chaos when
news from the north turned the tide of the Revolution.

While Howe was settling himself comfortably in Philadelphia with the handsome Mrs. Loring, Gentleman Johnny
had been running into strange wilderness difficulties and un-
orthodox American troops. On October 17, General Horatio
Gates reaped the reward of work done by General Philip
Schuyler, a New York patroon, and General Benedict
Arnold, a New Haven merchant. He accepted Burgoyne's
surrender of 6,000 men at Saratoga, brought France into the
war and sent a thrill of exultation through the country. The
exploit also sent Colonel Hamilton north on a delicate mission.

Washington could think of no one better fitted than his
youngest staff officer to induce a triumphant general to give
up a large part of his victorious army. Technically, of course,
the Commander-in-Chief had only to issue the order. Actually it was not that simple. Gates, vain and stubborn, was
basking in the glory of extravagant praise and cocking an
attentive ear to the many in and out of Congress who said
that the victor of Saratoga was better qualified for command
than the consistent loser from Mount Vernon. To compel

such a popular hero to part with a couple of brigades against his will might precipitate a crisis. Hamilton was to avoid that but get the men, and his instructions gave him the widest possible latitude.

Posting rapidly northward, he heard nothing but lush encomiums on the man he was to meet. However, a young Colonel who had remained unawed by Washington was not likely to fall victim to the glamor of a Gates. Pausing at Fishkill to demand that 1,000 of General Putnam's men be marched to Pennsylvania at once—an order given more peremptorily than the old wolf killer liked—he hurried on to Albany, where he had been invited to enjoy the hospitality of Washington's old friend, Schuyler.

At his first interview with Gates he employed tact, although he found it difficult in the face of that General's habitual sneering expression. He wanted two of the northern army's three brigades, but Gates, looking down his long nose at the small figure of Washington's emissary, refused to send more than one.

"The force of [his] reasons did by no means strike me," the twenty-year-old Colonel wrote his chief, "and I did every thing in my power to show they were unsubstantial."

Arguing politely, he found it hard to refrain from using the full powers with which he had been furnished, but youthful impetuosity was not one of his youthful faults. Reflecting—so he told Washington at some length—that Gates's popularity was too great to be defied with prudence, he accepted the offer of one brigade and reported that, added to Putnam's thousand, the total would not be far short of what Washington wanted.

Next day, however, he learned that Gates had detailed the smallest of his three brigades for the march, and proposed to keep a large force uselessly garrisoning posts that were not threatened. Obviously it was time to take a high tone with the hero, and Hamilton enjoyed that tone. But he was still prudent. "Having given General Gates a little time to recollect himself," as he wrote Washington, he prepared to exercise his authority, but so circumspectly that Gates, whose essential timidity he had shrewdly divined behind the sneers and bluster, need not feel goaded into defiance. He made it quite plain that he could go further, and then phrased his order for a stronger brigade in the form of a request already granted, writing:

"I indispensably owe it to my duty to desire in His Excellency's name that another may go instead of the one intended, and without loss of time. As it may be conducive to dispatch to send Glover's brigade, if agreeable to you, you will give orders accordingly.

"I have the honor to be,
"With real respect and esteem,
"Sir, your most obedient servant,
"A. HAMILTON."

"I approve entirely of all the steps you have taken, and have only to wish that the exertions of those you have had to deal with, had kept pace with your zeal and good intentions," Washington praised him.

A triumph over the hero of Saratoga was not the only pleasant memory that Hamilton brought back from Albany. The Schuyler hospitality had been delightful and the Schuyler girls were more charming than the Livingstons, to whom they were related. There was one for every taste. Angelica, witty, well-educated and well-read, was quite a lady of fashion and the belle of Albany. Gertrude was the family heroine, having rescued a baby sister during an Indian raid on their home and narrowly missed being tomahawked on her own staircase. Peggy was a flirt and a tomboy. But Colonel Hamilton, with judicious passion, singled out the plainest, quietest of the brood, Elizabeth.

She was not at all hard to look at, only plain in comparison with the beautiful Angelica or her cousin, Sarah Jay, who was lovely enough to be mistaken in Paris for Marie

Antoinette. Betsey Schuyler, six months younger than Hamilton, was small, with an attractive figure, large, dark eyes, a fine brown skin and black hair. While Angelica was acquiring great erudition at the finest of colonial seminaries for young ladies, located in New Rochelle, her sister was learning how to manage a household and take care of children, gaining practial experience from a swarm of younger brothers and sisters. Descended from the greatest Dutch families of the province—her mother was a Van Renssalaer, fourth in direct line from the first patroon—she was acknowledged in the family circle to be the best-natured and most modest of them all. Hamilton could admire these solid qualities, and the girl was prepared to adore the slim, handsome stranger with the beautiful manners, ready tongue and romantic uniform of his country's defenders.

Of course her father had a finer uniform, but General Schuyler was hardly a romantic figure, even to those who loved him. In his more martial moments, he suffered badly from gout and the most his friends could say for his very Dutch appearance was that, in spite of an enormous nose and small eyes, he had an honest face. He also had more ability than the description usually implies. He welcomed his old friend's aide heartily to the big, yellow, many-windowed Schuyler mansion, showed him the scar on the magnificent bannister where the tomahawk aimed at Gertrude had struck, and gave him some sound advice about Gates.

Riding back to headquarters, and being laid up on the way by a fever, the Colonel thought of Betsey Schuyler and decided to write. Her acquaintance and the success of his mission gave him cause to be well pleased with himself, which was fortunate since he and the men for whom he was responsible were joining the main army just in time to go into winter camp, and that camp was Valley Forge.

Eleven thousand men staggered over the icy roads into the snow-covered hills above Philadelphia. The staff, riding in behind them, could see the line of march traced in blood and hear Washington raging against the commissary, which had been paid for enough shoes, clothing and blankets for a bigger army. But money had been embezzled, stores sold to civilians and supplies left behind for lack of teams and wagons, while officers of the line bickered for their own saddle horses and elaborate baggage, each insisting that his and his State's prestige depended upon a showy mount and a pile of luggage.

While the soldiers were building log shelters and standing sentry with their feet in their hats to keep from freezing their toes, the General lived in a tent and kept Hamilton busy drafting sharp complaints to Congress. Alternately he stormed and pleaded, demanding action on behalf of "the naked and distressed soldiers." The eloquent letters were without effect, and by the time the huts were built—by all except some clumsy city fellows who were slow at this work —nearly 3,000 were unfit for duty because they didn't have enough clothes to go out in. By early February another thousand were in the same condition, not to mention the sick. Food was scarce; the splendid oaks of Valley Forge disappeared under the axes of the wood-cutting parties; the horses died of starvation faster than the weakened men could dispose of the bodies.

Even for the staff it was a bad winter. Early in January Mrs. Deborah Hewes moved out of her house—a solid, Pennsylvania stone building of two stories with a one-story wing —and Washington moved in with his family. Their main meal at three o'clock was often no more than a little meat, some frozen potatoes, army bread and hickory nuts for dessert, a meal the rank and file would have considered unbelievable luxury. Most of the time there was no wine at all, and the Commander-in-Chief, once so careful in the selection of his Madeira, was reduced to very plebeian toping, John Adams noted, and "entertains his friends with rum and water." Adams thought it a fine gesture of economy and patriotism. The staff thought it a terrible hardship.

There was, happily, a lighter side. Lady Washington arrived in camp in February and relieved the monotony of toddy with occasional parties at which she served tea and coffee. There was some informal dancing and cards, of which the General was fond, and singing in the evenings. Hamilton occasionally obliged with the one tune he knew, warbling without much beauty but with excellent gesticulation:

> 'Twas in the merry month of May
>   When bees from flower to flower did hum,
> Soldiers through the town marched gay,
>   The village flew to the sound of the drum.
>
> The clergyman sat in his study within
> Devising new ways to battle with sin;
> A knock was heard at the parsonage door,
> And the Sergeant's sword clanged on the floor.
>
> "We're going to war, and when we die
> We'll want a man of God near by,
> So bring your Bible and follow the drum."

The men, equally cheered by feminine companionship, freely sharing their discomforts with a horde of wives and others, sang more ribald numbers, were drilled incessantly in the snow by the newly-arrived Baron von Steuben and scoured the countryside for food. They found little, for Howe was paying gold for supplies, and before the winter was half over the once-rich farms were swept bare for many miles around.

But spring came early, and as the shad began to run in the Schuylkill, the food problem was solved. Even lightly clad men were venturing out of doors, playing at the father of baseball, with the father of his country taking a hand now and then, although most of his officers preferred a more gentlemanly form of cricket. There were foot races, with a young John Marshall winning the nickname of "Silver Heels" because of his fleetness and the white yarn knitted into his stockings, for the runner disdained shoes. Congress improved its time by banning theatricals and other frivolities in the army, but much sounder legislation had proved unenforceable. The General, who was moderately fond of the play, decided to use his dictatorship. He authorized performances in the Valley Forge bakeshop, where on May 11 he presided over "a numerous and splendid audience" that saw the officers present Addison's "Cato."

The British, meanwhile, were quiet, living high in Philadelphia and giving elaborate entertainments which were cherished in the memories of loyal maidens for years afterwards. At the time, though, some of them found it hard not to resent the fact that Sir William always made Mrs. Loring the belle of the ball.

While the Americans were being tempered in the hardships of Valley Forge and being whipped into an army by the Prussian thoroughness of von Steuben, Sir Henry Clinton replaced Howe in the British command. His generalship could devise no better plan than a return to New York, and in the midst of a June heat wave he abandoned Philadelphia. Washington followed cautiously, and as the long, red column of the enemy, encumbered by 1,500 wagons, crawled across the Jersey meadows, there was a council of war, "which," Colonel Hamilton protested furiously, "would have done honor to the most honorable society of midwives, and to them only."

The council's advice not to attack caused this outburst, but Washington for once rose to his aide's expectations by overruling the decision, and on one of the hottest, muggiest days anyone could remember the Battle of Monmouth was fought in vain.

Hamilton was in a state of great exaltation throughout the combat. Painfully hurt when his horse was shot and fell on him, he continued amid the confusion of that day of disobeyed or misunderstood orders to gallop with messages, seek information and inspire the despondent. His West Indies upbringing served him well, for while men were dropping faster from the heat than from the British bullets, he remained as active as if he had been cool. General Charles Lee, whose cowardice or jealousy or treachery in failing to attack as Washington commanded cost the Americans a victory, thought the young fellow in a "sort of frenzy of valor," but the General was in a bitter frame of mind. He had fallen back and, although not cursed for a poltroon then and there, as later legend had it, he could see Washington's displeasure. Drawing up his men on new ground, he voiced an earnest pledge to be himself the last to leave the field.

"That's right, my dear General," cried the excited Hamilton, flourishing his sword, "and I will stay, and we will die here on this spot."

"I am responsible for something more than my own person," Lee says he retorted. "When I have taken proper measures to get the main body in good position, I will die with you on this spot, if you please."

Neither of them died, although plenty of others did as the poor soldiers marched and countermarched through mud and sand with the famous Jersey mosquitoes doing terrible, impartial execution on both sides, adding to the tortures of thirst, for there was little water to be had all that brutally hot day. Next to the mosquitoes, the British had the best of it, for they were able to draw off unmolested at last, and continued to New York with their 1,500 wagons, while Hamilton flung himself on the bare ground under a tree beside Lafayette to sleep till morning. Not far away Colonel Aaron Burr, who had been in command of a brigade, was also seeking rude repose.

Recriminations, denials, accusations and Lee's court martial kept the Battle of Monmouth a live issue from then until one afternoon in December four men stalked with great solemnity into a little wood four miles from Philadelphia. Colonel John Laurens of the staff, seconded by Colonel Hamilton, had called General Lee to this spot to answer for alleged reflections on Washington "in the grossest and most opprobrious terms of personal abuse." A Major Edwards accompanied the General.

It was to be pistols, as usual, and Colonel Hamilton, participating in his first duel, did not like it. To his logical mind, it did not seem that Washington's honor, which was supposedly the subject of dispute, could be affected by the result of a silly brawl in this isolated glade. However, Laurens, a brilliant and companionable youth from South Carolina, "the Bayard of the Revolution," had become his best friend, and the code of gentlemen was not permeated with Hamilton's good sense. The reluctant second was obliged to agree to the barbarous terms of allowing the combatants to walk toward each other and shoot at will. He watched them hold their fire until they were no more than five or six paces apart. He heard two reports, so close together no one could tell who fired first. And he rejoiced to observe that it was the sarcastic General who had been hit.

The wound was slight, so slight that Lee was all for trying another round. But the code now gave Hamilton a gentlemanly excuse for interfering. He argued that honor had been satisfied, that only "personal enmity" could justify another shot. Major Edwards agreed, and he and Hamilton drew up a formal account of the meeting in which they paid delicate tribute to the conduct of their principals as "strongly marked with all the politeness, generosity, coolness and firmness that ought to characterize a transaction of this nature."

That is more than could have been said for most patriots in their public capacities. The army spent most of 1779 trying to keep alive while its masters in civil office fumbled with improbable theories of administration. Hamilton's clerical work increased, putting him in touch with more and more influential figures. He still wrote voluminously to the New York committee. Washington used Hamilton's French and tact to smooth over jealousies of and about the foreign volunteers and to negotiate schemes of co-operation with the new allies, whose fleet came into American waters this year.

He found time, too, to elaborate theories of credit (prompted by the complete chaos of revolutionary finance) and of government (prompted by the complete helplessness of Congress in getting the states to do anything they didn't like). He reflected on trade and banking and the military situation and even Negro slaves, "for the dictates of humanity, and true policy, equally interest me in this unfortunate class of men." His meditations on this last subject were embodied in a suggestion to his friend Jay, now president of Congress, that several battalions of black troops be raised by promising all volunteers their freedom at the end of the war.

"It is a maxim with some great military judges," he wrote, "that, with sensible officers, soldiers can hardly be too stupid; and, on this principle, it is thought that the Russians would make the best soldiers in the world, if they were under other officers than their own. . . . I mention this because I have frequently heard it objected to the scheme of embodying negroes, that they are too stupid to make soldiers. This is so far from appearing to me a valid objection, that I think their want of cultivation (for their natural faculties are as good as ours), joined to that habit of subordination which they acquire from a life of servitude, will enable them sooner to become soldiers than our white inhabitants."

Southern sensibilities prevented Hamilton's idea from being tried out, and he went back to his military duties, which consisted of attempting to help keep an army on foot. Without any fighting to speak of, the ranks were pretty thin when they went into winter quarters, at Morristown again. Here in the coldest weather ever known, so bitter that sleighs could be driven to Staten Island, the sufferings of Valley Forge were repeated. The staff, however, escaped the worst of them even more successfully than the year before. There was wine again, and a decent table where noble French volunteers were frequent guests and where Washington introduced a pleasing touch of informality by having his youngest aide preside. The lad did this "with an ease, propriety and vivacity" which gave Alexander Graydon "the most favorable impression of his talents and accomplishments."

The Vicomte de Chastellux was equally pleased by the manners of the company and noted with surprise that the table groaned under eight or ten dishes of meat and poultry, a variety of vegetables, pies and puddings, fruit and nuts. He was also astonished by the toasts, which continued for a couple of hours while the General cracked nuts and sipped his wine. The "healths" were set forth by one of the aides —on the day described by Colonel Hamilton—"without order or ceremony."

After a shorter interval than the Vicomte liked, he was called back to table for supper. This time it was only a snack and the toasts were equally light, in what Chastellux took to be the English manner. The claret and Madeira were good, each man pouring into tiny glasses "the quantity you choose without being pressed to take more." Then someone would propose an airy sentiment, the glasses would be raised and emptied and the talk resumed. The polished Vicomte thought it a charming custom, "only a sort of check in the conversation, to remind each individual that he forms part of the company."

Headquarters had greater attractions that winter than wine and Frenchmen. Liberty Hall was not far away, and the Livingston girls were as charming as ever. Lord Stirling's daughters were with him—he was a major general now—and Susan Boudinot lived nearby. For chaperons there were the watchful Martha and General Greene's wife. If there was a dearth of theatricals, the young people made up for it by dancing, sometimes for no better reason than to keep warm and because it was the cheapest recreation to be had. They saw no irony in the fact that one of the most popular tunes this year, when the big rooms of the lovely old Ford mansion were adorned for frivolity, was "A Successful Campaign."

His Excellency could cut a vigorous caper and sometimes joined the younger blades, making up in endurance what he might have lacked in grace. The night he and Mrs. Greene kept the floor together for three mortal hours on end without once sitting down lived in the memory of Harry Knox, and the lady's husband admiringly reported it as "a pretty little frisk."

Colonel Hamilton was no longer quite the slave of the Livingstons that he had once professed himself. His thoughts wandered even so far afield as matrimony, and he invited Laurens, making unsatisfactory war in the South, to find him a wife in the Carolinas. The specifications for the paragon were these:

"She must be young, handsome (I lay most stress upon a good shape), sensible (a little learning will do), well bred (but she must have an aversion to the word *ton*), chaste and tender (I am an enthusiast in my notions of fidelity and fondness), of some good nature, a great deal of generosity (she must neither love money nor scolding, for I dislike equally a termagent and an economist). In politics I am indifferent what side she may be of. I think I have arguments that will easily convert her to mine. As to religion, a moderate stock will satisfy me. She must believe in God and hate a saint."

These were not details that the intending husband made up in his head. He was painting the portrait of a living girl, and he had no need to look for her in the Carolinas. For General Schuyler's daughter had arrived to visit her father, who, although retired from the army into Congress, lent his civilian assistance to his friend the Commander-in-Chief that winter. The letter to Laurens was an admirably accurate description of Betsey. The suggestion that there might be such another in the South was no more than a bit of camouflage designed to disguise from the writer himself, perhaps, that he was about to sacrifice his bachelor freedom. At any rate, by the time he wrote, he had had ample opportunity to decide that he had found the one woman who would have been proud, able and willing to fulfill his notions of what a wife should be.

She had received several letters from the Colonel in the last year, and had heard her father speak admiringly of the lad's sound views on public affairs, which agreed with those of Schuyler. Now the young gallant's violet eyes gazed into her attentive face as he protested in sincere accents an undying affection. He danced and talked and walked and went sleighing with her every moment he could spare from the little log office where he worked. In a few weeks, inspired perhaps by the example of a brother officer, William Duer, who this winter married Lady Kitty Alexander, he was asking formally for her hand and receiving a cordial welcome into New York's aristocracy.

"You cannot, my dear sir, be more happy at the connexion you have formed with my family than I am," wrote the patroon. "Until the child of a parent has made a judicious choice, his heart is in continual anxiety; but this anxiety was removed on the moment I discovered it was on you she had placed her affections."

If it be true that a perfect match consists of one who loves and one who allows himself to be loved, this one was destined for success. Betsey, without desire or ability to shine in intellectual society, was blissfully eager to devote a lifetime to adoring the brilliant Alexander. Hamilton, never so amiable as when appreciated, was prepared to be as good a husband as his nature permitted, and an unfailing politeness, thoughtfulness and tact may wear as well as worship on the part of a husband.

This winter he even added the last, and actually wrote a bit of verse for her. Seventy-five years later their descendants found the scrap of paper, yellow and torn and slightly effaced but lovingly mended with tiny stitches of common thread, in a little sack that she had worn on a chain around her neck for three-quarters of a century. In the neat spidery hand-writing of the man who had died fifty years before her, they read:

Answer to the Inquiry Why I Sighed

Before no mortal ever knew
A love like mine so tender—true—
Completely wretched—you away—
And but half blessed e'en while you stay.

If present love . . . face
Deny you to my fond embrace
No joy unmixed my bosom warms
But when my angel's in my arms.

Thereafter he wrote to Betsey almost as often as to Jay or Duane of the New York committee. But if the world thought the penniless immigrant was marrying above himself, he had no such ideas, nor indeed had the Schuylers. It was he who condescended. True, Betsey was an eminently suitable match for the great man he proposed to be, but there were defects which even when most in love he set himself to correct.

"I entreat you, my charmer," he told her in one of his more amorous epistles, "not to neglect the charges I gave you, particularly that of taking care of yourself and that of employing all your leisure in reading. Nature has been very kind to you, do not neglect to cultivate her gifts and to enable yourself to make the distinguished figure in all respects to which you are entitled to aspire. You excel most of your sex in all the amiable qualities, endeavor to excel them equally in the splendid ones. You can do it if you please, and I shall take pride in it— It will be a fund too to diversify our enjoyments and amusements and fill our moments to advantage."

The happy girl, spurred by these admonitions and by a few more lover-like declarations, such as "I love you more and more every hour," did try. She found that he was right, as usual, and her spelling and grammar began to improve. For her part, she was not an exacting fiancée. She even delighted in the catalogue of qualities which Alexander listed as responsible for his mild infatuation.

"The sweet softness and delicacy of your mind and manners," he wrote, "the elevation of your sentiments, the real goodness of your heart—its tenderness to me—the beauties of your face and person—your unpretending good sense and that innocent simplicity and frankness which pervade your actions, all these appear to me with increasing amiableness, and place you in my estimation above the rest of your sex."

Love and the immense volume of the General's diplomatic and military correspondence failed to consume the young man's energies. He wanted to expend the excess on a sleigh-ride which Lord Stirling was planning over the bay to Staten Island with 2,500 men to surprise the British garrison there. Washington refused him permission, which was a bit of luck, for the raid was a failure and some five hundred of those who took part in it were listed as "slightly frozen." Hamilton, therefore, turned to more sedentary occupations.

His pen wagged on over a wide range of topics not immediately connected with his duties. One of the lighter compositions was an estimate of the enemy formed on a mission to arrange an exchange of prisoners. An admirer of English institutions, Hamilton was not much taken with English men, and in the midst of lavish hospitality, inspired partly by a desire to show the rebels what they were missing in their own poverty-stricken quarters, he wrote:

"Our interview is attended with a good deal of sociability

and good humor, but I begin, notwithstanding, to be tired of our British friends. They do their best to be agreeable and are particularly civil to me, but, after all, they are a compound of grimace and jargon and, out of a certain fashionable routine, are as dull and empty as any gentlemen need to be. One of their principal excellencies consists in swallowing a large quantity of wine every day, and in this I am so unfortunate that I shall make no sort of figure with them."

Dislike of an enemy was coupled with a soldierly distaste for speculators in army supplies. Rage against a particularly flagrant example, an attempt to corner the flour market, sent him back for a moment to his old trade of journalism, and over the signature of *Publius* he did all that words could do to shame the gambler, Congressman Samuel Chase. That type of business man, however, is not reached by phrases, even "an undisputed title to be immortalized in infamy" or "the peculiar privilege of being universally despised." Chase was a good deal more chagrined by the failure of the corner than by newspaper attacks.

His critic's next literary labors, always excepting the incessant Washington correspondence, were in a broader field. One of the reasons for the army's stagnation was the collapse of Continental finances. The currency issued by Congressional authority, backed by nothing except Congressional eloquence, was valued by a suspicious populace no higher than the oratory. French assistance was just beginning to make an impression, but local jealousies had nullified even reasonable Congressional requisitions. One shrewd French officer noticed that "this country suffers more from its internal management than from the war itself." Hamilton heard from Duane, who had been sent to Congress and could speak from the heart as well as from firsthand experience:

"To know the value of domestic enjoyment, next to headquarters, I recommend the chair at the Board of Treasury, for ten months of a session in which both our friends and foes are waging a successful war against the public credit."

Things were so desperate that the leaders, who professed to believe one-man control of any department smacked of tyranny, were preparing to sacrifice principle and give Robert Morris complete charge of the non-existent finances. Morris's reputation stood very high. He was an unusually successful merchant who had worked hard in committees and at the same time astounded the impressionable Chastellux by his knack for war profits, estimated by the Vicomte at £300,-000 to £400,000. It was characteristic of Hamilton that he supposed he could give this man lessons in political economy, and no less characteristic that he was right.

In a letter of some 8,000 words, complete with footnotes and citations of authorities, he outlined to Morris a comprehensive system of public credit to be founded on a foreign loan, a bank, a responsible minister of finance and some taxes in kind. The argument was reinforced with examples drawn from the history of European states and Adam Smith's new book, "The Wealth of Nations." Behind the quotations and the borrowings was a more acute understanding of the potentialities of the capitalist system than any other man in America possessed. Hamilton had already asserted that "a vast majority of mankind is entirely biased by motives of self-interest." Centralization of financial power working through that motive was what he recommended, for, he said:

"The safest reliance of every government is on men's interests. This is a principle of human nature, on which all political speculation, to be just, must be founded."

It was a principle to which he clung all his life, and the young economist further warned Morris:

"The only plan that can preserve the currency is one that will make it the *immediate* interest of the moneyed men to co-operate with the government in its support."

Hamilton thereupon proceeded to an analysis of inflation that anticipated all the wisdom of the next hundred years on the subject, but he was cautious about showering it unasked on Morris. Prudently he selected the pseudonym of James

Montague—a hint again of the Whig financial genius of the previous century—and proposed to avow his real identity "if I offer anything new and useful." Morris thought he did, and one more influential citizen had discovered the merits of Alexander Hamilton.

An even longer exposition of the staff officer's views went to Duane, but this time by request. It had needed little urging. The Colonel was writing to everyone he knew on the necessity for a strong government, one that would put some vigor into the lethargic conduct of the war. He even wrote of it to Betsey, who doubtless read with admiration if she didn't understand what he was talking about:

"I think our safety depends on a total change of system, and this change will only be produced by misfortune."

The letter to Duane went beyond the problems of credit and currency. It proposed a new form of national government, "a solid coercive union" which would consider the states as no more than convenient subdivisions for local matters. The author declared Congress "should have considered themselves as vested with full power *to preserve the republic from harm.*" It was a doctrine of implied powers in broadest form, but Hamilton argued that the word "government" means a complete sovereignty having the force of a law of nature. He scouted the theory that a sovereign, independent nation in Congress assembled could be prevented from carrying out a much-needed task for its citizens by any legal quibbles about spheres of authority. He professed contempt for the argument that the states were the sovereign nations. Again his composition bristled with historical precedents and made a deep impression.

The system, of course, was not changed, and a few days after he had sent his advice to Duane, the reformer was riding to Hartford in Washington's suite to confer with the Comte de Rochambeau, the French commander, on joint operations that might effect something great. But, as if to lend point to Hamilton's recent writings on finance, the entire resources of the headquarters staff, when pooled, amounted to $8,000 in Continental paper. Washington seriously doubted that it would be enough to buy food for the little party. Fortunately, the governor of Connecticut saved them embarrassment by issuing orders that they were to be treated as guests of the State, so the conference was held without interruptions from importunate innkeepers.

Returning with no prospects of wonderful achievements, the cavalcade rode in pleasant late September weather through scenery that might have caused them to exclaim in admiration if they had not been so used to it. His Excellency proposed on the way to inspect the important Hudson River defenses at West Point, a mere formality since the vigilant, efficient General Benedict Arnold was in command there, and Washington placed implicit confidence in him. Hamilton was ordered to go ahead to prepare for the General's reception, and he trotted briskly forward in the golden early sunlight of September 24, 1780, for his mission was unusually welcome. Arnold's headquarters were in the exceptionally comfortable Robinson mansion, Arnold's table was exceptionally elegant, and Arnold's wife exceptionally attractive.

IX

THE GENERAL LOSES HIS TEMPER

ALL THE DAYS OF HIS LIFE HAMILTON NEVER CAME AS SO UN-
desired a guest as on the morning he rode innocently up to
the Robinson mansion with a smile on his wide, well-shaped
mouth and an appetite for breakfast and harmless flirtation
in his well-groomed person. General Arnold, who had spent
the last few days arranging to let the British capture West
Point and perhaps Washington as well, had not expected the
Commander-in-Chief so soon. He was not ready, and before
he could adapt his plans to the situation he received news
that showed him he never could be ready.

From one of the advanced outposts came a message that
Major John André, the British adjutant, masquerading as a
Mr. Anderson, had been taken in civilian dress inside the
lines. Papers found on him were being sent forthwith to
Washington. Arnold knew those papers. He had written
them himself. They embodied a detailed plan for the betrayal of West Point, which would give Sir Henry Clinton a
chance to split the United States in half, as Burgoyne had
failed to do.

It was a brilliant, careful scheme to end a war, reunite an
empire and become a hero, but it was crashing in ruins because of an unlucky mischance. Washington would arrive at
any moment; Hamilton was walking in the garden. There
was a bare possibility of escaping the firing squad if horse
and boat were quick enough. In a way it was like the emergencies that had brought out Arnold's heroic qualities at
Ticonderoga, Quebec, Saratoga and Lake Champlain.

The big man with the limp acquired in the service of a

country that was to make his name synonymous with treason acted instantly. A word of farewell and explanation to his wife upstairs and he was gone, with the one scream she uttered before she fainted still ringing in his ears. Down to the river he rode, leaving a concerned Colonel Hamilton to worry about his lovely hostess's sudden indisposition.

Benedict Arnold was in his barge, urging his rowers to greater speed in the direction of the British frigate *Vulture* when the Colonel's puzzlement was resolved into horror. The papers for Washington had been delivered to the aide, and he was reading the story of a hero turned villain. Furiously he set out in pursuit, racing his horse madly as far as Verplanck's Point. It was too late. The *Vulture* with Arnold on board was dropping down the river to New York. Pausing to send off some instructions for repelling the scheduled attack on West Point, although he rightly doubted that the British would attempt it now, Hamilton came back to Arnold's late headquarters to find bedlam.

Washington was there, pale and ominously calm as danger always encountered him, giving orders to put the defenders on the alert, to push new redoubts to completion, to hasten the reinforcements Hamilton had already requested. Messengers mounted and galloped away. Officers addressed each other in incoherent rage, unable to express their fury and shame. And in her room Peggy Arnold, roused from her faint, was shrieking that George Washington had come to murder her infant.

Neither then nor later did the men who discussed that blasted career care to inquire just why Benedict Arnold turned upon the cause he had done so much to promote. Resolutely they ignored the shabby treatment with which Congress had rewarded his most glorious deeds, the shameful petty persecution with which little politicians had dogged him, the gradual conviction that such men could never govern a country and that it were better to return to British rule under guarantees against tyranny. They made no allowances for the effect upon his sentiments of an adored young bride with the loyalist views of her well-to-do Philadelphia family. They simply set him down as the blackest traitor since Judas and exhausted ingenuity in seeking epithets strong enough to describe him.

Hamilton felt and spoke with the rest. But the Colonel, always clear-sighted in estimating the limitations of his own sex, never could command the same sound judgment where women were concerned, especially if they were pretty. A good-looking girl, in his eyes, was invariably as good as her looks, and by that standard Peggy Arnold was a paragon of all the virtues. Hamilton, who was to be deceived by lesser charms than those of the golden-haired beauty who raved and moaned that she was the victim of a plot, was stirred to anguished sympathy.

"Every thing affecting in female tears, or in the misfortunes of beauty; every thing pathetic in the wounded tenderness of a wife, or in the apprehensive fondness of a mother; and, till I have reason to change the opinion, I will add, every thing amiable in suffering innocence; conspired to make her an object of sympathy to all present," he told Laurens.

Next day the susceptible Colonel offered his utmost services to the stricken Peggy, who was by no means certain how much of her share in the conspiracy was known. He wrote to Betsey, sure that she would understand the nobility of the sentiments that moved him:

"She received us in bed, with every circumstance that would interest our sympathy, and her sufferings were so eloquent, that I wished myself her brother, to have a right to become her defender. As it is, I have entreated her to enable me to give her proofs of my friendship. Could I forgive Arnold for sacrificing his honor, reputation, and duty, I could not forgive him for acting a part that must have forfeited the esteem of so fine a woman."

It is a pleasing coincidence that a few days later Colonel

Aaron Burr was subjected to the same affecting scenes, and reached a different, more cynical and more accurate conclusion. Burr, quite as interested in feminine charms as Hamilton, was to amass an even more imposing array of conquests, but there is no record that any woman ever succeeded in deceiving that gay spirit. Peggy Arnold, traveling by easy stages to her family in Philadelphia, stopped off at the home of Mrs. Theodosia Prevost, who had won the gallant Burr's vagrant heart. That gentleman, coming to call, was struck with the artificiality of the Arnold hysteria. Later he noted that in a moment of confidence the lovely Peggy confessed to Mrs. Prevost that she was weary of playing the hypocrite. Burr formed the very shrewd notion that it was largely owing to her "great persuasion and unceasing perseverance" that Arnold had been seduced into becoming a traitor.

Meanwhile Colonel Hamilton's sympathies were being kept alive by the sad plight of Major André. There, but for his brains, was just such a man as Hamilton aspired to be and very nearly was. André, handsome, brave, possessed of a pretty wit, pleasing voice, facility in producing the minor literature of the day, a talent for drawing and exquisite taste in dress, was the complete gentleman of his time. That such a dainty fellow should die shamefully on the gallows saddened more callous natures than Hamilton's. Washington's aide was assiduous in little attentions to the prisoner, and he vainly pleaded that the spy be shot instead of hanged.

Washington, indeed, was reluctant to do either. He wanted Arnold, not André, and he cherished a faint hope that, facing ignominious death, André might be persuaded to request Clinton to make the exchange. Hamilton was assigned to the mission, but for once he begged off. He did not want to be thought so mean himself as to urge meanness on another.

"I confess to you," he told Betsey, "I had the weakness to value the esteem of a dying man, because I reverenced his merit."

Others undertook to advance the suggestion, only to be

repulsed with quiet scorn, and André went firmly to his fate
—another victim, his tearful executioners declared, of Arnold's baseness.

"Never, perhaps, did any man suffer death with more
justice, or deserve it less," Hamilton cried.

Tragedy, however, could not becloud the sympathetic
Colonel's horizon for long. He was to be married in two
months, and he wished to bring his bride a more brilliant
title than that of military secretary. In November he was
importuning Washington for an opportunity "to act a conspicuous part in some enterprise that might perhaps raise my
character as a soldier above mediocrity." There was an independent command over some two hundred men going, and
Hamilton thought he had earned it. Washington, who
needed his secretary, refused, and the friendly Lafayette suggested that he might be joined with the venerable Franklin
in the embassy to France. This was for Congress to reject,
which it did at once, for the candidate was known only to a
few members, and he had offended several of these—Chase,
for example.

Actually Hamilton did not try for this place, since he knew
Laurens wanted it so that he might have a chance to work for
the liberation of his father, then imprisoned in the Tower
of London. The Bayard of the Revolution was appointed,
and his former second rejoiced, for of all the men he ever
met—great, wise, brave, talented, witty, learned and amiable
—Laurens was the only one who extorted from the Creole
immigrant a genuinely friendly devotion. He was kind and
considerate to many; he produced enormous stacks of letters
to an astounding variety of correspondents, but to the South
Carolinian alone could he write, the occasion being his comrade's departure from the staff, in this vein:

"Cold in my professions—warm in my friendships—I wish,
my dear Laurens, it were in my power by actions, rather than
words, to convince you that I love you. I shall only tell you,
that till you bid us adieu, I hardly knew the value you had

taught my heart to set upon you. Indeed, my friend, it was not well done. You know the opinion I entertain of mankind; and how much it is my desire to preserve myself free from particular attachments, and to keep my happiness independent of the caprices of others. You should not have taken advantage of my sensibility, to steal into my affections without my consent."

Not even to make Betsey an ambassador's wife would he press his claims to a post his friend was seeking, but never again did he allow himself to be put in such a position by the ties of friendship. When Laurens was killed in battle at twenty-eight, Hamilton mourned him more sincerely than a brother, but did not replace him.

It was a somewhat disgruntled lieutenant colonel who took leave in December and rode north to Albany for his wedding. Disgruntled, that is, so far as professional prospects were concerned, for he had no doubts about the wisdom of his matrimonial venture. He had been, he confessed, "from a rational sort of being and a professed contemner of Cupid metamorphosed into the veriest inamorato." That was an exaggeration, but he was able to control his dissatisfaction as he came into the Schuyler mansion, where a few days before Christmas, 1780, he made Betsey the proudest girl in America.

It was, everyone agreed, a brilliant wedding and an ideal match. James McHenry, the young Irish army surgeon turned aide de camp, tuned up his lyre to the breaking point, called on all the Muses and poured forth a lyric to Hymen in which Love, Genius, Plutus, Prudence and a dozen more symbolical personages tumbled in incongruous, verbose confusion to the close:

> All these attendants *Ham* are thine,
> Be't yours to treat them as divine;
> To cherish what keeps love alive;
> What makes us young at sixty-five;

What lends the eye its earliest fires;
What rightly managed still inspires.

Wedded bliss had either dulled the bridegroom's critical
faculties or rendered him for the moment more kindly than
usual in his verdict on a friend's literary output, for he
replied:

"I see by perseverence all ladies may be won. The Muses
begin to be civil to you, in spite of Apollo and my prognosis.
You know I have often told you, you wrote prose well but
had no genius for poetry. I retract."

The mood of gentle tolerance—and lapse from the best
form of spelling—did not last. Returning to the army after a
brief wedding trip, the young husband was less than ever satisfied with what seemed decidedly a "groveling condition"
for a Schuyler son-in-law. It could not be said that marriage
made him arrogant; he had been that before. The "bastard
brat of Scots pedlar" had come far to be able to enter so distinguished a family, and nothing showed the distance as
much as the fact that not a single member of his circle who
wrote about the wedding hinted that Hamilton had improved his social position or acquired valuable connections.
In a few years he had so impressed his personality upon his
friends that they took for granted his being a great man.

If there was an exception to this opinion, it was Washington. Not that the General doubted his aide's talents, but he
insisted on employing them where they would do the most
good. That was a duty, and His Excellency had very uncompromising notions about duty. That he had grown fond of
the lad did not enter into the matter. Neither did the young
fellow's repeated requests for a transfer. Neither did the fact
that he had become the son-in-law of the only man to whom
Washington at this period subscribed himself "your affectionate." Hamilton was put back to his papers and driven
hard, while distaste for his position swelled within him.

February 16, 1781, began like any other day at New Windsor headquarters, full of troubles, worry and bad news for the General, full of work for the aides. Hamilton, running downstairs to send an important letter to the commissary, passed Washington and was told to report back at once. On the way he was stopped by Lafayette for "about a minute on a matter of business." Then, excusing himself "in a manner which, but for our intimacy, would have been more than abrupt," he ran up the steps. At the top of them, not in his room as usual, stood a Commander-in-Chief in a towering passion. For it was only over trifles these days that Washington dared seek the relief of temperamental outbursts, and his staff, more often than not, was the butt of them. Now he loomed over the little Colonel, his face pale so that the small-pox scars stood out in bolder relief. The fine figure seemed to swell, the powerful hands clenched and the never very strong voice took on an unaccustomed resonance.

"Colonel Hamilton," he stormed angrily, "you have kept me waiting at the head of the stairs these ten minutes. I must tell you, sir, you treat me with disrespect."

To both Washington and Hamilton, that was a more serious charge than an irreverent generation might imagine. The younger man, feeling that an injustice had been perpetrated upon him, nevertheless retained his capacity for rapid calculation. It was a chance he had been waiting for, and so, drawing himself to his full height until the top of his head almost reached His Excellency's chin, he replied, "without petulancy, but with decision," he thought later:

"I am not conscious of it, sir; but since you have thought it necessary to tell me so, we part."

"Very well, sir," snapped the General, "if it be your choice."

For a moment Hamilton, rosy, boyish and very serious, confronted the full fury of a famous temper. Then the pair separated with great dignity, and it is tribute to Washington's good sense and good nature that he quickly swallowed both anger and pride and made overtures that almost amounted to an apology.

"In less than an hour after," Hamilton recorded complacently, "Tilghman came to me in the General's name, assuring me of great confidence in my abilities, integrity, usefulness, etc.; and of his desire, in a candid conversation, to heal a difference which could not have happened but in a moment of passion. I requested Mr. Tilghman to tell him—1st. That I had taken my resolution in a manner not to be revoked. 2d. That, as a conversation could serve no other purpose than to produce explanations, mutually disagreeable, yet I would be happy if he would permit me to decline it. 3d. That though determined to leave the family, the same principles which had kept me so long in it, would continue to direct my conduct towards him when out of it. 4th. That, however, I did not wish to distress him, or the public business, by quitting him before he could derive other assistance by the return of some of the gentlemen who were absent. 5th. And that, in the mean time, it depended on him, to let our behavior to each other be the same as if nothing had happened. He consented to decline the conversation, and thanked me for my offer of continuing my aid in the manner I had mentioned."

Oddly enough, it was Hamilton who professed himself the injured party. He was to grow accustomed to vicious and violent attacks and be able to ignore them, but he never lost a keen sensitiveness to imagined slights. There was the less excuse for this emotion in the present instance because, he wrote Schuyler, his resignation was "the deliberate result of maxims I had long formed for the government of my conduct."

"I always disliked the office of aid-de-camp," he added, "as having in it a kind of personal dependence. . . . I was always determined, if ever there should be a breach between us, never to consent to an accomodation."

Consciousness of being in the wrong peeps through his

sneering references to "the Great Man" in an account of the split to McHenry, and even more in the version of the affair which he thought it necessary to furnish Schuyler. He complained that Washington was "neither remarkable for delicacy nor good temper." He accused his chief of "self-love," predicted that he "would never forgive me for what it would regard as a humiliation." And then he flung out:

"For three years past I have felt no friendship for him and have professed none. The truth is, our dispositions are the opposites of each other, and the pride of my temper would not suffer me to profess what I did not feel. Indeed, when advances of this kind have been made to me on his part, they were received in a manner that showed at least that I had no desire to court them. . . .

"You are too good a judge of human nature not to be sensible how this conduct in me must have operated on a man to whom all the world is offering incense."

In an almost painful effort to be fair, he went on in a tone of childish condescension that is one of the few signs in his correspondence at this time that he was only twenty-four:

"The General is a very honest man. His competitors have slender abilities, and less integrity. His popularity has often been essential to the safety of America, and is still of great importance to it. . . . I think it necessary he should be supported."

It was well for the angry young man's future career that his splenetic analysis of Washington's character was almost wholly mistaken.

X

FAMILY MAN

IF HAMILTON EXPECTED HIS FRIENDS TO RALLY ROUND WITH praise for his haughty rejection of the General's advances, he was disappointed. Carefully avoiding any encroachment on his tender dignity and all appearance of dictating where he might consider his honor to be involved, they nevertheless indicated quite plainly their disapproval. Lafayette and Tilghman argued that he held his pride too high. Washington was still in a forgiving mood, and Schuyler wrote cautiously:

"I do not mean to reprehend the maxims you have formed for your conduct. They are laudable, and, though generally approved, yet times and circumstances sometimes render a deviation necessary and justifiable."

Schuyler thought the present was such a time. Hamilton himself knew it was, for only a few weeks earlier he had written:

"I find our prospects are infinitely worse than they have been at any period of the war, and unless some expedient can be instantly adopted, a dissolution of the army for want of subsistence is unavoidable. . . . We have never experienced a like extremity at any period of the war."

Even his own arguments could not move him. He knew as well as Schuyler where he was most useful, but nearly four years under the orders of a greater man than himself brought out the worst traits in Hamilton's character. He chafed under "the groveling condition of a clerk," resented reproof as an insult and rejected the most well-meant advice with scorn if it did not agree with his views.

In this mood, he went home to Betsey and begot himself
a child. But domesticity was only briefly consoling. Soon he
was writing Washington that he was still a lieutenant colonel
and wanted a command in some light corps. He dreamed yet
of an exploit to make him famous, and therefore sought a
post with troops usually used on detached service where a
colonel could accomplish something great on his own. In refusing the request, the General stooped to what was for him
a detailed and friendly explanation. He could not, he wrote,
push a brevet staff officer into a line command over the heads
of deserving men. He begged Hamilton to believe that no
personal feeling entered into this decision.

Disappointed, the Colonel turned to the arts of peace. He
began a series of newspaper articles on the virtues of a government that would really govern. Against the general opinion that a patriot owed first allegiance to his state, the young
man who had no state put forth strong national views and
called them those of *The Continentalist*. At the same time he
was preparing a 15,000-word guide to financial success for
Robert Morris, who had at last taken over the so-called treasury as its sole head. Perhaps Congress had been scared into
this step by a demonstration of the Philadelphia citizenry,
who, underscoring the worthlessness of the currency, paraded
a wretched cur through the streets tarred and plastered with
Continental dollars instead of the more valuable feathers.

Urging the steps that Morris was already preparing to take,
Hamilton drew an analogy from Montague's financing of
King William's wars, and pointed out:

"A national debt, if it is not excessive, will be to us a national blessing. It will be a powerful cement to our Union."

"I esteem myself much your debtor for this piece," Morris
replied.

Refreshed by these literary exercises, Hamilton returned
to the assault on Washington's principles against promoting
former staff officers over those in the field. Repulsed again,
he determined to leave the delights of a renewed honey-

moon, and rejoined the army to press his claims to active service in an honorable position. He had so little success that in July he resigned his commission, but Tilghman brought it back to him, promising in the General's name speedy participation in field work of an interesting nature. For the army was going to move at last in a joint operation with the French aimed at Washington's old antagonist, Cornwallis, who had been fencing with Greene in the South.

A place could be made for Hamilton in this enterprise. He was very happy about it, gay and excited, but there was a moment when he remembered that he was a prospective father and had a wife who might worry about him. So in August he put his tongue in his cheek and wrote Betsey that honor and duty alone called him to Virginia.

"I cannot announce the fatal necessity, without feeling everything that a fond husband can feel," he added. "I am unhappy; I am unhappy beyond expression. I am unhappy, because I am to be so remote from you; because I am to hear from you less frequently than I am accustomed to do. I am miserable, because I know you will be so; I am wretched at the idea of flying so far from you, without a single hour's interview, to tell you all my pains and all my love. . . . I must go without seeing you—I must go without embracing you;—alas! I must go."

Actually he was in the highest spirits on the six weeks' march, interrupting his happy visions of war and fame only to write to Betsey in September:

"Let others waste their time and their tranquillity in a vain pursuit of power and glory; be it my object to be happy in a quiet retreat with my better angel."

The next month he was hotly resenting an attempt to replace him in the post of most danger at Yorktown, where the unfortunate Cornwallis was bottled up between a French fleet and the allied army. The Colonel won the right to storm a British redoubt which prevented the besiegers from making their circle complete, and on the night of October 14 he earned his little moment of martial glory. Charging at the head of his regiment, he had himself boosted to the top of the earthen slopes of the defense through a brief but hot fire, the first man to stand on the redoubt. It was an easy, quick victory with the loss of only four wounded in his command. Good husband that he had become, he reported to Betsey:

"Two nights ago, my Eliza, my duty and my honor obliged me to take a step in which your happiness was too much risked."

Five days later he watched Cornwallis's sword being surrendered while 8,000 British soldiers and sailors laid down their arms. Hamilton decided to follow their example. The war was over, although peace was still to be formalized, a process that took more than a year. But when the redcoats passed submissively between the long lines of their French and American conquerors, thirteen colonies had achieved their independence. What they would do with it was another problem. What was to become of the men who had won it was equally pressing.

In Hamilton's case the personal factor actually overshadowed for a time the temptations of public life. He was nearly twenty-five, a family man with very firm objections to being supported by a father-in-law, but positively less able to afford domestic luxuries than he had been at fifteen, no better qualified for a profession—except that of arms, which would be useless in the piping days of peace—than he had been when he paced Batteau Street as a student. The task of readjustment after six years of war bewildered a great many of the heroes, but Hamilton decided his future without delay. Like a good many of his colleagues, he proposed to exchange his high-collared blue army coat for the sober black of the law.

The ceremonies attending the surrender of Yorktown, therefore, did not detain him, and he was in Albany, hard at the study of his chosen profession, when his son was born in January, 1782. They named the boy Philip for his grand-

father, and the actuality of parenthood was an additional
stimulus to his father's achieving a quick civilian career.
Hamilton had known what it meant for a child to be dependent on the charity of relatives, and he did not propose to
have that happen to his own.

Methodically as he had crammed knowledge into his head
at King's, he pored over legal tomes, and gave thanks that
his health, which had been delicate at intervals ever since
the fever caught on his mission to Gates, was improving under a regimen prescribed by McHenry. The fellow aide, a
better physician than most of those in active practice, had ordered a diet of plain meats and vegetables, tea and water for
his drink and only three glasses of wine a day. After his stomach returned to normal, the patient was to follow his own
judgment, "for the man who has had ten years experience in
eating and its consequences is a fool if he does not know
how to choose his dishes better than his Doctor."

The diet agreed with Hamilton so well that he was in the
midst of most of the festivities by which Albany celebrated
victory. The little town was very gay that winter. It housed
a good many refugees from Manhattan, which was still in
British hands, but after Yorktown they knew it was only a
question of time before they would return to their homes
and perhaps repay with interest the hardships they had undergone. None of them was merrier than Alexander Hamilton and that other precocious veteran, Aaron Burr. The two
were the life of a dozen parties and became sufficiently intimate to rejoice together because the legislature had disbarred
all Tory lawyers in the State. Since most of the older men
with lucrative practices fell under the ban, there were golden
opportunities waiting for newly qualified patriots.

Two vivacious colonels in their middle twenties, conscious of exceptional talents, surveyed this field with pleasure. They were so much alike that it was inevitable they
should get on well—until acquaintance became too close,
when the similarities of temperament would begin to grate

upon each other. But in Albany in 1782 they were friends.

Seen in company, they appeared to be two different styles of the same model. Much alike in figure, one was dark, the other fair. Burr's black eyes were as large and brilliant as Hamilton's violet ones. His high forehead, straight nose and smiling but firm mouth gave him an expressive charm. Both young men concealed the color of their hair with powder and wore it clubbed behind. Both affected meticulous neatness of dress in bright but not gaudy colors.

Both were in a hurry to get into paying practice, Hamilton because he hated his little family's dependence on Schuyler, Burr because he wanted to get married. The fundamental good judgment which the elder of these two invariably displayed in his appraisals of women had led him to fall in love with the plain Mrs. Theodosia Prevost, some years his senior, widow of a British army officer, mother of growing children and without any fortune to speak of. Like Hamilton, he was adored by his future wife. Like Hamilton, he reciprocated by urging the poor woman to improve her mind. Like Hamilton, his conjugal attitude was distinguished by unwavering courtesy, thoughtfulness and as much fidelity as he could muster. All in all, there was little of old Jonathan Edwards, that "unspottyd lamb of the Lord," in his grandson. But from the second President of Princeton, he had inherited pedagogic instincts that neither ambition nor passion could submerge.

Distractions from study were not altogether social and domestic. Hamilton thought about his military duties for a time, but on March 1 wrote to Washington that he saw no prospects for usefulness in the field.

"The difficulties I experienced last campaign in obtaining a command, will not suffer me to make any further application on that head," he complained, a little maliciously, and then proceeded to resign his pay but not his commission, just in case there should be a call he might wish to answer.

At about the same time he wrote to a friend:

"You cannot imagine how entirely domestic I am growing. I lose all taste for the pursuits of ambition. I sigh for nothing but the company of my wife and baby. The ties of duty alone, or imagined duty, keep me from renouncing public life altogether."

The obstacle to renunciation was an offer from Morris. The Financier wanted Hamilton to take the post of receiver of Continental taxes for New York. He accepted after some bickering over remuneration and assurances that the job need not interfere with his studies. He was to get one-fourth of one per cent. of the New York quota whether or not he collected the entire $373,598, making the pay $934. But he did not take up his duties until he had been admitted to the bar in June.

That a few months of reading should qualify an attorney was not as surprising as it might have been to those who knew only that the general rule was three years' study. The rule was honored largely in the breach when applied to talented heroes in those troubled times. Burr had received his license a few months earlier with no greater preparation. John Marshall, the fleet young soldier of Valley Forge, had his law certificate signed by Governor Thomas Jefferson of Virginia after a desultory reading of Blackstone and six weeks of lectures at William and Mary, where the future Chief Justice's notebooks evidenced more devotion to the charms of the fair Mary Ambler than to torts and replevins.

Hamilton had a solider foundation of legal learning than either Burr or Marshall. He had studied to such purpose that he was able to prepare a little textbook as he went along, and it was so well done that, without any later revision, it was used by several generations of law students.

The author, however, did not put his new knowledge to immediate use. He made a gallant effort to earn his $934, and to that end attended the New York Legislature's session at Poughkeepsie. In spite of all he had witnessed of state reluctance to share the Continental burden, he thought so well of

himself that he really believed the New Yorkers would surrender $373,598 to his eloquence. Most of them, however,
could remember when the entire budget of their province
had been no more than £4,000. The idea of paying Congressional requisitions, furthermore, seemed to many to be a
negation of the whole Revolution. They had fought and won
a war against taxes aggregating a good deal less than $373,
598. Besides, there were more congenial matters for legislation. There were Tories to be ruled out of the professions,
estates to be confiscated, jobs to be distributed, public lands
to be disposed of.

The solons admired the young Receiver's fresh enthusiasm
in the abstract. They rewarded it by passing his draft of a
resolution recommending a convention to prepare a better
union of the states, for most of them looked upon this document as no more than a pious hope. But when Hamilton offered them a neat, co-ordinated system of taxation, with definite sources of revenue allotted to his office, he found that his
lucidity of argument and fervent pleas were ignored. It mattered little to the gentlemen at Poughkeepsie that the army
was decaying in its camp, that convalescent soldiers discharged from the atrociously mismanaged hospitals had to
beg their food in the streets, that a member of Congress was
penning the vicious arraignment:

"Want of Fidelity, Honor, and Humanity in the Doctors
and avarice in the Suttlers, has Slain ten Soldiers to the Enemies one."

To correct this situation, Hamilton once again betook
himself to the press. He supplemented newspaper articles
with private letters to influential men. A few paltry thousands were all he could squeeze out of New York for Morris,
a disappointment which left him lamenting:

"Experience is a continual comment on the worthlessness
of the human race; and the few exceptions we find have the
greater right to be valued in proportion as they are rare.
I know few men estimable, fewer amiable."

That last was sheer bitterness; he knew many amiable men and enjoyed their society in Albany that autumn while he took his first cases and discovered that he had as much instinctive grasp of the law as of business, and that the combination could be very valuable to his clients.

He also learned that his failure with the legislature had not been personal. Members, recalling the persistence and importunity of the Receiver, decided that those qualities might be useful in representing New York in Congress. Perhaps there was something in the fact, too, that he was Schuyler's son-in-law. At any rate, they gave him Schuyler's seat, and summoned him to the temporary capital to get his instructions. It was during this trip that the almost forgotten days of the West Indies were revived in his memory, along with an unpleasant reminder of his illegitimacy. St. Croix, however, seemed very far away, and it was almost with an air of detachment that he reported to Betsey:

"I omitted telling you of a disagreeable piece of intelligence I have received from a gentleman of Georgia. He tells me of the death of my brother Levine. You know the circumstances that abate my distress [one of them was that he and his mother's eldest son had never met] yet my heart acknowledges the rights of a brother. He died rich, but has disposed of the bulk of his fortune to strangers. I am told he has left me a legacy. I did not inquire how much."

Hamilton's heart acknowledged, too, closer family ties than his relationship to Peter Levine. He remembered that he had a full brother, not to mention a parent, and of a sudden he became concerned for those two relics of his West Indian life. He managed to get in touch with his younger brother, James, a true son of their father, somewhat impoverished and confident that a change, any change, would raise him quite suddenly to prosperity. Alexander replied to an expression of these dreams with an offer of £50, advice to remain single if it was not too late and exhortations to "exert your industry for a year or two more where you are." After that he proposed to bring James to the United States and settle him on a farm, a prospect which was not sufficiently alluring to tempt the younger from his islands. Softened by his own paternity, Alexander asked somewhat anxiously:

"What has become of our dear father? It is an age since I have heard from him, or of him though I have written him several letters. . . . My heart bleeds at the recollection of his misfortunes and embarrassments. Sometimes I flatter myself his brothers have extended their support to him, and that he is now enjoying tranquillity and ease; at other times I fear he is suffering in indigence."

Neither of the James Hamiltons could overlook the opportunities inherent in such tender solicitude. Both became consistent borrowers and, it must be said, equally consistent in forgetting to repay. Their benefactor was not meticulous in such matters and never seemed to mind. He was savoring the unfamiliar joys of domesticity, and found them so delightful that he fell into the usual habit of proud fathers, expatiating on the wonders of his seven-months-old offspring and bragging:

"He is truly a very fine young gentleman, the most agreeable in his conversation and manners of any I ever knew, nor less remarkable for his intelligence and sweetness of temper. . . . It is agreed on all hands that he is handsome; his features are good, his eye is not only sprightly and expressive, but it is full of benignity. His attitude, in sitting is, by connoisseurs, esteemed graceful, and he has a method of waving his hand that announces the future orator. He stands, however, somewhat awkwardly and as his legs have not all the delicate slimness of his father's, it is feared he may never excel as much in dancing, which is probably the only accomplishment in which he will not be a model."

Hamilton was still in the same mood in November when he resumed a neglected correspondence with Lafayette by writing:

"I have been employed for the last ten months in rocking

the cradle and studying the art of *fleecing* my neighbors. I am now a grave counsellor-at-law, and shall soon be a grave member of Congress. The Legislature, at their last session, took it into their heads to name me, pretty unanimously, one of their delegates.

"I am going to throw away a few months more in public life, and then retire, a simple citizen and good *paterfamilias*. I set out for Philadelphia in a few days. You see the disposition I am in. You are condemned to run the race of ambition all your life. I am already tired of the career, and dare to leave it."

This preview of Lafayette's fate was clairvoyant. The strangely modest estimate of his own desires could only have been due to an upset stomach, a rarely indulged mood of profound discouragement or a momentary yielding to the convention of disclaiming extravagant aims. Whatever the cause, the insincerity was plain, and did not impose for a moment on the Marquis. Hamilton had not spent six years of his young life in helping to set up a new nation only to retire from competition for positions of power in it. He was aware, more than most of his fellow fighters for independence, that the task of consolidating present gains would be at least as difficult as revolution. He was aware, too, that there were wide, probably irreconcilable differences in the ideas for which the revolutionists had fought.

His own strength in the coming conflict of principles was in large part the thorough understanding he had of his own political philosophy. Others who had not thought their doctrines through to logical conclusions might be swayed this way and that in the struggle. Hamilton, with a clear view of his goal, was not to be diverted from it by opportunist considerations. He knew exactly where he wanted to go, and the Continental Congress's session of 1783 lay in his path.

XI

GENESIS OF A REACTIONARY

AMBITION, LOGIC AND TEMPERAMENT HAD TURNED HAMILTON into a rebel. They never made him a radical, and, like most men of conservative instincts, the more he saw of liberals the less he was attracted by their philosophy. He was as much interested in progress as they, but there were no left turns for him on the march toward an orderly, prosperous society.

"Our separation from the mother country cannot be called a revolution," he once said. "There have been no changes in the laws, no one's interests have been interfered with, everyone remains in his place, and all that is altered is that the seat of government is changed."

This was decidedly an over-simplification. Certainly many of the delegates who gathered in Philadelphia with young Congressman Hamilton in 1783 thought they had made a revolution and were by no means willing to refrain from interference with certain interests. Their chief business at his first session, however, was to wrangle over the diplomatic miracle which Franklin, Adams and Jay had wrought—a treaty of peace so favorable to the thirteen states that it was understandable only on the theory that Great Britain was too thoroughly disgusted to bargain about terms. But in signing it the envoys had violated their instructions to accept no settlement that did not include France.

Gratitude to the ally who had made the American victory possible dictated this, but few nations can afford the luxury of gratitude and fewer still indulge in it. French policy had been governed by a desire to weaken England rather than by sheer love of liberty and America. There were men in Con-

116

gress, however, who knew so little of statecraft that they wished to reject the treaty forthwith. Hamilton was not of their number. Arguing on behalf of ratification, he maintained that it would be folly to sacrifice substantial national interests to a Quixotic loyalty to King Louis. Fortunately the opening of negotiations for a general peace in Europe obviated the need for putting Congressional idealism to the test, and the treaty went through.

Hamilton did not find the attitude of his colleagues toward domestic problems any more consistent with his notions of duty and propriety. He complained that there was no money to meet the national debt, no inclination to pay off the army with anything more substantial than kind words, no desire to grapple boldly with pressing issues. The new member, who had hoped that Congress only needed a strong lead—to be supplied by himself—was soon writing ruefully to Washington:

"We are a body not governed by reason or foresight, but by circumstances."

This was after he had seen twelve states agree to a general customs levy to provide a steady revenue for the Continental government, only to have the measure blocked by the veto of the great and sovereign independency of Rhode Island. Hamilton had listened to member after member declaiming about rights and needs and sacrifices, each of his own community, but hardly anything about broad national problems. The New York delegate's pet proposals for retaining a portion of the army, disbanding the rest with full pay and asserting some authority over the states were heard with admiration for the way he expressed them, and with complete indifference to the principles he expounded.

Overwhelmed by the futility of it all, he was in no frame of mind to adhere strictly to the niceties of political ethics. Always willing to take a shady short cut to an obviously desirable destination, he suggested that Washington use the well-known discontents in the army to threaten Congress. A little mutiny, nothing serious but sufficient to frighten honorable members, of whose courage Hamilton had formed a low estimate, would serve. His Excellency, however, was no more avid of dictatorship in '83 than he had been in '76. It was not for nothing that even in the midst of his greatest triumphs and at the height of his martial fame, the expression "citizen and soldier" was frequently on his lips. It was not for nothing that this most retiring of successful generals put "citizen" first—and meant it.

Mildly he pointed out to his former secretary that mutiny could not be turned on and off at will. An angry army let loose upon its ungrateful masters was not likely to permit itself to be used to effect Hamiltonian policies and then submit meekly to civilian law and order.

Washington's heroic abnegation was beyond Hamilton's powers. Nor was he the man to achieve effective leadership in so fumbling a body as the Continental Congress. He believed its narrow-minded talkers had to be driven, not led. They opposed to his utmost efforts a stubborn stolidity against which mere brilliance battered in vain. Deliberative assemblies are by nature distrustful of the flashing mind that leaps unerringly to its conclusions. Successful parliamentary chieftains who have this quality hide it as thoroughly as they would a moral scandal. Hamilton's arrogance, his almost insulting assumption that lesser men should accept humbly the logic of his ideas, hardly endeared him to colleagues whose prejudices against his policy were far stronger than mere reason. His orations were persuasive, powerful and nullified by an inability to conceal a sense of superiority.

Congress was glad to make use of his literary ability in such matters as a letter to recalcitrant Rhode Island. He was called on again when a small band of soldiers, far removed from Washington's personal influence, rose against injustice and scared the delegates out of what small portion of common sense they possessed. Frantically they called on Pennsylvania to furnish militia for their defense, and when the local

authorities declined, it was Hamilton who drafted the dignified rebuke that almost hid the Congressional jitters from
public view. These services, which seemed to the delegate
himself to be worthless, inspired the partial McHenry to assure him:

"Were you ten years older and twenty thousand pounds
richer, there is no doubt but that you might obtain the suffrages of Congress for the highest office in their gift."

That, however, would not have been high enough for
Hamilton. His disgust for the system of rule by Congressional petition—"influence is not *government*," Washington
put it neatly—had grown in Philadelphia. Seen at first hand,
the impotence of the Confederation was disheartening, but
there was one gleam of hope. He found a Virginia Congressman who shared his views and could defend them as well.
James Madison, whose thirty-two years had been devoted to
study from earliest boyhood, had spent the revolutionary
years in legislative halls. From his books and his colleagues
he had drawn lessons in national principles.

Small, frail, with unimpressive features lit by pale blue
eyes, he wielded a pen as effective as Hamilton's. He could
sway an audience, too, without eloquent flourishes, speaking
quietly as if addressing each auditor in intimate conversation. Unlike his New York colleague, he could carry that tact
into the lobby. He understood that votes are gained by organization rather than by pyrotechnics on the floor.

He and Hamilton were much together that session. The
Virginia planter and the New York lawyer discovered some
congeniality in tastes. Both loved reading and talk. Both
were temperate in an age of heavy drinking. Both wore a
grave air in public and relaxed into genial wit in private.
But the important similarity was that both went home in
1783 convinced that their country was in greater danger
from internal weakness than it had ever been from British
force.

"We have now happily concluded the great work of independence," Hamilton informed Jay, "but much remains to be done to reap the fruits of it. Our prospects are not flattering. Every day proves the inefficacy of the present Confederation."

Madison was writing in the same vein, yet the two greatest constructive thinkers of the country did not reach quite the same conclusions from these premises. In the seclusion of his study and the society of the Virginia aristocracy, Madison was working out a system based on what the eighteenth century had learned from Rousseau to regard as the nobility of human impulses. In the hurly-burly of New York law, business and politics, Hamilton was carrying his low opinion of mankind to its logical end—a conviction that the stupid, vulgar masses should be ruled for their own good by the few "estimable" men, who must be tempted to the task by solid rewards. At twenty he had written perhaps the most liberal sentiment of his life:

"That instability is inherent in the nature of popular governments I think very disputable. . . . A representative democracy, where the right of election is well secured and regulated, and the exercise of the legislative, executive, and judiciary authorities is vested in select persons, chosen really and not nominally by the people, will, in my opinion, be most likely to be happy, regular and durable."

At twenty-six he still endorsed this view, but with reservations. He now emphasized vesting authority in "select" persons, and was not so particular about how they were chosen, for he had observed that in what he considered popular assemblies, "the inquiry constantly is what will *please*, not what *benefit* the people."

The New York Legislature, which inspired this comment, had no pretensions to speaking for the majority of the State's adult citizens. There were high property qualifications attached to the franchise for the Assembly, higher ones for Senate and Governor. Perhaps ten per cent. of the white adult males qualified to vote for Senator. The authors of the

Declaration of Independence had not meant its high-sounding phrases to apply to the landless poor in the North any more than to Negroes in the South. New York was typical of all the states in that its new republican government was designed for the use of its principal property interests. Therefore, even the legislature was not to be permitted to exercise all the power that seemingly was vested in it. Real control was transferred to an inner group, and this by the deliberate aim of the framers of the state constitution, the chief of whom, Jay, summarized his statecraft in the short and simple dictum:

"Those who own the country ought to govern it."

That was the thought that governed creation of a Council of Appointment consisting of the Governor and four Senators chosen by the Assembly. Every state officer except the lieutenant governor and treasurer, including many who now would be regarded as county or municipal servants, were named by these five. The result was America's first political machine based on the spoils system, and the only unforeseen circumstance was that it had fallen into the hands of Jay's opponents. George Clinton, a bright-eyed, jovial ex-brigadier who conformed to a later generation's notions of a professional politician, slipped into the governorship and wielded the patronage club so dexterously that he held the job for eighteen years without interruption.

Contrasting the strong hand of Clinton with the feebleness of Congress, Hamilton could only regret that the Governor's principles did not entitle him to inclusion in the select ranks of the estimable few. For Clinton was one who thought he had taken part in a revolution. So far as he looked beyond the retention of power, he was a believer in states' rights and liberty. This last was a word Hamilton thought much abused. Freedom you couldn't use meant little to him, and he held that government exists for the purpose of maintaining rigid order, protecting property and promoting prosperity, not merely guaranteeing an abstraction. Furthermore, to

Hamilton's restless mind, the property represented by commerce was of more interest because more progressive than
static agrarianism. The merchant, the financier and the
manufacturer, he thought, were the men who owned the
country and ought to enlist the co-operation of the statesman. Agriculture might be left to farmers.

Cherishing these views, he entered New York City at the
end of November, 1783, on the heels of the British evacua-
tion. For the moment he was content to earn a living and
keep up just so much active interest in public affairs as
would enable him to seize an opportunity for promoting the
ideas which were then described as "continental" as opposed
to "provincial." His observation post, being both his home
and office, was on Wall Street at the corner of Broad, a location which did not then bear quite the significance that it
later attained. Wall Street itself was the center of fashion, a
pleasant thoroughfare of solid, almost stately residences, each
with its trees and gardens behind, and the spire of Trinity
Church towering over the whole.

The city had deteriorated to a miserable shabbiness since
Hamilton's student days. The blackened scars of two destruc-
tive fires and the almost equally blighting effects of a military occupation of seven years had left the town of twenty-
odd thousands uncomfortably conscious of having lived
through a war. A momentary revival of trade, perplexing
problems of titles thrown into confusion by the Revolution,
a lush crop of claims and counter-claims for war services and
damages and the necessity for new contracts to rebuild the
city opened a welcome field for litigation. Counselor Hamilton found clients crowding upon him with a rapidity which
most fledgling attorneys experience only in dreams.

The business acumen which had enabled him to handle
Cruger's manifold interests to advantage served him well in
his profession. Soon he was the favorite adviser of New
York's merchants, but he did not specialize and practiced
impartially in cases ranging from knotty points of inter-

national law to wills, assault and petty theft. By the time he had been in practice six months only Aaron Burr could dispute his title to leader of the city's bar. Before a year was out he was taking in students at $150 a year each. He handled so many cases he should have grown rich quickly, but in one respect Hamilton was modest. His fee for an office consultation at this time was £1-10s; for court work he charged £5 a day, not notably cheap for legal services but a good deal less than some of his rivals asked.

Mercantile magnates were attracted by his fervent stand for the sanctity of property more than by the modesty of his fees, and more still by his success in winning cases that involved the defense of personalty from the "anarchic tendencies" of the times. He gained a great deal of fame by defending a rich, unpopular Tory from a poor widow who invoked a Trespass Act newly passed to do for landlords what the disbarring of loyalist attorneys had done for Hamilton. It provided that patriots might collect rent for the use of their property during the British occupation even though the tenants had already been obliged to pay the military. The test of the law was cleverly contrived to make use of popular sympathy for a poor woman who sought justice and back rent from one who was little better than a traitor.

It was a congenial case for Hamilton, since it gave him an opportunity to expound his favorite doctrines—the rights of the rich and the existence of a higher civil power than local government. He won his case on the argument that the Trespass Act violated the peace treaty and that every state was bound by the agreement with Great Britain.

As a pleader, the victor was exercising his talents on behalf of Baron von Steuben, setting himself up as the guardian of a cosmopolitan gentleman exactly twice his age. The Baron was displaying at once the peculiar incapacity of a successful soldier for civil life and a helpless charm that aroused Hamilton's protective instincts. Von Steuben was for long intervals a guest in the Wall Street house, and his host pursued with energy the hopeless task of obtaining from Congress a satisfactory pension for the drillmaster of the Revolution.

Partly in line of professional duty he was also founding a financial institution on the principles he had once expounded to Morris, and putting into its charter a clause that gave the Bank of New York a monopoly in its field. So far as sharing in the investment was concerned, he was the agent of his brother-in-law, John Church, Angelica Schuyler's wealthy English husband, but he had put his influence, eloquence and commercial genius to the task of defeating an agrarian plan for a land bank, a favorite fallacy of farmers who always want to have their land and spend its value too. Hamilton was on the original board of directors of the Bank of New York, but only held the place for the absent Church.

The background for these legal-financial acrobatics was one of increasing bitterness among those citizens Hamilton had once supposed capable of creating a "happy, regular and durable" republic. Many of them were just beginning to realize that the ideals they had fought for had been lost, while the principles of the "moneyed men" triumphed. Even that triumph began to seem a little hollow, for business again was bad after a brief spurt at the war's end, jobs were scarce and one of the earliest New York crime waves swept the city in the summer of 1784, with five men sentenced to death on a single day for robbery and burglary.

The newly appointed Mayor, Hamilton's old correspondent Duane, had his watch stolen, but recovered it and saw the thief branded with a T on the left thumb. Duane, however, was not a popular figure, although a conspicuous one in his gilded and monogrammed coach rolling grandly through the mud, garbage and refuse in the streets as he scattered pigs, dogs and pedestrians alike. There was an ugly spirit abroad, a premonitory rumbling of worse to come and all caused, old Robert Livingston thought, by "restless mecannicks who wish to ingross all to themselves." What most of them wanted was work, but their muttered protests against being left to starve struck fear into the well-to-do, who knew that under similar conditions they would show fight and were inclined to credit the poor with their own ruthless ferocity. However, Duane suavely announced that a "Bridewell is fitting up for the reformation of manners," and the popular discontents smoldered and almost died as rebuilding in the burned out sections of the city relieved unemployment.

There was nothing in the national outlook to offer any encouragement to a lover of order and commercial progress. Robert Morris, who had almost succeeded in pulling Continental finances out of the mire, so that even Thomas Paine exclaimed in approval, had become disgusted with the helpless ignorance of his master, the Congress, and resigned. His place was far from filled by a board of three, and Congress itself was roaming from place to place, hoping perhaps that a change of climate might lend it some strength. More than ever a querulous debating society, it was avoided by many of its own members and for long periods was unable to assemble a quorum for the consideration of resolutions. The remnants of its currency were sunk to worthlessness; its debts were regarded as repudiated.

The only bond that held the states together at all, a common enemy, had been relaxed, and the thirteen sovereign powers were giving a striking imitation of the Italian principalities at their jealous worst. Disputes over navigation of waterways waxed hot. Boundaries and claims to western lands were subjects of bellicose bickerings that sometimes went beyond words to blows. Incipient tariff wars broke out. Some observers thought it only a matter of time, and not long either, before England would be gathering thirteen repentant colonies back into the imperial fold.

The prophets of doom were so loud that they successfully obscured the actual insignificance of their number. Franklin, full of years and wisdom and tolerance, thought the country was exceptionally prosperous and remarked that there never was a time when some individuals did not complain.

"It is always in the power of a small number to make a great clamor," he added shrewdly.

The small number at this time were of imposing influence. They were the big merchants, the wealthier planters, the masters of inherited fortunes invested in negotiable paper— perhaps 160,000 men altogether—all worrying about their threatened domination. The vast majority of the nation's 3,000,000 inhabitants remained entirely disinterested. Workers, slaves, those small farmers who were really independent, owing no one and with an assured market, cared nothing and thought as little about their national government, whether strong or weak. No amount of propaganda could stir them to action for or against any such abstraction as a theory of administration. There was no appeal in it to their interests, and their emotions were untouched.

The favorite lawyer of New York, the lover of order, the admirer of the aristocratic Whig oligarchy watched critically the development of what his clients called chaos. He noted the widespread apathy and the limited enthusiasm. Entering upon an extensive correspondence with business leaders in the chief trading ports from Boston to Charleston (a correspondence he continued all his life) he reached the conclusion that in these men of affairs alone resided the will, the power and the cohesion necessary to establish a form of government that would give Alexander Hamilton's talents full scope. The representative democracy which he had once thought "most likely to be happy, regular and durable" was proving in actual practice, as he saw it, to be most miserable, eccentric and ready to fly to pieces because of its inherent centrifugal discords.

Busy with law cases, dinners, political articles, friends and family—Betsey presented him with a girl in '84—he was working out a class theory of government in which he recognized the principle that later became known as economic determinism, a clear-sightedness which he shared with Madison. But he went beyond the Virginian when he declared:

"All communities divide themselves into the few and the many. The first are the rich and well born, the other the mass of the people. The voice of the people has been said to be the voice of God; and however generally this maxim has been quoted and believed, it is not true in fact. The people are turbulent and changing; they seldom judge or determine right. Give therefore to the first class a distinct, permanent share in the government. They will check the unsteadiness of the second, and as they cannot receive any advantage by a change, they therefore will ever maintain good government."

Men who believed that "the rich and well born" had quite sufficient power were suspicious that the organization through which Hamilton's idea of a permanent share in the government would be carried out was already in existence. This was the Society of the Cincinnati, which owed its inspiration to Harry Knox's literary mind. Reviled as both a pitiful and a dangerous attempt to saddle an hereditary aristocracy upon a free people, the founders of the Society actually had such hopes. Only commissioned officers in the Revolutionary forces were eligible, and their membership was to descend from eldest son to eldest son, a restriction which must in a few generations reduce it to a sufficiently aristocratic exclusiveness. Marking the extinction of professional jealousies, Washington was elected as president general and Horatio Gates as vice president general.

Hamilton was an early member, but his ideal of government envisaged a House of Lords, a Senate, a Council by whatever name it might be called, chosen on somewhat more substantial grounds than possession of an army commission. He was active in the Society, seeing at once that it could become a useful political instrument, but not inclined to push it beyond that point.

In the earliest period of his disgust with the Articles of

Confederation, he had said that things would have to get worse before the country could be ready for the painful effort of making them better. As Congress drifted into New York in 1785 for its usual futile session, he thought things were quite bad enough. The Continentalist might make a play to turn influence into government. To those who gave all their loyalty to a state, to the debtors and small farmers and artisans, to the poor and the incompetent, to libertarian philosophers, it would seem a reactionary regime, only to be established by overthrowing the existing government. But Hamilton was prepared to shoulder the responsibilities of his reactionary principles. The youth who had been converted to rebellion against King George could not be expected to cavil at a little rebellion against the Continental Congress.

XII

FOUNDING FATHER

As the war of independence began with no other aim than to reform British imperialism, so the overthrow of the Continental Congress originated in an effort to make the Confederation work. For several years petitions, resolutions and memorials in favor of a general tariff, a unified currency and country-wide commercial regulations had been showered on Congress. They were met by denunciations of customs duties as a plot to raise the cost of living and by calls for more paper money so that poor men could settle their debts. In many sections the radicals who took seriously the promises and phrases of '76 were growing in influence and numbers. General Harry Knox, alarmed in every inch of his great bulk, summed up their vociferations in a letter to Washington, saying:

"Their creed is that the property of the United States has been protected from the confiscation of Great Britain by the joint exertions of all, and therefore ought to be common property of all. And he that attempts opposition to this creed is an enemy to equity and justice, and ought to be swept from off the face of the earth."

This doctrine terrified men who thought they owned the country, leading them to thoughts of anarchy and the breakdown of civilization. Such perils, as well as possible remedies for the faults of the Union, were sometimes discussed at Mount Vernon, where men of substance from every state, calling on the hero of the Revolution, were entertained with solemn hospitality and drawn out as to their views on the

129

state of the nation. Congress, it was plain, could do nothing for itself. Men of good will would have to act.

The opportunity, partly fostered by these conversations, came when Virginia, smitten with a sudden access of broad-mindedness after concluding a peaceful settlement of differences with Maryland, proposed a conference of all the states for the purpose of a general commercial appeasement. There was nothing revolutionary in the invitation, but some of those who were behind it saw a chance to discuss more than trade.

Among these was Hamilton. He was the most active of the New Yorkers supporting the call, and was rewarded by being selected as one of the State's delegates. Leaving his family, newly augmented by a son named for himself, he set out through the heat of late summer, 1786, for Annapolis. The road was long and bad, the inns atrocious and infested with fleas. But sometimes the delegate was entertained at private homes, and then there would be high talk far into the night. Among his hosts there was unanimity on one point that could hardly fail to commend itself to a traveler. The clamor for internal improvements—better roads and that new craze, canals—was loud among all classes. Obviously these projects could not be undertaken by the states except on short and isolated routes. The need for a central government with money or a binding agreement between local authorities was apparent.

Hamilton rode into Annapolis prepared to work the transportation argument for all it was worth. But it was worth nothing. Eight states had ignored the convention from which so much was expected. The few delegates who did attend deliberated briefly, and then Hamilton prepared a call for another meeting. This time there was to be a definite program for forcing reforms upon the reluctant nation in the name of order and prosperity. But the purpose was shrouded in the statement that the delegates would assemble in Phila-delphia in the following May "to take into consideration the situation of the United States, to devise such further provisions as shall appear to them necessary to render the Constitution of the Federal Government adequate to the exigencies of the Union, and to report such an act for that purpose to the United States in Congress assembled as, when agreed to by them and afterwards confirmed by the Legislature of every State, will effectually provide for the same."

If there were those who thought this meant only what it said, Hamilton was not of their number. He was out for something more than revision of the Articles of Confederation. And as he jogged northward he met news that convinced him it was now or never. For in that autumn, the people of western Massachusetts had risen behind a rough and ready leader, Daniel Shays. The old soldiers had taken up their old muskets against the old grievance, taxes. They asked no more than they thought they had been promised in the Revolution. But to Hamilton, and to the whole class to which he had allied himself, they seemed to threaten all law, all order, all property. And, although the Massachusetts authorities quashed Shays' Rebellion in a sharp fight that was mostly a rebel rout, Continentalists argued that the incident demonstrated the need for a stronger government.

To the political powers in New York, however, it demonstrated no such thing. Clinton, who had his own customs service well staffed with jobs for his supporters, wanted to keep it. He was willing to allow Congress a revenue, he said, but wished his men to collect it. Hamilton, deciding that the popular governor should be taught no political machine can defy the sentiment of a unanimous commercial interest, got himself elected to the Assembly in order to administer the lesson.

His first step was a skillful feint away from his real objective. As soon as the 1787 Legislature was organized, Assemblyman Hamilton introduced a bill to give Congress a definite grant of money. With daring restraint, the author had made it as mild as could be without sacrificing the national treasury to the local lassitude which had hitherto kept it empty. As debate on this perennial proposal droned on, it became apparent that if the measure failed this time, the avowed aims of the Confederation were hardly worth the paper on which the Articles were written.

But Clinton would not give up his grip on the customs patronage, and as the bill went down to defeat, even the most ardent states' rights man saw that some revision in the national government would have to be admitted, unless the Union was to break up into thirteen discordant, warring pieces. Congress itself was stirred sufficiently to place the stamp of its reluctant approval on the Annapolis invitation.

Therefore, when Hamilton offered his next resolution, calling for five delegates to be sent to Philadelphia, there was little opposition. The Clintonians were satisfied to reduce the number to three. Immemorial etiquette of legislative bodies decrees that the proposer of such a resolution must have a place on the delegation, a tradition which alone was responsible for sending Hamilton to the convention, since the Clintonians easily outvoted his friends. For colleagues they gave him Robert Yates and John Lansing, loyal followers of the Governor and sparkling legal lights of the State.

They were shrewd men, but they did not realize that revolutionary plans were maturing in the handsome head of their companion. They had not taken seriously his analysis of the desperate nature of public affairs, which indeed was not at all obvious that spring. Business, perhaps, could have been better, as it always can, but there was brisk building activity again in New York, and the city had never been gayer. Even Governor William Livingston of New Jersey, whose pre-war hospitality at Liberty Hall had delighted a young Creole from St. Croix, thought New Yorkers were setting too lively a pace, considering the parlous nature of the times.

"My principal secretary of state, who is one of my daughters," he complained, "is gone to New York to shake her heels at the balls and assemblies of a metropolis which might as well be more studious of paying its taxes than of instituting expensive diversions."

But Mr. Livingston was an old man, bowed down with the cares of ten years in the executive chair. The more resilient Hamilton saw no harm in dancing while the politico-economic fabric of the Livingston world grew frayed and tattered. There were, after all, only a few weeks for the shaking of heels before both the young dandy and the old Governor would be off for Philadelphia, where at the end of May they and fifty-three other citizens, all of them with what Jay would have called a stake in the community, gathered to carry out "the greatest work ever struck off at a given time by the brain and purpose of mankind."

Ambitious the fifty-five were, but not so ambitious as all that. They had come together in Independence Hall to solve some very pressing and immediate problems affecting their own class particularly and the country in general. Hard-headed and practical almost to a man, they were not working out an ideal for future generations to live by. They were dealing strictly with the present, and soberly suspected that contemporary difficulties would be too much for them without worrying about those to come. It was hardly an auspicious omen that Rhode Island in the prickly pride of her splendid isolation and self-sufficiency had refused to send delegates.

The eminent respectability of the convention hid from posterity and to some extent from themselves that its members were engaged in a high-minded conspiracy to overthrow their existing government. For very early in the proceedings it was obvious that Mr. Hamilton's invitation to consider amendments to the Articles of Confederation had been eye-wash. The majority were plainly bent on a complete new system, and for that reason decreed that the sessions should be held in secret and without any official record. They did not propose to have their labors interrupted or influenced by popular clamor. They knew that if their real purpose should become known, they might not be allowed to finish.

Surveying his colleagues, the youngest of their number was not greatly impressed with the assembled genius. But he was pleased to note that a broad cross section of the country's property interests—and nothing else—sat around him. A nation builder who held that any administration ought to "make it the *immediate* interest of the moneyed men to co-operate with the government" was encouraged by the solid property represented in Independence Hall.

There were thirty lawyers, advisers to the most influential moneyed men in America, to make up the majority of the convention. With them were eleven great mercantile magnates, seven proudly wealthy planters, two busy land speculators, two gentlemen of independent fortunes variously invested, two physicians and the venerable Franklin, who defies classification. At eighty-one, the Doctor stood on the extreme left, as opinion went in that group. His feeble old voice was lifted almost alone in mild praise of a genuinely democratic system, for of all those busy, practical men, the one who had been busiest and most practical entertained the highest hopes for a real popular government. Age and experience had their brief say through him and quavered into silence.

It was fitting that the opposite extreme should be taken by youth. Hamilton at thirty opposed to Franklin's democracy a republican ideal so oligarchical that, even in the privacy of the convention, few of those who agreed with him dared avow it.

Around him the fathers of a new country were taking a paternal attitude in settling their child's fate. Washington, as calm as on the march to Trenton, presided with immense dignity, declining to enter the debate but watching and listening, quite prepared for the worst. Little Madison, busy with his notes, ready to leap into any discussion, had come with a plan as completely detailed as Hamilton's and far more likely to prove acceptable. Gouverneur Morris, bright, cynical and aloof, shared with his friend Hamilton a belief in aristocracy, even an aristocracy of money, and a blunt determination to defend it. The stubbornly optimistic Franklin with bland benevolence shining from the broad face above the plain, dark clothes, clung to the manner of Poor Richard, informing his juniors that some of the greatest rogues he ever met were the richest rogues, a pleasantry that went down but ill in a body that included Robert Morris, Carroll of Maryland, the Pinckneys of South Carolina.

An American convention that could not be swayed by a Franklin would hardly surrender its judgment to a Hamilton. But the youngest of fifty-five was not dismayed by odds, and one day in June Washington graciously gave the floor to the delegate from New York. He held it for five hours, pouring forth, with only occasional glances at a few pages of notes, the Hamiltonian ideal of government. Erect—men noticed that day how straight he bore his five feet seven—the still rosy cheeks flushed with enthusiasm, the eyes starry with love of an idea, the fine hands moving gracefully in semi-concealment among the lace ruffles, the neatly powdered hair drawn back smoothly from the high forehead, Hamilton appealed deliberately, with all the fervor of eloquence, patriotism, high-minded virtue and studied idealism to the baser impulses of mankind.

"In short," says his brief of this part of his speech, "to interest all the *passions* of individuals."

Into his five hours he packed all the learning and all the thinking he had done since as a clerk in Cruger's store he had discovered economics.

"Society," assert the notes from which he spoke, "naturally divides itself into two political divisions—the *few* and the *many*, who have distinct interests.

"If government in the hands of the *few*, they will tyrannize over the many.

"If the hands of the many, they will tyrannize over the few. It ought to be in the hands of both; and they should be separated."

This separation of powers was one of the rare points on which the fifty-five were pretty well agreed. The studious

Madison had pondered it well, and as his friend from the Congress of '83 unleashed his eloquence, the Virginian's pen raced over paper.

In the first place, the spokesman of the moneyed interest proposed a lower house to be chosen by the suffrages of all free adult male citizens, and so far his scheme was as much as the radical Franklin asked. But what Hamilton really thought of this twig of government appeared more plainly later, when he sneered:

"Can a democratic assembly who annually revolve in the mass of the people, be supposed steadily to pursue the public good?"

So he set off against his concession to democracy a Senate chosen for life by voters who could satisfy stringent property tests. Over both was set a President, also chosen for life under an extremely complicated system of electors. The suffrage for these electors was to be limited to men possessing the then extremely high property qualification of "an estate of inheritance or for three lives in land, or a clear personal estate of the value of one thousand Spanish milled dollars of the present standard."

Hamilton's executive was vested with powers that led an English commentator to remark with some astonishment that the ex-rebel held ideas on the authority of a chief of state at least as arbitrary as those of George III. Hamilton's President, a monarch in all but name, was to veto legislation and appoint department heads without reference to the Senate. He was to appoint also the governors of the states and the officers of the militia. Hamilton was still foreigner enough to have no provincial loyalties and wanted every attribute of sovereignty removed from the states. Throughout his long disquisition, he told his colleagues frankly that the British model was the best then existing in the world, and, strengthened and improved as he suggested, would end their difficulties.

The great effort, the most brilliant feat of sustained intelligent oratory Gouverneur Morris ever heard, won no converts. The debate rolled on, four months of it, and although he missed no more than five weeks in two trips home to attend to the more pressing claims of his law practice—one of his problems was the tangled affairs of Baron von Steuben, still genial, affectionate, deserving and poor, still pursuing his mirage of a pension in vain—Hamilton took little further part in it. He was, however, alert to the real meaning of the struggle as the representatives of land and commerce, big states and little states, city and country, North and South wrangled, pleaded and slowly reached out for compromise, so slowly that by July Washington himself was fearful of failure, writing:

"I *almost* despair of seeing a favorable issue to the proceedings of the Convention, and do, therefore, repent having any agency in the business."

Through all the confusion of conflicting ideas, one principle was constant. The fifty-five—among whom was none who in his person embodied the interests of the small farmer, the debtor, the mechanic or the laborer—were striving always toward a system based on safeguarding the rights of property. Sometimes, when delegates seemed momentarily to forget this, Hamilton injected a few words into the debate, as when he said:

"The difference of property is already great among us. Commerce and industry will increase the disparity. Your government must meet this state of things, or combinations will in process of time undermine your system."

The convention, in due course, took heed and gradually there emerged a practicable framework, largely on the model which Madison had brought to Philadelphia. Neither in the finished document nor in the ocean of words that went into its making was there much preoccupation with the liberty of the individual, the rights of man or the aspirations of free peoples, which in the Constitution itself were dealt with summarily in a preamble. "Men who own the country," recognizing the existence of evils threatening their material dominion, simply drew up a prescription to alleviate those evils.

It was, perhaps, fitting that to the most coldly realistic of their number, the cynical Gouverneur Morris, they assigned the task of polishing the composition. Morris gave it a thoroughly hard, high polish, too, one that was to survive the legalistic friction of generations of judicial quibbles. It was a fine job, but surely the draftsman's ready tongue must have strayed into his cheek when he penned the initial phrase, "We the People of the United States." For the people had had so little to do with the pages that followed that they were as yet entirely ignorant of the contents. Drawn up by extra-official delegates appointed without any general election, the document was to be presented in the familiar form of a dictator's coup d'état. Ignoring the existing constitutional method, which called for approval by Congress and each of the state legislatures, the convention had, without authority, ordered special ratification assemblies to vote yes or no, and nine states were to be enough to put the Constitution into effect. Success alone could justify such high-handed usurpation, and Hamilton expressed the only grounds for optimism when he unenthusiastically closed his share in the debate with:

"No man's ideas are more remote from the plan than my own are known to be; but is it possible to deliberate between anarchy and convulsion on one side, and the chance of good to be expected from the plan on the other?"

The argument was not unanswerable. Sixteen of the delegates obviously thought there could be an alternative, for on September 17, 1787, when those who were not too greatly disappointed in their work signed Mr. Morris's elegant literary exercise, "We the People" was seen to consist of thirty-eight names. Yates and Lansing had left in disgust more than two months earlier, and the sovereign state of New York is represented on the bulwark of liberty by a single signature: Alexander Hamilton.

XIII

THE FEDERALIST

"BETTER THAN NOTHING," HAMILTON REMARKED CURTLY BUT
in private of the document that was one day to command a
veneration those who composed it reserved for Holy Writ.
Few of his contemporaries were any warmer in their praise,
so it was as well that most of the Constitution's leading defenders were lawyers, accustomed to making the best possible
pleas for causes that inspired in them a devotion rather less
than ardent.

Fortunately, too, the same chilling indifference operated
to some extent on the other side. Since the wisest jurists have
disagreed profoundly as to just what the Constitution means,
there could be little hope that the voters to whom it was
submitted for a yea or nay decision—in the best manner of
a dictator's plebiscite—would understand it any more clearly.
Furthermore, Mr. Morris's polished phrases offered no hold
for the grip of spontaneous mass emotions. In the great bulk
of the populace, the campaign was productive only of apathy.

Within the limits of those immediately affected, the opposition was sufficiently hot. The class represented in New
York by Clinton was aroused to a defense of jobs and prestige. The philosophical advocates of weakness in the central
government elaborated their attenuated theories. States'
rights extremists muttered fearfully of tyranny. The cowed
but sullen followers of Shays, dreaming wistfully of unlim-
ited paper money and the virtual extinction of all debt, were
vociferous, if no longer dangerous. The combined total of
the dissenters heavily outnumbered the 160,000 who have

been estimated as having a material stake in the proposed regime.

Clinton's legislature, reluctantly authorizing the election of a convention to consider ratification, took the unprecedented step of enfranchising for this single occasion all free men. This sacrifice of cherished property qualifications was obviously made in the belief that the poor would oppose the aristocratic aspects of the Constitution once these were pointed out to them. Actually the poor scarcely bothered to vote at all, but that was not foreseen.

Hamilton, surveying the odds, refused to admit discouragement. Some of the other founding fathers were worried about New York. Neither the richest nor the most populous of the states, its geographical position gave it a good deal of importance, for if New York held aloof, the new nation would be split in half. British military experts had contended that such a division would have proved fatal in the Revolution. It would also be a death blow to reconstruction.

The forces that Hamilton set himself to organize were small but powerful. Schuyler, dragging the other Hudson valley patroons in his wake, was a dogged, blind follower of his son-in-law. The clan of Livingston threw its numbers and widely assorted talents into the scale. The merchants, land speculators and holders of Continental securities were ready with votes and influence and money. Up-State New York has been beaten by weaker combinations.

The campaign, however, opened on a regrettably vulgar plane. The opposition—men always suppose it is the other side that starts this sort of thing—refused to keep the argument on the high level of the practical issues, and Hamilton was having his first experience of a place so prominent that its occupant becomes a target for the mud of his foes. Taking the lead in the ratification fight, he was denounced alternately as a base-born adventurer and a dangerous aristocrat. His refusal to pretend a patriotic attachment to New York was sneered at as ingratitude to the community that gave him bread. His admitted admiration for the British political system was twisted into treasonable plotting to overthrow the republic and place King George's second son on an American throne. His activity in the Cincinnati was construed malevolently as aiming to convert that self-styled patrician order into an engine of despotism. This whispering campaign gained force and scope, until at last the calumny touched his military record. Only then did he call for help, and got it from Washington.

"As you say," wrote the General, "it is insinuated by some of your political adversaries, and may obtain credit, 'that you *palmed* yourself upon me, and was *dismissed* from my family,' and call upon me to do you justice by a recital of the facts; I do, therefore, explicitly declare, that both charges are unfounded. With respect to the first, I have no cause to believe that you took a single step to accomplish, or had the most distant idea of receiving an appointment in my family till you were invited thereto. And with respect to the second, that your quitting it was altogether the effect of your own choice."

Slander did not prevent Hamilton from presenting a serene face to society. He became an inveterate diner-out that season, his clear, rapid speech dominating the conversation at New York's best homes. He jested lightly with Burr, turned the solemn formality of Jay and Duane to laughter, exchanged ready banter with Troup and Morris. His humor, lively enough to amuse a generation that had chuckled with Dr. Franklin, never earned him the name of a wit, but that is a title that goes with a gift for unkind, easily remembered sneers at other people, and Hamilton had no petty malice. When he wished to blast a character, he unlimbered the heavy artillery of thunderous invective, never the popgun of sarcasm or epigram. His sayings were not repeated as often but were as well-liked as those of more ill-natured gentlemen.

His talk this winter was merry, inconsequential as he sat

at table. But when the ladies, duly complimented and flattered, had withdrawn, he guided the men toward politics, expounding the virtues of "better than nothing." Madison was a visitor to the city, and his quiet voice chimed in, emphasizing his friend's more staccato phrases, capping his jokes with anecdotes which, the hearers agreed, no one told so wittily as the bald little Virginian.

Then Hamilton was off on his professional rounds, for his practice could not be neglected, no matter how perilous the political outlook. At the common tables where the attorneys gathered after their court battles on the circuit, in the inns and country homes of the patroons, at taverns where the dryness of the law was alleviated by heroic potations, he talked incessantly about the Constitution. He spoke, more glowingly as he warmed to his subject, of its potential benefits. He answered objections. He persuaded, pleaded, bullied, persisting doggedly in the face of what he secretly thought an appalling stupidity and blind prejudice. And on an October day, dropping down the Hudson from Fishkill in one of the little sloops which experienced travelers preferred to the jolting stages, he had an idea for lifting the campaign to the intellectual heights the magnitude of the issue deserved. In the little cabin, he pulled paper to him and wrote:

"To the People of the State of New York:"

Thus was born *The Federalist,* and as the glorious panorama of the river slipped past unnoticed and the water slapped a soothing accompaniment on the sides of the boat, Hamilton's pen traced steadily the neat straight lines of one of the world's greatest politico-literary masterpieces, orderly as his thoughts, firm as his will, clear as the alternative he outlined with incisive strokes. By the time he reached New York the article was finished, and in his mind was the plan for a series of papers that would exhaust the subject.

A busy lawyer, pestered by clients and actively organizing a political party, needed help, and Hamilton found it in Madison and Jay. There were no men in the country capable of worsting this triumvirate in honest argument on political, economic and juridical issues, and the plan commended itself to each of them. The field was carefully divided. Jay, who was in charge of foreign affairs for the Confederation, was to deal with international aspects. Hamilton was to expose the country's need for a strong government, and allay fears of too strong a government. Madison, who had seen more of his ideas embodied in the Constitution than any other man and therefore had more paternal affection for it, was to explain the constructive virtues. That rigid scheme was not adhered to very strictly. Jay was in poor health all that winter and contributed no more than five of the eighty-five numbers. Madison, who had to return to Virginia to lead his own ratification fight, wrote fourteen by himself, may have done twelve others in whole or part and composed three with the assistance of some notes from Hamilton. At least fifty-one were the sole work of the original projector, and all were signed *Publius.*

Appearing on the average of one every three days in New York papers, from which they were widely copied, the essays achieved the highest aims of journalism. They treated a current problem in the light of eternal truths, giving to the arguments of 1787 an immortality that has been acknowledged by constitution makers ever since. Few authors of other fundamental laws display as much sense as *The Federalist,* but they all draw on that work whose literary quality is as remarkable as its logic.

Especially in Hamilton's contributions, the dry, dead stalks of political economy come alive in a ferment of seething ideas. He could take the conflict of abstractions and turn it into something as exciting as a duel. There is suspense as the struggle sways this way and that, but the Right always triumphs in the end. For Hamilton, while presenting the opposition's thesis with a force few of its supporters could have supplied, kept in reserve the telling blow that exposes the inner futility of an outwardly unanswerable argument.

A professional writer would be content to rest a claim to immortality on fifty-one numbers of *The Federalist*. But Hamilton tossed them off as a sideline in the midst of what seemed more pressing occupations. There was no time for revision or much correction. Fortunately, the articles needed neither, for the thought could not have been better arranged, and the style—admirably clear and strong, alternately fire and ice—is as near perfection as mortal authors can come.

The series was so powerful that it actually won converts, and among these was Alexander Hamilton. Approaching the Constitution as "better than nothing," he found in his exhaustive analysis possibilities that had been easy to overlook. The form of the new government was far from that authoritarian oligarchy which he had envisioned as operating high above the ignorance and prejudices of the masses. But as he considered how the new system must work out, he realized that it contained hidden reserves of strength.

These came to be employed so exactly as *The Federalist* predicted that the articles often read like a summary of subsequent United States history, the reader becoming conscious only at intervals and with something of a shock that *Publius* was writing before the event, not after it. To one gifted with so much foresight, it was obvious that the administration proposed would easily "make it the *immediate* interest of the moneyed men to co-operate with the government." Once these two had been joined, Hamilton was willing to take the chance on mere mobs or idle theorists being able to put them asunder. And so it was with real conviction that in the last number of *The Federalist* he summed up his views of the Constitution:

"I am persuaded that it is the best which our political situation, habits, and opinions will admit, and superior to any the revolution has produced."

Among the lesser by-products of *The Federalist* was a contribution, not permanent, to political manners. The earnest devotion of *Publius* to reasoning and facts lifted the whole

PARADE IN HONOR OF THE ADOPTION OF THE FEDERAL CONSTITUTION, 1788

Constitutional debate several degrees in the scales of intelligence and politeness. As the articles succeeded each other with cumulative power, the electorate was less frequently called upon by its other mentors to judge the merits of the case by considering that Hamilton was a foreign adventurer of uncertain parentage, that Madison was a slave-owner who wanted to assure a market for the increase of his human cattle in the Carolinas and Georgia, that Clinton was a narrow intriguer seeking a selfish provincial dictatorship. All those things were still said, of course, along with a thousand other irrelevancies, but with diminishing conviction and effect.

The issue was not settled altogether by reason, slander or economic pressure. There were the usual social influences, the swaying of whole families by careful words at table or in the drawing room, and Hamilton spoke many of them. That spring he went about in society alone, for Betsey was expecting another child in April. James Alexander Hamilton was born less than two weeks before the election of delegates to the ratifying convention, of whom his father was one.

It was well that the novelty of parenthood was wearing thin, for Hamilton had small time for family pleasures. At night when he got home from a party he would be at his desk by the only light on Wall Street, hastily preparing a brief or another number of *The Federalist*. At dawn he would snatch a little sleep before embarking on the next day's round of court work, writing, conferences and carefully designed chit-chat.

Electioneering was so intense that both sides expected a record vote. Both were pouring liquor down the throats of supposedly doubtful freemen. Masters were warning their servants how to vote. Campaign funds were raised, with as much as £20 a head collected from leading men. Jobs were promised lavishly, and Clinton's remarkable patronage machine was running at top speed. Only when it came time to count noses was it seen how little real interest the Constitution aroused in the general public. Fewer than 3,000 of New York's adult males bothered to show up at the polls, and under the pressure of commerce, the menaces of employers and the stimulant of staggering potions, the vote was almost unanimous for delegates pledged to ratification. Clinton himself polled only 134, while Duane, at the top of the Federalist ticket, had 2,680.

Up-State, as usual, had a different view of its interests. There, the result was a complete defeat for the new form of government, and as he prepared to take his seat in the convention, which had been summoned to meet in Poughkeepsie, Hamilton wrote to Madison that the enemies of the Constitution had swept the State.

"They have a majority of two-thirds in the Convention, and, according to the best estimate I can form, of about four-sevenths in the community," he said, adding quite calmly that he expected the session to last until ratification should be accomplished.

On June 16, 1788, the New York City delegates set sail for Poughkeepsie in a body, saluted by the booming of cannon and cheered by a noisy crowd. Next day, without guns or cheers, the convention was organized, and Hamilton found himself the leader of a band of nineteen. Clinton and Melancthon Smith, an orator of considerable provincial fame, commanded a compact majority of forty-six.

The odds, to the shrewd eyes of Hamilton, were not as unequal as numbers seemed to make them. The delegates, although elected for their opposition to a central government, were not mere instruments for recording the will of their constituents. They were supposed to think for themselves. Their thoughts, furthermore, were less important than the acts of others. If they could not be convinced by arguments, they might be swayed by facts. One of these was that nine states could put the government into effect, and then what would happen to an isolated province? More immediate was the warning that New York City might secede, and that threat, which was to be treated lightly by later generations when the metropolis wearied of being outvoted by Up-State farmers, had substance in the days of the Confederation. An independent free city at the mouth of the Hudson could have slapped handsome customs duties on every ounce of goods that came to or from the hinterland.

That was the foundation of Hamilton's confidence as the debate on the Constitution got under way, clause by clause, as if nothing had ever been written on the subject. Erect and alert, with a clear voice that never tired, he was on his feet hour after hour, nearly every day, answering objections, explaining, protesting. Jay's long, thin figure rose to support him, and Chancellor Robert Livingston, regarded as an old man because he was already an old judge at forty-two, exercised his judicial learning on the same side.

Day by day the debate waxed keener and of less imporance, for the deeds of other states were louder than the words of New York. One by one they were falling into line, while Hamilton was sending off expresses to Madison urging that he rush news of Virginia's ratification even if he had to reverse the charges, for the influence of the largest state of all might be decisive in Poughkeepsie. Actually it was New Hampshire that provided the needed spur, for when word of her acceptance came down on June 24, it was plain that the new government was going into effect, and Hamilton could see the fear of it growing on his opponents.

He and his eighteen colleagues, therefore, were in jolly mood as the convention adjourned for a Fourth of July celebration. Each of the two parties maintained its own table, and at each Independence was solemnly toasted in thirteen different varieties. Politely the two factions exchanged copies of the sentiments to which they drank, and most of the delegates emptied glasses to all of them at both dinners, while guns boomed and drums rattled in appreciation of each toast as it was read. Poughkeepsie had a safer, saner Fourth than Albany, where rival mobs tried to fight the Revolution all over again with bayonets, stones and clubs.

Next day the debate was resumed, with an added acidity in the speeches because of yesterday's wine, but news of Virginia's ratification ended the contest. Ten states had agreed "to form a more perfect Union, establish Justice, insure domestic Tranquillity, provide for the common defense, promote the general Welfare, and secure the Blessings of Liberty to ourselves and our Posterity." New York could do no less, although it hardly seemed in good taste to yield to fear. Much more graceful to bow to the force of argument, which was done, 30 to 27, on July 26, Melancthon Smith courteously explaining that Colonel Hamilton's powerful expositions had entirely convinced him.

New York City was willing to take Mr. Smith at his word. Intoxicated with the thought of a trade boom and the hope of being the seat of the new government, the metropolis put its soul into a fitting commemoration of the event, which was said to "give the first polish to the noble statue formed by the late glorious Revolution." The result completely delighted every man, woman and child in town except Colonel Bauman, who had arranged some very spectacular fireworks, only to see them outshone by a particularly brilliant full moon. Nothing like that day's procession had ever been seen in New York. There were flags and eagles and figures of Fame announcing through trumpets the dawn of a new era. There were thousands of marching men in militia companies, clubs and business groups. There were floats in which every trade gave a symbolical representation of its own adherence to the Constitution.

But the masterpiece of the whole parade, everyone agreed, was a splendid model of a frigate, thirty feet long by twelve wide, manned by forty men and tugged by ten white horses from the fields where a City Hall would one day be built, to the Bowling Green. She was rigged as for sea and armed with thirty-two cannon, real ones that roared salutes to the answering crowds. And the name of the ship, in honor of him who had done more than any other New Yorker to make this celebration possible, was HAMILTON.

XIV

INTERLUDE IN WALL STREET

The year after the victory parade was a period of what passed for idleness and relaxation in the life of Alexander Hamilton. He was occupied only with his increasing law practice, voluminous correspondence on organizing the new government, the leadership of a party facing a bitter struggle for control of New York and attendance at a session of the Continental Congress, to which he had himself elected in order to supervise that body's self-extinction and the selection of his city as the temporary capital. These added up to so little for his restless energy that Angelica Church heard in London that her "petit Fripon" was getting fat and losing his good looks from sheer laziness.

"He will be unable to flirt as Robert Morris," Angelica warned her sister; "pray, Betsey, make him walk, and ride, and be amused."

Angelica's rumor was a base slander, her warning unnecessary. Her brother-in-law preserved a very fine figure indeed, amused himself hugely and his capacity for flirtation was unimpaired. His habit of walking, which she supposed given up, had proved to be attended with some inconvenience, for he still talked aloud to himself. One day at Kinderhook a storekeeper refused to change a $50 bill for him, and when some of the bystanders after Hamilton's departure asked if the money were counterfeit, the proprietor explained that it was only the poor gentleman's mind that was bad. One of the store loafers remarked that he seemed sane enough.

"That may be," was the retort, "he probably has his lucid intervals, but I have seen him walk before my door for half an hour, sometimes stopping, but always talking to himself, and if I had changed the money and he had lost it I might have received blame."

Schuyler heard the story and repeated it to Betsey with great glee. His son-in-law took heed. A rising man, one who aimed, too, at control of a nation's finances, could not afford a reputation for eccentricity in money matters, much less outright lunacy. Thereafter Hamilton made it a point to confine his solitary walks to his library, where his soliloquies would be heard by none save sympathetic ears.

The first election under the Constitution consumed some of his surplus leisure. He took the stump in 1788 in a campaign that won for the Federalists, as his party began to be called, four of New York's six seats in the House of Representatives. He also added his mite to the flood of letters that inundated Mount Vernon to sweep Washington from his retirement into the Presidency.

"I take it for granted, sir," he wrote, "you have concluded to comply with what will no doubt be the general call of your country in relation to the new Government. You will permit me to say that it is indispensable you should lend yourself to its first operations. It is of little purpose to have *introduced* a system, if the weightiest influence is not given to its firm establishment at the outset."

Despite the confident tone, he later presented several additional, nicely reasoned opinions on why the General should allow himself to become the first citizen of the republic he had done so much to create. That settled at last, he turned back to state politics. He wanted to end Clinton's domination in order to get a legislature that would send well-intentioned men to the Senate. Without ceremony he rejected a Federalist candidate for Governor in order to win votes from Clinton with a moderate of the popular party. For this, he selected his convention colleague, Yates, and enlisted in the campaign committee so various a lot as Burr, Troup and William Duer, Lady Kitty Alexander's husband, then rising to eminence as a financier and speculator. Clinton scraped through by the narrow margin of 6,391 to 5,962 in a State of 324,270 population, and lost control of the Legislature. That body was so divided among factions that it elected no Senators at all.

New York, therefore, was not represented in the Upper House when the time came to inaugurate the new government on March 4, 1789. Other states had been equally dilatory, and individuals more so, with the result that only six Senators were in the city on time. Representatives were equally scarce, and the eager mouthpiece of Massachusetts conservatives, Fisher Ames, unable to exercise his oratory because there was no quorum, thought the country had gone to a great deal of trouble to clamber from the frying pan into the fire.

"The people will forget the new government before it is born," he mourned.

By April 2, however, enough legislators found their way to New York to organize Congress, count the electoral vote and discover that George Washington had been chosen President by unanimous vote and John Adams Vice President somewhat less overwhelmingly. The notice did not take the principals by surprise, and they did not imitate Congressional delay in reaching their posts. In the midst of an April shower three weeks later, the whole city and a good proportion of the rural population crowded into the tip of Manhattan to see Washington land at Murray's Wharf from an elegant barge, which the municipality had sent for him.

As the tall figure in the blue and buff which he had made famous during the Revolution strode down Pearl Street, disdaining a coach, to Samuel Osgood's big square mansion on Cherry, "the shouts of the populace drowned the combined noises of the mechanical devices." Martha was hardly missed. While the war raged, it had been her custom to remain at home in the fighting season, and this was just another campaign to the Washington family.

The equipment for peace, however, had been supplied more lavishly than that of war. New York, proud of its growing population, now passing the 35,000 mark, had outdone itself to welcome the new government. The new Federal Hall opposite Hamilton's house was one of Major L'Enfant's better architectural pieces, with graceful pillars, well-proportioned chambers and a splendid marble lobby, the whole reckoned as well worth the £20,000 it cost. Although not quite finished, its main rooms with their crimson draperies were ready for the practice of government.

On April 30 the Hall was tastefully decorated and the entire city dressed in its best for Washington's inaugural. Flags and banners hung from all the houses—more than 4,000 of them in a metropolis that had pushed its way for more than a mile up Broadway. Big as the town was, it was too small for the visitors. The boarding houses were full of Congressmen, empty rooms in any home were snatched by job hunters and the merely curious. And still the crowds came in, so that pretty Bertha Ingersoll wrote:

"We shall remain here, even if we have to sleep in tents, as so many will have to do."

Miss Ingersoll was spared the inconvenience, but the competition for quarters was so keen that the thrifty New Yorkers could not resist temptation. Soon there were complaints, initiated then and revived regularly for the next one hundred and fifty years, that shops and inns profiteered shamelessly on innocent visitors. Almost before it started, the new government was being urged to flee from the city of dreadful prices and reckless extravagance to a simpler, cheaper capital.

The cost of living, however, was ignored as this Thursday dawned, fair and mild, to usher in the first act of the great American drama. There was no role as yet for Alexander Hamilton, and he waited quietly in the wings until his part should be written. In point of fact, he stood on his balcony opposite Federal Hall enjoying an excellent view of the ceremony, impressive in its brief solemnity as Chancellor Livingston administered the oath of a Washington whose dark brown suit, white silk stockings and silver buckles had been made, the newspapers noted with fond approval, in America. The streets, as far as could be seen along Nassau, Broad and Wall, were jammed, workmen in leather breeches squeezed against gentlemen in satin smallclothes, and all, Mr. Hamilton observed, cheering like good Federalists.

The central figure bowed gravely and departed to the seclusion of the temporary executive mansion on Cherry Street, but the celebration was less restrained without him. By ten at night the streets were so crowded there was scarcely room for the pigs and none at all for coaches. Visitor and native alike had turned out in full force to admire the illuminations and the immense transparencies hung between houses—one of Fame descending from heaven to crown Washington, another showing the hero posed under a figure of Fortitude with House and Senate grouped around him and Justice and Wisdom surmounting the whole.

There had been hopes of an inaugural ball, too, but without Martha it was not deemed quite proper. However, a brave substitute was held in the Assembly Rooms on Broadway on May 7, and Mr. Fenno in his *Gazette* waxed almost lyrical in attempting to describe the "consummate taste and elegance" of the ladies. Hamilton and Betsey were there, conspicuous among the bright throng of which one of Fenno's journalistic rivals reported:

"Joy, satisfaction and vivacity was expressed on every countenance."

Probably the reporter had not seen President Washington. The General, uncomfortably conscious of setting precedents at every turn, was trying to observe some advice on etiquette which he had solicited and obtained from Hamilton. Neither of them thought it odd that one born into the Virginia aristocracy should request a former West Indian clerk to settle nice points of conduct for a nation's ruler. The former clerk, with obvious pleasure, had drafted a lengthy paper on the need for a "high tone" in the executive department. Regretting that public opinion would not tolerate as high a tone as was theoretically desirable, he commended the President to a formal dignity that was well suited to the character of the man, but hedged him about with restrictions to which the master of Mount Vernon was little accustomed.

Hamilton liked the idea of formal levees at which, once the guests had been assembled in proper order, the President might make an entrance, "to remain half an hour, in which time he may converse cursorily on indifferent subjects, with such persons as shall invite his attention, and at the end of that half hour disappear." Presidential entertaining in the grand manner was to consist of not more than four large affairs a year, but weekly dinners for six or eight, "to be confined essentially to members of the legislature and other official characters," were permitted. Remembering from his staff days how Washington would sit by the hour after a meal cracking nuts and sipping wine and encouraging informal talk, the arbiter of etiquette added sternly:

"The President never to remain long at table."

This last was one of the few points His Excellency ignored, but he restricted executive dinners as Hamilton suggested, and admirably dull they were, too, long silences being broken after the cloth was removed by a sudden flurry of polite sentiments.

"Such a buzz of 'health, sir,' and 'health, madame,' and 'Thank you, sir,' and 'Thank you, madame,' never had I heard before," noted Senator Maclay of Pennsylvania, but the animation died quickly and there was silence again while the host "played with the fork, striking on the edge of the table with it."

Washington, poor man, was more than bored and worried. He was sick, too, but as long as he was able he lived up nobly to the specifications his one-time secretary had drawn.

That young man was not so solemn. He and Betsey entertained in far more lively fashion, by no means confining their guests to "official characters." The beaux and gallants buzzed at their house as busily as did the Congressmen at Washington's dinners, and with a sprightlier tone. Mrs. Hamilton's fine eyes and graceful manners won their admirers, but more young men came to gather around her pretty sisters and cousins. Angelica Church had come home again with what the old-fashioned Walter Rutherfurd called "a late abominable fashion from London, of Ladies like Washwomen with their sleeves above their elbows." A great many women spent more than their husbands could afford in an effort to look as much like a washwoman as the lovely Angelica, while less hidebound gentlemen vowed that Mrs. Church's bare arms were entrancing.

"If there is a town on the American continent where English luxury displays its follies, it is New York," wrote a French visitor, Brissot de Warville, after a tour of the country. "You will find here the English fashions. In the dress of the women you will see the most brilliant silks, gauzes, hats and borrowed hair. Equipages are rare; but they are elegant. The men have more simplicity in their dress; they disdain gewgaws, but they take their revenge in the delicacies of the table."

The simplicity of masculine attire was purely relative. Another writer was complaining that a tailor had to be an upholsterer to pad his clients out into the modish shape, and one purveyor of suitings advertised this selection of colors to discriminating gentlemen: "Bottle green, batswing, navy blue, parsons gray, changeable pearl, scarlet, light blue, light green, London smoke, purple, mulberry, garnet, sea green, mouse's ear, pea green, drake's head." It was small wonder the world of fashion presented a colorful picture, but it was not as English as Warville supposed, for British visitors thought the styles copied from the French. Perhaps they were only American.

Dancing and dining were not the sole diversions. The city

boasted 330 taverns and twenty-two churches. There were elegant concerts and theatrical offerings in the red wooden theater on John Street. Cock-fighting and cards were still favorite amusements, and the hangings at the gallows in the fields off Broadway were considered as recreational for all save the principals. The eternal gullibility of New Yorkers was catered to by strolling exhibitions of freaks, among them a new microscope said to magnify a common louse to twelve feet long (three shillings that treat would cost you) and "a Male and Female of the surprising species of Ourang Outang or the Man of the Woods" (chastely clad in a girdle of fig leaves in the wood cuts reproduced in the papers).

Pessimists like Senator Maclay looked upon the follies and extravagances of New York as an appropriate setting for the new government. At first glance it seemed to be as futile as the Confederation. The pressing need was for a revenue, but Congress, in which merchants held an unusual proportion of seats, gently dallied with a tariff bill while members imported huge stocks and raised the prices in accordance with duties they expected to levy. The organization of executive departments was secondary only to taxes, but the Senate spent weeks in debating how the President should be addressed, whether as "Excellency" or "Majesty" or "Highness," and whether a sergeant-at-arms might be called Usher of the Black Rod after the British example. Equally fatuous, the rugged levelers screamed that republican institutions could not survive ordinary parliamentary politeness, and the uncompromising Maclay registered horror when a Bishop was denominated as "Right Reverend."

The wheels of government ground on remorselessly, and ground amazingly little, but Hamilton from his place as a bystander was not as worried by the scantiness of the output as some of the laborers in the field. He was waiting for the bill creating a Treasury Department, for Washington had asked him to preside over it, Robert Morris having declined to submit to another experience of republican finances. Hamilton's study of probable Constitutional development had convinced him in advance that a Congress without a guide is a ship of state without a rudder. The superiority of the Constitution over the Articles of Confederation was that it provided a potential pilot. The man who proposed to fill that position had already divined what later generations learned from experience—that when Congress is dominant or left to its own devices the government is weak and static without aim or discernible progress, but that when the executive takes control things may happen, either for good or ill.

Action was what 1789 demanded, but until he could direct it, Hamilton was content to employ his energies in trying again to elect a couple of United States Senators. The New York Legislature was called into special session for this purpose in July.

The earlier deadlock had been caused by Hamilton's presumption in demanding the election of his father-in-law and Rufus King, a youngish man who had inherited one fortune and married another. The Legislature was willing to accept Schuyler, but King was a stranger. He had moved to New York from Massachusetts only after the constitutional convention, and was to an even more marked degree than Schuyler the personal nominee of Hamilton. Members thought one Senatorship to a family was quite enough. The Livingstons were especially resentful, for they held that their services to the Constitution merited at least a seat in the Upper House. But Hamilton wore them all down in the end by sheer stubbornness and Schuyler and King came to the Senate in time to help pass the bill creating the Treasury Department. The vote on this measure, interrupted by an August heat wave that killed twenty New Yorkers in a week, came on September 2, and nine days later Alexander Hamilton took office as Secretary.

"I hazard much but I thought it an occasion that called upon me to hazard," he wrote Lafayette.

Next day the gargantuan Knox became Secretary of War,

and the Cabinet was completed within two weeks with Thomas Jefferson as Secretary of State and Edmund Randolph, another product of the Old Dominion, as Attorney General.

Hamilton was not particularly interested in the personalities of these colleagues. And, as he bowed to the task of giving the Constitution a twist to the right, it seemed to him of even less importance that George Clinton had moved to recover the position he had so nearly lost at the last election. The Governor had been alarmed by the strength of the coalition Hamilton brought into the field against him, but it was a very loose federation, easily broken up by an astute politician. Within two weeks of Hamilton's plunge into the Treasury, Yates was immobilized by elevation to the State's highest judicial post and Burr enticed into neutrality if not friendship by appointment as Attorney General.

Even if he had thought these political manipulations in his home state might one day concern him, the Secretary could hardly have spared the time to oppose them. For he was in the spotlight of the national stage, performing an extremely difficult juggling act in the presence of a critical if breathless audience. The rest of the show was forgotten, for all men knew this single performance would determine the length of the run. With an unexpectedly keen appreciation of its own supernumerary part in the drama, Congress passed a resolution calling on the Secretary to report on the state of the public credit, and adjourned until the following January. So once again the candles flickered until dawn in a house on Wall Street, and *The Daily Advertiser,* with somewhat premature enthusiasm, sang brightly:

> . . . young Hamilton's unshaken soul
> the wayward hosts of anarchy control.

Unfettered by Congressional advice, the Secretary set himself to making the Treasury Department the kind of a government organ that most of the founding fathers had thought too extreme. Always in the back of his mind was the memory that the British Prime Ministry had developed from the accretion of power in the hands of the principal officer of finance. He knew, as did Madison and plenty of their contemporaries, that the Constitution had been designed to solve certain economic difficulties. Hamilton assumed this was the Treasury's job. As he organized that department with his left hand, and set it going on the routine of collecting revenue with an efficiency hitherto unknown in America, he was perfecting a broader policy. What he had been unable to win by persuasion in Philadelphia, a determined man in power might accomplish by indirection in New York.

Ten years of correspondence, debate and pamphleteering should have acquainted anyone interested in the subject with Secretary Hamilton's views on finance, credit, taxes and public policy in detail. The leaders of Congress, particularly, knew exactly what he thought about government of the people by the people. They were familiar with his thesis "that no plan could succeed which did not unite the interest and credit of rich individuals with those of the State."

Madison, now the chief figure in the House of Representatives, was thoroughly informed as to Hamiltonian principles and was better equipped than most to understand them. When Washington's choice of a Treasury head was announced, the Virginian characterized his late collaborator as "best qualified for that species of business, and on that account would be preferred by those who know him personally."

Appreciation was mutual, and as he sat at his mahogany desk elaborating a system of government, Hamilton supposed that their old relationship would continue. "Might I ask of your friendship," he wrote, "to put on paper and send me your thoughts" on problems of revenue and credit. Three years later, explaining that he had counted very definitely on "the firm support of Mr. Madison," the Secretary added: "Aware of the intrinsic difficulties of the situation, and of

THE FIRST CABINET, AN ENGRAVING FROM THE
PAINTING BY ALONZO CHAPPEL

the powers of Mr. Madison, I do not believe I should have accepted under a different supposition."

As far back as the letters to Duane and Morris, in the series of *The Continentalist* and, more recently and completely, in *The Federalist,* he had outlined his very practical beliefs. That he would fight for redemption of every borrowed dollar, a single stable currency, a central banking system and government support for commerce and industry had been proclaimed as publicly as his illegitimacy, his predilection for aristocratic forms, his distrust of the people. It was not his fault if the latter points were more widely current in some parts of the country.

It needed no indiscreet or corrupt hints from him to send the price of the despised Continental securities soaring. His friends, personal and political, knew what was in his mind, and a great many of them proceeded to capitalize their knowledge. They knew, too, that the avowed aims of the Constitution makers was to re-create the value of this paper. Indeed, the whole literature of the ratification pamphlets for a year had teemed with promises that the new instrument would protect the public creditor.

Clever speculators, therefore, leaped into the market while there was yet time. Soon the scrip was up to forty-five cents in Philadelphia, New York and Boston, but news traveled slowly in the West and South where no man had heard of Hamilton or his views on public credit. There the paper could be bought at ten cents or even lower. Long before the Secretary finished his report, express riders were galloping into the wilderness to offer poor men a few cents for scrip that had already risen to half of par, and the wily Jeremiah Wadsworth freighted two fast sloops with coin for a paper chase in out-of-the-way Southern ports.

Hamilton, fully aware of what was going on, made no move to check the gamblers. Concentration of the national debt in a few well-disposed hands was an essential part of his plan, deliberately encouraged, for he proposed to make the

national debt the foundation stone of national finance and
national prosperity. It was a daring innovation, since few
in that age realized that a nation in borrowing from its own
citizens is in a different position from an individual who has
borrowed from another.

The value of the scrip as an instrument of national policy
depended upon the securities being held by the influential
few. How else was he to "make it the *immediate* interest of
the moneyed men to co-operate with the government"? Hardship might be worked on the innocent who had supported
the Revolution in its darkest moments. The innocent might
cry out that they had been robbed. But to Hamilton that
mattered little if he obtained for his administration the enthusiastic support of the compact band of capitalist entrepre-
neurs who alone could be expected to appreciate the beauties
of a class-conscious government.

Undeflected by abstract theories, he saw that the backing
of the masters of money, the masters of trade and the masters
of land must be thrown behind any centralized system that
would rule and not merely influence, and of these the planters and patroons were least interested. No other classes were
powerful enough even if they could be aroused, and Hamilton was the last man in America to want to rouse the unpre-
dictable masses.

His personal attitude toward speculation was rather complex. He owned $800 worth of public securities and never
tried to get more. But his brother-in-law, John B. Church,
was one of his best clients and Hamilton, as his man of business, handled thousands of dollars' worth of scrip for him.
Schuyler also profited enormously. Yet the Secretary understood quite well the delicacy of his position, and his public,
even his semi-public, utterances were superbly moral.

"I am sure you are sincere when you say that you would
not subject me to an impropriety," he replied to Light Horse
Harry Lee, a friend of army days, who had asked about a
probable rise, "nor do I know that there would be any in an-

swering your queries. But you remember the saying with regard to Caesar's wife. I think the spirit of it applicable to
every man concerned in the administration of the finances of
the country. With respect to the conduct of such men, *suspicion* is ever eagle-eyed. And the most innocent things may
be misinterpreted."

There is no need to value too highly the purity here displayed. Hamilton's objects were obtainable without telling
the Lees of Virginia how to make a fortune. He could see
that without any other assistance from him than his known
views and tenacity, the national debt was finding its way into
the hands where he would have put it in the first instance,
where as a brevet lieutenant colonel he had urged Morris to
put it. The Secretary could devote himself to making use of
the holders.

He ceased for a time to be an assiduous diner-out. Parties
at his own home were infrequent. He read hardly anything
unconnected with his office. Indeed, the organization of the
department and the preparation of his report occupied him
so completely that Oliver Wolcott, coming from Connecticut
to assume the position of Auditor of the Treasury, thus described one of New York's leading dandies:

"From the appearance of Col. Hamilton, I think him a
very amiable, plain man."

The amiability never wavered, but Wolcott discovered
that the plainness was an erroneous first impression. Hamilton was seen, elaborately garbed in bright coats somewhat
longer in the skirt than most, at such occasions as a Presidential visit to the wax works. He was in the theater on the historic November night when Sheridan's "The Critic" melted
Washington's gravity into laughter.

Hamilton had given up most of his practice, but he had to
keep a few clients like Church, for he had saved little and
the needs of a family of six, coupled with the display demanded of his official position, were hardly met by his salary
of $3,000 a year, a sum that showed how far Congress was

from sharing his views on the Cabinet rank of a finance minister, since it had fixed the rewards of the Secretary of State
at $3,500. Hamilton was not alone in his opinion of the fig-
ure a nation's rulers ought to cut, although Wolcott was expecting to save a third of his $1,500 salary despite the greater
cost of living in New York, and had written to his wife:

"The example of the President and his family, will render
parade and expense improper and disreputable."

General Knox was equally attentive to the Presidential
example, but he knew how many horses and servants Washington brought with him and what a shipload of furniture,
plate, pictures and linens Martha had sent ahead of her for
the house in Cherry Street. So the Secretary of War, with a
family no larger than Hamilton's, was spending more
than $4,000 a year just to maintain his house, his coach and
his five servants. Of course his Lucy—grown so fat that John
Adams's daughter exclaimed, "I am frightened when I look
at her"—was addicted to flamboyant, unsuitable and expensive costumes, but a Secretary of the Treasury could hardly
allow himself to be outshone by a Cabinet colleague.

Hamilton and Betsey kept their end up, and if they did
not run into debt very much, the credit was hers. She had
learned early in her married life that Hamilton's mind was,
as the phrase went, too enlarged and grand to concern itself
with a petty household budget. He was always owing comparatively trifling sums, which gave him a great sympathy for
men who had borrowed more than they could pay. One of
his favorite works of art was the portrait of Betsey done while
Ralph Earle, the artist, was in debtors prison. Her example
stimulated enough other women to brave the conventions
and the gloomy cells so that the painter was able to earn his
way out of jail.

Hamilton never came close enough to that predicament to
worry him, but the financier, tossing millions back and forth
with easy dexterity, balancing national accounts, gauging potential revenues to a hair or calculating estimates to a nicety,

could never keep his own quite modest personal records straight. Betsey, however, was not a Schuyler and a Van Rensselaer for nothing. Her capable little hands sorted out his muddled statements; she saw to it that bills were paid or plausibly postponed, stretched the family income to surprising limits and won from James McHenry the enthusiastic encomium:

"She has as much merit as your Treasurer as you have as Treasurer of the wealth of the United States."

XV

CASH AND CREDIT

"ALL THE PERPLEXITIES, CONFUSION AND DISTRESS IN AMERICA, arise . . . not from a want of honor or virtue, so much as from downright ignorance of the nature of coin, credit and circulation."

Thus John Adams summarized the troubles that confronted Hamilton. The Boston patriot was writing to Jefferson, on whom the words of wisdom were wasted, for the sage of Monticello shared to an almost painful degree that "downright ignorance." But the "Duke of Braintree," as satirists soon began to call the Vice President because of his pomposity, vanity and faintly ridiculous insistence on titles and ceremonious modes of address, was a political philosopher of the stature of either Hamilton or Madison. When self-esteem, against which he struggled in vain all his ninety years, did not becloud his judgment, no one saw the truth more clearly.

His perspicacity in this instance was proved by the reception of Hamilton's "First Report on the Public Credit." Ready on January 9 for submission to the second session of Congress, it was designed for oral delivery in the manner of a British Chancellor of the Exchequer presenting a budget to the Commons. That was the method taken for granted, but Congress decided not to extend the courtesies of the floor to the Cabinet. The House was in no mood to copy Parliamentary procedure, and even Hamilton's close supporters felt their dignity obliged them to dispense with ministerial leadership. Others were frankly afraid the Secretary's eloquence would sweep them off their feet.

Five days of unremitting labor put the report into shape to

be read by others, and on January 14 Congress realized it had
a master, a leader who would guide its vacillating footsteps
toward a very different form of government than the old
Confederation. Not even the deadly monotone of the clerks
could disguise altogether the inflammatory nature of Hamilton's lucid exposition of national needs. It was revolutionary,
or at least counter-revolutionary, yet no one could quarrel
openly with the purpose of his program, which he put forward as:

"To justify and preserve the confidence of the most enlightened friends of good government; to promote the increasing respectability of the American name; to answer the
calls of justice; to furnish new resources both to agriculture
and commerce; to cement more closely the union of the
States; to add to their security against foreign attack; to establish public order on the basis of an upright and liberal policy:—these are the great and invaluable ends to be secured by
a proper and adequate provision, at the present period, for
the support of public credit."

He offered to achieve these benefits through a national
debt of such colossal magnitude that some of the listeners
seemed to see the overwhelming burden of it crushing the
taxpayers of remote generations into helpless misery. For
Hamilton proposed to refund at par the entire mass of Continental obligations, domestic and foreign, and to assume on
behalf of the Federal government all the outstanding war
debts of the states as well. This made the stupendous total of
nearly $70,000,000, and even disinterested men soberly feared
that this was more than a population of 3,000,000 could
ever pay.

The report was not content with a moral plea for good
faith. It contained provisions for a sinking fund, a schedule
of taxes to finance the plan and a clause that not more than
two per cent. of the principal could be paid off in any one
year. The author was so far from sharing popular doubts of
the nation's financial ability that he was afraid the bonds

might be redeemed too rapidly, and he had use for a consolidated debt. Under his scheme, it was to serve as the credit basis for new capitalist enterprise, the nucleus of government support to the expanding forces of individual initiative.

The Senate, true to its oddly autocratic star-chamber methods of secrecy, which were supported by some of the loudest mouthers of democratic ideals, heard the report behind closed doors in an "awful silence." The egalitarian Maclay, representing the small farmers of western Pennsylvania, was "so struck of an heap" that he was unable to find words to record his feelings in his diary. But Maclay was out of touch with current events and entirely ignorant of the published works of Alexander Hamilton. For months, therefore, Maclay had been puzzled by the rise in scrip, apparently supposing it to be one of those mysterious workings of the vile capitalist that pass common understanding.

"The report from the Treasury explained all," he now discovered.

The Senator was in the lower House to observe how that body received Hamilton's wisdom. He noted with disapproval that most of those in the packed galleries wore the pleased look of speculators. To the suspicious Pennsylvanian, his gloomy nature rendered more irascible by gout and an uneasy feeling that the world was unwilling to govern itself according to his homespun political ideas, a smile was the sure mark of a gambler in public paper. He must have been nearer right than usual this time, for many exuberant spirits in the audience could not wait in silence for the report to be finished. As soon as they heard the essential paragraphs about refunding, they scrambled out into Wall Street for an impromptu celebration of the fortunes they had made. Their joy was reflected in the faces of the Representatives, nearly half of whom were holders of scrip. Only a few of these thought it necessary to lie about their operations, for the notion that a statesman should not profit by his vote would have seemed Quixotic to most.

The Secretary of the Treasury was the hero of the hour, and for a short time he basked in the sun of what seemed universal approval. Even Madison praised the report, seeing no flaw as yet. The objectors were few and obscure or, like Maclay, refrained from public expression of their feelings, although the Senator, after a day to recover from the shock, confided to his diary:

"The business of yesterday will, I think, in all probability damn the character of Hamilton as a minister forever."

Neither friends nor foes seemed to grasp thoroughly just what the Secretary was driving at. The first group saw that he was bent on restoring the credit of the United States, or rather creating it. His enemies observed that he was enriching a class that is never popular. Few were aware that he was aiming beyond that, although he had made himself sufficiently clear to any not blinded by the downright ignorance of which Adams complained.

His report went further than details of financial practice. It outlined a system of practical administration in which the trading interests and the advocates of continental expansion would be linked to a strong central government by bonds of material gain that only revolution would be able to break. It was usual for the proponents of this theory to argue that politics is a business, best operated by business men, and that the prosperity of their class will be reflected in benefits to all the people. Hamilton, whose goal was the same as that of men who talked in this vein, was not deceived by their talk.

He had no delusions that a merchant was any more altruistic than a mechanic or a farmer. Furthermore, he seriously doubted the success of a political system founded on altruism. His wide reading had revealed no instance of such a thing being tried, much less proved. His was not the type of mind that could derive pleasure from the experiment, and his all-too-well-founded opinion of the essential baseness of man's nature would have made him a sorry leader for such a cause.

Disdaining visionary schemes, he had a very clear idea of the sort of a state he meant to build, but he had to do it with the tools at hand. There was neither time nor material nor (in him) patience for the elaboration of new machinery. Surveying the 3,000,000 inhabitants of the United States with an impartially distrustful gaze, he found there were in general just two kinds of men who could be induced to work for his principles. These were the merchant-financiers and the speculators in western lands. They alone stood to gain substantially and immediately from the existence of a strong central government.

The great disfranchised masses were of no account in the political scale at all, useless then and for years afterward to any party. Economically they were a tool, not a force, for they were unorganized, helpless. Even the planters who set themselves up as champions of democracy were far from willing to admit working people to a share of the government.

"Notwithstanding all the scoffing and reproaches against us as slaveholders, the cause of republicanism in this country is connected with the political ascendancy of the southern states," argued one eminent Virginian. "Freemen cannot be employed generally in laborious and servile occupations, without debasing their minds."

No one save a dreamer would have thought, then, of establishing a firm, progressive government on the weakness of the bewildered many, and Hamilton saw no visions. The small farmers were of as little value to him. Their views were of necessity limited to their immediate needs and desires, a narrow outlook that scarcely transcended county let alone state boundaries. The great eastern land barons, patroons and planters, had rallied to the protection of property, but by property they meant their acres, their timber, their slaves and their serfs. They had no interest in the development of their country as a mercantile power. They looked with positive distaste on westward expansion, for that might lower the value of their eastern holdings. They misliked the embryonic industry that fired Hamilton's imagination, for that might tempt tenants to leave the land.

The only men, then, who really "thought nationally," as Hamilton would have put it, were the merchants, financiers and land grabbers. All of these needed a strong Federal government in their businesses. The merchants had to have thirteen united states in which to operate freely, and they wanted a powerful administration to safeguard their shipping abroad. The financiers would be ruined without the protection of a stable currency and banks which they could control free of political interference. Obviously one government was better for them than thirteen. The land grabbers could realize their potential fortunes only if the nation grew sufficiently to send the population increase out to reclaim the wilderness. That migration, too, depended on canals and roads which only a rich national regime could build; the extinction of Indian claims and raids, which only a strong executive with ample authority could achieve; a confirmation of title, which would be easier to obtain from a central land office than in the midst of conflicting pretensions of eastern states.

Hamilton cherished no illusions as to the integrity, patriotism, good faith or even good sense of the class upon which he deliberately builded a new nation. He was well aware that the big shipping interests, the Cabots and Tracys and Peabodys, had made their fortunes as privateers and had the morals of the pirates from whom they were ethically descended. He knew how these men gambled with the lives of their crews, sending out rotten, leaky ships for the chance of doubling or trebling their investment on a single voyage. He thoroughly understood his own clients, the merchants, with their tricks of adulteration, counterfeiting and false grading, so that dealing with them was an exciting battle of wits. He was acquainted with the ruthlessness of the land grabbers in defrauding Indians and immigrants alike.

But, such as they were, he had only them to work with, and the accuracy with which he gauged their price could be measured by the adulation that went up from the jubilant scrip holders laughing and shouting in the crisp January air of Wall Street. They were snatching at immediate profit and singing the praises of Alexander Hamilton.

That young man accepted the encomiums gracefully, smiling and loquacious, but watchful. For underneath the happy cries of the speculators his keen ear detected a rumble of discontent. In a few days old soldiers and backwoodsmen were growling that they had been swindled. Patriots who had taken Continentals in the dark days, and probably cheated the army at the time, wailed that they had been robbed by a little ring of insiders led by the Secretary of the Treasury. In the taverns there was menacing talk of a "corrupt squadron" of Congressmen and gamblers. Hamilton disposed of such grumblings with a shrug of his well-tailored shoulders. He was not bothered by the outcry of the moment. He was quite sure it could not affect his funding bill.

His confidence was based partly on the fact that at least twenty-nine of the sixty-four members of the House held public securities. Sixteen of the twenty-six Senators were in the same fortunate class. On the initial bill, that providing for the redemption of Continental paper at par, the only objectors at first were the loud but insignificant minority represented by Maclay who opposed funding altogether and a louder, even less significant group in favor of repudiation. These gentlemen, screaming that poor men had been cheated and would now be taxed to make crooked gamblers rich, stormed through days of debate. They were answered with contempt, but suddenly a new note was struck in the House, so quietly that Hamilton was one of the few who understood at once that it constituted a threat to his entire program.

It came, most unexpectedly to the Secretary, from James Madison. He was a Virginia planter, of course, but Hamilton had thought he would rise superior to his class interests in support of the strong government both had sought. Madison, however, did not mean by this quite the same thing as did his collaborator of *The Federalist*. Furthermore, he was most unfavorably impressed by the unctuous greed of his friend's eulogists, and his sense of justice had been outraged by the sharp practices of the speculators. So on a February day he rose to offer in his weak but oddly arresting voice a plan that would save the credit of the nation and wreck Hamilton's scheme for linking the rich to the state. Madison suggested simply that original holders of scrip be paid at par. All others were to receive the highest market price prevailing before Hamilton's report, the balance to be paid to the first creditor of the government.

Taken off his guard by this flank attack, Hamilton scurried about, rallying his forces. His busy little figure was seen darting from man to man in the lobbies. The sour Maclay raged at finding him closeted with a Senate committee, practicing heaven knew what black arts on the guileless solons. Betsey's budget was upset again to provide tasteful little dinners where men with votes were exposed to the Hamiltonian charm and logic. The "corrupt squadron" was drilled and exhorted, and on February 28 its disciplined ranks rode down the unorganized opposition. Hamilton's funding bill was law, and he could turn to the part of his program that he had always expected to rouse a storm.

This was the assumption by the national government of state debts incurred in the Revolution. It was opposed by states' rights men who realized that taxation to pay them off would add to the Federal power. It was opposed by the advocates of repudiation. It was opposed by an important group from states which had no debts to assume. Virginia and several other Southern states had liquidated their war costs and saw no reason why their citizens should be taxed to help pay the debts of Massachusetts. This last fraction of the opposition contained several who had fought valiantly for the funding bill.

In the House the debate took on a note of hysteria. The virtues and sufferings of old soldiers were hashed up again.

The stories of speculators swarming into the hills and forests in search of state scrip were repeated, with all too much accuracy. Charges of outright bribery were bandied about and, in spite of the tradition that a vote is an article of commerce, under which most of these men grew up, proved baseless. Subtler influences were at work, however, such as Robert Morris's offer to let Maclay in on some of the great financier's land speculations. The press was so full of arguments and scrip quotations that toward the end of March *The Daily Advertiser* could find room only for the barest mention of a really important event:

"On Sunday last, arrived in this city, Thomas Jefferson, Esq., Secretary of State for the United States of America."

Hamilton, redoubling his lobbying efforts for assumption, paid almost as little attention to the new arrival as had the newspapers. When they met at a Cabinet session, each was mildly pleased to find that the other lived up to his reputation. There was nothing in Jefferson's manner to cause the Secretary of the Treasury any alarm. Almost as tall as the President, Jefferson owed most of his slender height to exceptionally long, clumsy legs. Carelessly dressed, his dark red hair combed loosely off a broad forehead and tied at the back of the neck, he gave the impression of being a contemplative soul. The wide face with the rather pale blue eyes, long chin and high cheekbones was plain and unassuming. He was by nature retiring, and one of the best-known stories about him illustrated a tactful modesty that Hamilton never tried to emulate.

"You replace Doctor Franklin, I hear," the French Minister of Foreign Affairs had said politely when the new envoy first came to the court of King Louis.

"I succeed him; nobody could replace him," Jefferson replied.

Of course the Secretary of State was known for more than courtesy and tact. Author of the Declaration of Independence, Governor of Virginia when the State was abolishing such relics of feudalism as primogeniture, diplomat, philosopher and writer on innumerable speculative topics, he possessed learned accomplishments which Hamilton respected. But the younger man was as yet unaware that his new colleague planned to put his theories into practice. For the time being he seemed nothing like so dangerous as his bosom friend, Madison.

That gentleman, with what Hamilton could only regard as treason to their common aims, was putting backbone into the fight against assumption. The motley hosts of disorder gathered around the slight figure, and when the tidal wave of argument receded at last to leave the field clear for a vote, Madison carried the day by 31 to 29.

If Hamilton needed any proof of his thesis that all men are ruled by interest and that moneyed men in particular would support only that government which gave them profits, he got it in defeat. His old friend, Representative Elias Boudinot, speculator now in scrip and land, was shaken from his allegiance to the brilliant schoolboy who once had lodged in his home.

"His wrinkles rose in ridges," Maclay reported maliciously, noting also that Senator Schuyler's "hair stood on end, as if the Indians had fired at him."

Theodore Sedgwick of Massachusetts, called to order in the midst of a furious diatribe against demagogues, clapped his hat on his head and stalked out of the House. Speculators, facing a net loss on the state bonds they had been buying so gleefully, muttered that the Federal regime was hardly worth while. Let it go the way of the Confederation and good riddance.

Hamilton alone remained serene. There were more ways than one to get his program through a House whose resistance he had been prepared to circumvent from the start, since from the start he had expected no other conduct from a popularly elected body. Many of its foolish members thought the location of the permanent capital was as important as assumption, and the site was to be chosen at this session.

The Secretary, unfettered by preferences, saw with pleasure that the Representatives of every section were intriguing in this matter with a fervor that matched their denunciation of gamblers. Washington favored a site near Georgetown in Virginia; Morris was for Philadelphia; Maclay liked the idea of a capital on the Susquehanna, near where he lived and owned land. Baltimore, New York and the Falls of the Delaware had their local advocates. Surely out of that conflict it should be possible for an impartial man to salvage a valuable assumption bill.

Negotiations were opened with Morris, Maclay and others. Morris had already delivered all the votes he could command. Maclay refused to be tempted. But in the office of the Secretary of State there toiled a man very busy with the organization of a new department, a man who admitted knowing nothing of finance, a man whose attachment to his state was close, a man whose character Hamilton thought he had read at a glance. So one morning as Jefferson was calling to see the President, he was waylaid by the Secretary of the Treasury. The dandy of the Cabinet craved a few moments of his colleague's time.

Together the awkward, secretly bewildered Virginian and the plausible little New Yorker walked up and down Broadway before Washington's door—the executive mansion had been removed to the Macomb house—the attentive but somewhat uncomprehending red head bowed toward the powdered coiffure. For half an hour Hamilton expounded the needs of the country, not knowing that his companion had already expressed the tentative conclusion that it might be better to accept assumption than risk the funding bill altogether and thus sacrifice national credit.

"He painted pathetically the temper into which the legislature had been wrought," Jefferson wrote years later, when he felt his share in the business needed justification; "the disgust of those who were called the creditor states; the danger of the secession of their members; and the separation of the states. He observed that the members of the administration ought to act in concert; that, though this question was not of my department, yet a common duty should make it a common concern; that the President was the center on which all administrative questions ultimately rested, and that all of us should rally around him, and support with joint efforts, measures approved by him; and that, the question having been lost by a small majority only, it was probable that an appeal from me to the judgment and discretion of some of my friends might effect a change in the vote, and the machine of government, now suspended, might be again set in motion.

"I told him that I was really a stranger to the whole subject; that, not having yet informed myself of the system of finance adopted, I knew not how far this was a necessary sequence; that, undoubtedly, if its rejection endangered a dissolution of our union at this incipient stage, I should deem that the most unfortunate of all consequences, to avert which all partial and temporary evils should be yielded. I proposed to him, however, to dine with me the next day, and I would invite another friend or two, and bring them into conference together; and I thought it impossible that reasonable men, consulting together coolly, could fail, by some mutual sacrifices of opinion, to form a compromise which was to save the union."

The conference was held, and Hamilton was never so persuasive as at table. Over the wine the bargain was struck— two votes for assumption and a capital on the Potomac. The latter part of the deal was put through on July 16 by the discipline of the "corrupt squadron," whose members voted to a man for the site of the future Washington. Five days later assumption was reintroduced in the Senate, passing over Maclay's dazed and sputtering protests by 14 to 12. The fact that the President favored the bill was stressed heavily as Hamilton had stressed it to Jefferson, and Maclay exclaimed:

"The President has become, in the hands of Hamilton, the dishclout of every dirty speculation, as his name goes to wipe away blame and silence all murmuring."

Murmuring was not really silenced when the new bill came down to the House, but Representatives Richard B. Lee and Alexander White of Virginia changed their votes— "White with a revulsion of stomach almost convulsive," Mr. Jefferson remembered—and Hamilton's program for capitalist domination of the government was saved, 32 to 29. Twenty-one of the majority were speculators.

Once again the press broke out in a rash of panegyric. Moneyed men exclaimed in admiration. Even Madison submitted with good grace. And Hamilton made no secret of his own feelings, betraying what Maclay thought was a "boyish, giddy manner" at a celebration of the Pennsylvania delegation. It was quite a party, costing the careful but gouty Senator 28 shillings and a two-day headache. The young Secretary joked and bubbled over with good spirits, drank sparingly and escaped a hangover.

But he was not resting on his laurels. He had just begun to earn the gratitude of the class to which he had attached himself. While the legislators scattered to their homes, to meet next in Philadelphia, the capital for ten years while Washington was being created out of a swamp and a forest, he retired to his study. There, alternately pacing the floor and bending over his papers, he built the superstructure for the framework of government which his "Report on the Public Credit" had erected on the foundation of the Constitution.

XVI

THE LADIES, GOD BLESS 'EM

THE LABORS OF SUMMER AND AUTUMN, 1790, SENT HAMILTON to Philadelphia for the last session of the first Congress armed with the materials for a burst of creative effort that amazed his contemporaries. He arrived, also, with an accumulated craving for the pleasures of the flesh which the gossips found no less remarkable.

He seemed to find time for everything. The Secretary's neat person, usually accompanied by Betsey, who was enjoying a brief respite from child-bearing, was seen at levees, balls and theaters. He made the rounds of Philadelphia fashion, and became one of the minor terrors of husbands—without Betsey. He directed in lordly style the party maneuvers of the "corrupt squadron." He completed the machinery of his own department and began to tinker with that of others. He demonstrated that if Mr. Jefferson took first place at formal receptions, Colonel Hamilton was prime minister in the Cabinet. He continued his paternal guardianship of the elderly Baron von Steuben, so that the genial disciplinarian told people proudly:

"The Secretary of the Treasury is my banker—my Hamilton takes care of me when he cannot take care of himself."

That strain on Betsey's budget was relieved when Congress awarded the old soldier a pension and a grant of land, and his young benefactor went on with his work of placing control of the government so firmly in the hands of his moneyed men that no mere agrarian political ascendancy would ever be able to dislodge it.

The debt settlement had gone far to effect this, but there

was more to come. In rapid succession, Hamilton sent down reports on improving customs receipts and protecting what American industry existed, on disposing of public lands, on a mint, on an excise on spirits, and finally on a national bank. Every one of them built up to the Hamiltonian idea of government, but the last two, the taxing power linked to a central credit system, guaranteed that form of government.

The excise, unpopular as it was, went through with little opposition that Hamilton regarded as serious. The noes in the House were twenty, nineteen of them from the South and West where many farmers had no other way of getting their crop to market than by converting it into whisky. But, adding these taxes to the customs, Hamilton had tapped the two great, readily collectible revenues available, and secured for the government money, which is power. He did not fail to notice that there was a party line beginning to form, and those nineteen agrarian votes brought the first plain division of Congress into Federalists and Democrat-Republicans.

The Bank of the United States completed the split, for it tied the interests of the moneyed men to the state with a grip which agrarians feared instinctively. Opening new credit facilities to commerce and offering an improved circulation medium, it would have attracted mercantile support on those grounds alone. But Hamilton went further. He threw national credit and national cash into the bank to be used within extremely broad limits at the discretion and for the benefit of its private directors. Nor was this disguised.

"To attach full confidence to an institution of this kind," he declared bluntly, "it appears to be an essential ingredient in its structure that it shall be under a *private* not a *public* direction—under the guidance of *individual interest,* not of *public policy.*"

Small wonder Maclay noted that the merchants and speculators in the Senate were "magnetically drawn to the contemplation of the moneyed interest." For Hamilton was giving them the government's money to work with. In addition he had prepared such a scholarly defense of a banking system in general and a central bank in particular that a great deal of the opposition was diverted by the hope that the whole country would share in the benefits accruing to the capitalists.

Indeed, Hamilton's glowing analysis of what state banks had done in the past and could do in the future was so convincing that even Madison did not care to meet the issue directly. Crusty John Adams might have done it, for he was dazzled only by his own eloquence, and Hamilton never converted him from the opinion:

"Banks have done more injury to the religion, morality, tranquillity, prosperity, and even wealth of the nation than they can have done or ever will do good. They are like party spirit, the delusion of the many for the interest of a few."

But Adams was immured in the silence of the Vice Presidency, emerging only in the disguise of *Davila* in the newspapers. Congressional opposition, declining the issue of whether a bank was desirable, preferred to take its stand on the ground that it was unconstitutional. Madison made a stirring appeal to the House not to overstep the bounds set forth in the fundamental law, and nowhere in that document was there express authority to establish a national bank. The leaders really did not expect to defeat Hamilton on this point in a Congress where trade was so strongly represented, and Jefferson was considering whether some coup could not be effected to increase the agrarian representation in Congress, "which may put that interest above that of the stock jobbers."

The bill went through smoothly enough, but there was hope of a veto, and the real test of strength was in the struggle to win Washington. He had doubts on the Constitutional question, and called for Cabinet opinions. Jefferson and Randolph put the case for strict construction and Madison, at the President's request, wrote what amounted to a veto message.

Hamilton, scribbling in great haste, drafted a defense of the implied powers of the Constitution that foreshadowed the decisions of the Supreme Court and was thought worthy to stand beside the more deliberate opinions of John Marshall. The arguments were old to Hamilton. He had wanted even the feeble Confederation to seize greater authority than he claimed under the Constitution. He had held then, and now repeated, that a sovereign nation by definition possesses the attributes of sovereignty and by implication must have the right to provide for the welfare of its citizens. This was a view congenial to Washington. He signed, permitting the country to develop in the direction of genuine national strength and unleashing a burst of speculation in stock of the new bank.

"Of all the shameful circumstances of this business, it is among the greatest to see the members of the Legislature who were most active in pushing this job most openly grasping its emoluments," mourned Madison.

Hamilton, despising the gamblers quite as thoroughly as any southern planter, was confirmed in his view that it is the part of statesmanship to use the ignoble impulses of mankind to achieve the form of government which alone may keep those impulses under control. He wrote in positively Jeffersonian vein denouncing the "confederated host of frantic, and, I fear, in too many instances, unprincipled gamblers." But he did not believe in burning down the house to get rid of the rats. On the whole he was satisfied that he had given muscles and nerves to the inadequate skeleton of the Constitution until it was able to carry a tolerable load of government.

So, in spite of incessant writing and argument and persuasion and the thousand details of organizing an internal revenue service, he enjoyed life in the big city with its brick houses and pavements, so much neater and cleaner than New York. He and Betsey had taken a rather larger place than they could afford, a solid, comfortable mansion with handsome gardens on Third Street at the corner of Walnut, in what was called "the court end of town." Washington had rented Robert Morris's home nearby, and the Hamiltons were in the very cultivated throng that gathered around Martha for plum cake and tea on Friday evenings. Elsewhere a more robust hospitality was dispensed, and Abigail Adams, mourning the lost beauties of her New York home, Richmond Hill, was abusing Philadelphia in general, its frightfully high prices not the least, but adding:

"I should spend a very dissipated winter, if I were to accept one half the invitations I receive."

Others welcomed dissipation, and Hamilton was one. His temperate mode of life relaxing somewhat, he was seen to be "liquorish" at various parties about town, and some prudent men with pretty wives gave the Secretary of the Treasury a wide berth. The city being twice the size of New York, there was a corresponding social activity. There were real salons, and Morris and the William Binghams were drawing on two of the largest fortunes in America in keen competition for the honor of giving the most elaborate dinners.

Anne Bingham won easily over the stout and unflirtatious Morris, who soon gave over the rivalry. Daughter of the Financier's partner, Thomas Willing, the lady brought to her entertaining the shrewd qualities of her father. She brought, too, great beauty, charm and tact. Tall and slender, displaying on formal occasions rather more or her bosom than New England Puritans thought proper, she had returned from a few social triumphs in Europe with the ambition of being a queen of society. She perfected what some of her friends remarked upon as the pretty and fashionable art of cursing daintily. Her home was designed for pomp and ceremony; her life was governed by the craving to preside over a brilliant salon; even her death at thirty-seven was due to her insistence on resuming the whirl of parties too soon after giving birth to a child.

But this winter of 1790-91, Mrs. Bingham was in excellent

health and introducing new Continental customs at the big house on Third Street. Here there was sparkling if idle talk, the sort of conversation men rehearsed in advance, and gambling for stakes that reached into hundreds of dollars. Only a few were still shocked by the facts of life, and even well-brought-up girls were permitted to hear stories indicating that their married friends produced children through another medium than the kindness of storks.

The talk, however, was bolder than the arts dared to be, as the traveled Harry Hills learned when he brought from Europe a marble Venus to adorn his home. She created so much comment that he was obliged to have her clothed. He chose a frock of Grecian design, and thereafter the cold marble features were displayed to the world above tasteful folds of decent green silk.

In a circle that tolerated bawdy stories but shrank from marble nudity, Hamilton moved with a sure social sense. He was gifted with an instinct for knowing how far he might go. Duller and less accomplished men noted with disapproval that his conversation, especially with women, was "very trifling." But the women liked it—one, at least, missed his "agreeable nonsense" when he was absent—and he had no difficulty in responding adequately to the toast when, as was frequently the case in an age of politeness to and contempt for their sex, the sentiment was:

"The Ladies, God bless 'em!"

His talk was not always trifling, even in moments of relaxation. He was elected to the American Philosophical Society in January, and thereafter the meetings of that learned body were enlivened by a memory stored with vast miscellaneous reading since student days.

Gaiety at the Hamilton home was less elaborate but rather more spontaneous than at the larger affairs of Mrs. Bingham. The Secretary's sisters-in-law were with him again, and stood in mighty little awe of the great man. They chaffed him familiarly and were so careless of his dignity that Peggy

Schuyler—"a wild young flirt from Albany," someone described her—could take joy in a large company in adorning his careful costume with a bow dropped from Angelica's shoe and dubbed him knight.

"Not of the garter," objected Mrs. Church.

"True, Sister," retorted the pert Peggy, "but he would be if you would let him."

Hamilton's dignity, however, was proof against such foolery. He was even able to maintain it in the face of gossip that linked his name with other women than the beautiful Angelica, until he himself had to confess to the truth of the charge "that I had nothing to lose as to my reputation for chastity."

What did destroy his self-possession for a moment was news from New York. There, while he flirted with Mrs. Bingham, explained the Constitution to Washington and prepared to collect an excise from hot-headed backwoodsmen, a sudden upheaval in the political world upset his calculations. It was not really as wonderful as it seemed to Hamilton, but he had supposed New York to be eating out of his hand despite the existence of two powerful dissenters. The peculiarities of the suffrage in his state made family influence of unusual importance, so that one of the exaggerated sayings of the day was:

"The Clintons have *power*, the Livingstons have *numbers*, the Schuylers have *Hamilton*."

The Secretary of the Treasury had no doubt he outweighed power and numbers. But when the Legislature met in January to choose a new Senator—Schuyler having drawn one of the short terms necessary to carry out the provision of one-third of the upper house being elected every two years—something went wrong. There had been no hint of organized opposition; Schuyler's name was the only one presented, and yet the Legislature inexplicably rejected him. Inexplicably, that is, in Philadelphia. New York knew that Hamilton's high-handed manner of forcing Rufus King upon it two years ago had alienated the whole clan of Livingston.

Out of that obscure jumble of intrigue and vote-trading came the inevitable compromise, and Aaron Burr emerged as Senator from New York. He and Hamilton passed as friends. They had appeared together in court. They exchanged visits and dinners and little courtesies. Betsey and the accomplished but invalided Mrs. Burr were on excellent terms. The new Senator, more than most, graced that social sphere in which the Secretary delighted. For all that, Hamilton realized, Burr was dangerous. The fellow was brilliant and seemed to Hamilton to be unscrupulous. He was as attracted by and even more attractive to women. He commanded large fees, earned them quickly and spent them easily. He read widely and to good purpose, and the really great ambition of his life—unknown to his whole generation —was to prove by means of his adored little daughter, Theodosia, that women can have brains and souls. For that he would cheerfully have sacrificed the world.

None of these factors were the cause of Hamilton's uneasiness. He was surrounded by men as unscrupulous and ambitious as he supposed Burr to be. What made that brilliant son of Puritans a menace was the very doubtful orthodoxy of his ideas. It was not at all certain that Burr believed wholeheartedly in anything except Theodosia, and certainly he was no bigot on the sacredness of property. The people meant a great deal more to him than the credit of governments, the rise and fall of securities or even the inviolability of land titles. It was bad enough for Madison and Jefferson to set the landed interest up against the moneyed interest. But at least the basis of their party was property. Who knew what Burr might set up?

However, a single Senator, even a Burr, was not likely to do serious damage once the whole fabric of Hamiltonian finance had been woven into the governmental structure. The Secretary of the Treasury, setting up the Bank of the

United States—the fact that speculators were heavily represented on the directorate did not escape censure—and working out the routine of his expanding department, found that
he did not have enough to do. His successes had for the moment overpowered his enemies, and Adams could find no
more exciting news to write Jay than:

"The winter is very mild; Politicks dull, Speculation
brisk."

Such being the case, Hamilton was a little bored, in a
mood to be interested in the story of a pretty woman or to
devise some new scheme for augmenting the power of his
country and his class. It was like him to find time for both.

The United States, he thought, ought to become a great
industrial as well as a great commercial power. Therefore he
set himself to working out a program, writing to business
men for information, ordering every Treasury employee to
gather data on local manufacturing enterprises, however
small, and pondering the share government ought to take in
promoting factories. He was hard at it when on a summer's
day in 1791, a Mrs. Maria Reynolds, young and lovely and
in obvious distress, called to see him.

Leading her into a room apart from his family, the Secretary listened to a tale that is one hundred and fifty years
older now, but even then was of sufficient antiquity. It seems
that Mrs. Reynolds had a brute of a husband who abused her
and left her. All she wanted was to return to her family in
New York, and she had come to the gallant Colonel Hamilton, as a fellow New Yorker of known greatness of heart, to
provide the means for the journey. The story, as has been
said, was old, but Mrs. Reynolds was not.

"I replied," Hamilton recorded, "that her situation was
a very interesting one—that I was disposed to afford her
assistance to convey her to her friends, but this at the time
not being convenient to me (which was the fact) I must request the place of her residence, to which I should bring or
send a small supply of money."

The social gaiety of Philadelphia had waned with the hot weather, and life was a little dull. So that evening the Secretary of the Treasury was climbing the steps of a rather inelegant lodging house not at all in the "court end of town." The fair Maria met him at the head of the stairs and conducted him into what proved to be her bedroom. He handed over a banknote at once, but "it was quickly apparent that other than pecuniary consolation would be acceptable."

The gallant fellow was too much a gentleman to deprive distressed womanhood of any sort of consolation. He did it so acceptably that nothing more was heard about the unfortunate lady's desire to return to friends and family in New York. Instead it was Betsey who departed, happy and unsuspecting, to take her little brood of four on a visit to her father in Albany. Thereafter Hamilton's meetings with his new mistress took place in his own home.

He was no longer bored. Maria and the even more fascinating problems of industrial development saw to that. The vision of mills humming with machinery tended by the busy hands of women and little children, who would thus augment the income of the honest husbandman, floated before him far oftener than the fair features of Mrs. Reynolds. Eagerly Hamilton elaborated the broad theory of protection, subsidy, privilege and exploitation, but when it came to the point he was not content with theory. So while he wrote his "Report on Manufactures" for submission to Congress, he was busily organizing an experimental corporation to prove his point.

The information he was collecting from all over the country was helpful both to the report and the company. Soon he settled on New Jersey for his test factory, and one day Washington himself rode out to the falls of the Passaic, where his young friend pointed out with kindling enthusiasm the excellence of the site and the advantages to be derived from the production of needful and desirable articles. The placid rural setting, one day to become the city of Paterson, was approved and Hamilton returned to Philadelphia and Mrs. Reynolds, to draft a prospectus for the Society for Establishing Useful Manufactures.

This was entirely a labor of love. Hamilton was doing the work, but was not to share in the profits. True to his principles, he was leaving profits to men who need such stimuli. The ambitious project called for a corporation with a capital of $500,000—only three companies in the whole country, all of them banks, had as much—and its products were to include textiles, paper, shoes, wire, pottery, printers' supplies and beer. New Jersey was induced to contribute a charter that was to irk future generations, and abdicated quite a good deal of the state's sovereign powers. The corporation received, in exchange for nothing, a monopoly, immunity from taxes, wide powers of condemnation, the privilege of operating a lottery and exemption from militia duty for its employees. Thus encouraged, moneyed men led by Duer rushed for the stock and the prospectus was so persuasive that the actual subscription aggregated $625,000.

Well pleased, Hamilton polished off his notes on the theory of such enterprises, and on December 5 the House was listening to what none of the members realized was an alarmingly prophetic document. Hamilton's "Report on Manufactures" opened a vista of protective tariffs, special privilege, subsidies and dizzy profits. It noted with approval that in British factories most of the operatives were too young for useful farm work, but in 1791 child labor was regarded as a very fine thing, even by thinkers whose professed love for common men was greater than Hamilton's.

Meanwhile the liaison with Maria was proceeding in the direction that a really shrewd gallant—Senator Burr, for example—might have foreseen. The abusive husband had turned up seeking a reconciliation, and Maria wondered whether she should grant it.

"I advised to it," said Hamilton, "and was soon after informed by her that it had taken place."

It was not so complete that the fond wife gave up her handsome little lover, and at one of their meetings she told him that James Reynolds was engaged in speculation in public securities and knew something about a Treasury leak. It was just at this time that the boom in bank stock was causing Hamilton most concern. In the same week, somewhat relieved by a lull in the storm, he was warning Duer, who had been his assistant at the Treasury for a few months and was now one of the most active and wealthiest plungers in the New York market:

"If the infatuation had continued progressive and any extensive mischiefs had ensued, you would certainly have had a large portion of the blame."

The prospect of discovering a means to check the speculation prompted the Secretary to send for Reynolds. The man —Hamilton's impression of his utter villainy is, perhaps, not reliable—declared he had received a list of claims from Duer, which was of little importance if true, since Duer had been out of the department too long for any data of that kind he might have taken with him to have current worth. But Hamilton did not say this aloud for "it was the interest of my passions to set value upon it." He was not sufficiently carried away, however, to yield to Reynolds's plea for a job.

At this late date Hamilton began to have suspicions. Characteristically, he believed the man capable of anything, but thought the young and pretty woman might really be fond of him. As he had had no doubts that Peggy Arnold was a pure innocent in the treason of her husband, so he found excuses for Maria Reynolds, so fair and sorrowful and yielding. And, between indecision and passion, dreading the springing of a trap and not quite convinced that there was any basis for his fears, he continued his visits to the shabby boarding house, for Betsey was home again, until in mid-December he received a communication which he deciphered with difficulty.

"I have not tim to tell you the cause of my present

troubles," he read, "only that Mr. has rote you this morning and I know not wether you have got the letter or not and he has swore that If you do not answer It or If he dose not se or hear from you to day he will write Mrs. Hamilton he has just Gone oute and I am a Lone I think you had better come here one moment that you May know the Cause then you will the better know how to act Oh my God I feel more for you than myself and wish I had never been born to give you so mutch unhappiness do not rite to him no not a Line but come here soon do not send or leave any thing in his power"

Hard on the heels of this missive came a letter from the anguished husband, who spelled only a little better than his wife. He had found a note from Maria to her lover. On being taxed with it she broke down and confessed all, and he (Reynolds) was a broken man but "determined to have satisfaction. it shant be onely one family thats miserable."

The blackmail threat was plain enough, and Hamilton bowed to it. There was nothing else to do. If he allowed the scandal to break, Washington and Adams probably would turn from him in disgust, Betsey be wounded to the depths of her nice little mind, the whole pack of agrarians scream with coarse joy, the aristocratic Bingham salon jest with subdued but more barbed mockery. And the whole edifice of extra-constitutional authority for government and mon-eyed men might come tumbling down upon a disgraced, ridiculous Secretary. Of course there were plenty of tongues wagging about his supposed amours, but as Hamilton said himself "there is a wide difference between vague rumors and suspicions and the evidence of a positive fact." Some years later, when recalling the anguish of his unaccustomed hesitation, he added:

"No man not indelicately unprincipled, with the state of manners in this country, would be willing to have a conjugal infidelity fixed upon him with positive certainty. He would know that it would justly injure him with a considerable and respectable portion of society; and especially no man, tender of the happiness of an excellent wife, could, without extreme pain, look forward to the affliction which she might endure from the disclosure, especially a *public disclosure* of the fact. Those best acquainted with the interior of my domestic life will best appreciate the force of such a consideration upon me.

"The truth was, that in both relations, and especially the last, I dreaded extremely a disclosure—and was willing to make large sacrifices to avoid it."

Therefore he sent again for Reynolds. Unsavory negotiations proceeded for several days with the fellow taking a tone that was at once nauseating and inconclusive, for he well understood the value of keeping his victim in suspense: "But your being in the *Station of life* you are induses me to way every Surcomcance well." After some almost Oriental huckstering, that careful consideration boiled down to a demand for $1,000, for which "plaister for his wounded honor," as Hamilton called it, he promised to quit the town and his wife and "leve her to Yourself to do for her as you thing proper."

It was cheap, but the Secretary of the Treasury, the founder of a nation's credit, a bank, a funding system, a mint and a gigantic industrial corporation, had considerable difficulty in scraping the money together. He managed it at last, however, in two installments, and, filing the correspondence and receipts among his very secret papers, devoutly prayed that he had heard the last of the affair Reynolds.

XVII

GENTLEMEN FROM VIRGINIA

Hamilton had other matters to worry him than black-mail. The amazing success of his program held in it the seeds of opposition. The very firm foundation he gave to the government furnished a solid platform on which the wrestling match of principle might be staged. Now a champion had arisen to challenge him, and Thomas Jefferson was a more formidable opponent than he looked, more formidable than Madison, more formidable than Hamilton ever realized.

The Virginian had watched with increasing alarm the progress of Hamiltonian policies. His admitted ignorance of finance could not blind him to the trend of financial policies whose operations he did not thoroughly understand. The rise of merchants, speculators and eastern moneyed men to power was profoundly disturbing to this product of what was then the frontier, for Jefferson had grown up on the Allegheny slopes in a land of log cabins and buckskin breeches. But he had not stayed there. He had traveled and studied, so that he brought to the science of government the maxims of political philosophers superimposed on the prejudices of a western farmer. He brought, too, an unrivaled talent for organization. He drilled no "corrupt squadron." For him, the far more difficult task of disciplining an entire army.

He had been at it for a long time before Hamilton realized that the rather retiring Secretary of State, who avoided crowds and public appearances and speeches, was a serious antagonist. But gradually it became apparent that Jefferson had ambitions and governmental ideas. That they were more

193

flexible than Hamilton's gave them no greater attraction in that young statesman's eyes. That they had their first appearance in the form of attacks by lesser men on the bank, the funding operations and even the monopolistic charter of the Society for Establishing Useful Manufactures did not disguise their inspiration.

A paper boom again was raging in New York, an obvious target for the fire of Jeffersonian orators and pamphleteers. The ostentation of the newly rich provided ample material for the sarcasm of agrarians, but when moneyed men took up a subscription to have Hamilton's portrait painted by the accomplished John Trumbull, the shafts began to be aimed more directly at the Secretary of the Treasury. Both sides were drawing their ranks closer for a new battle preliminary to the coming elections. Jefferson, writing innumerable letters of advice and exhortation, conferred personally and at length with Congressmen and editors, governors and judges, travelers and planters. Hamilton did his training for the fight in, of all places, the arms of Maria Reynolds.

Looking back on his folly, he was unable to explain satisfactorily to himself or anyone else just what impelled him to return to that shabby bedroom. No doubt the obvious beauties of the seductive matron were a powerful attraction. But there were plenty of weak and willing women in Philadelphia who did not have blackmailing husbands. Nor does the style of her wooing seem calculated to stir the passions of a man of sense or taste, for she wept, lamented, implored and made a general nuisance of her supposedly breaking heart. At the same time the crude invitations of her husband should have warned the most unwary, for only two weeks after Hamilton had paid over the last of the $1,000, Reynolds wrote:

"I have not the Least Objections to your Calling. as a friend to Boath of us. and must rely intirely on your and her honnor. . . . So dont fail in Calling as Soon as you Can make it Conveanant. and I rely on your befriending me if there should anything Offer that would be to my advantage."

This in itself would not have lured Hamilton to the Reynolds rooms. It took several epistles from Maria. She expressed herself as "ready to Burst with Greef" and scarcely able to "rise from My pillow wich your Neglect has filled with the shorpest thorns" and "I shal be misarable till I se you," but the missive that finally brought the errant lover to heel ran:

"alas my friend what can [I] ask for but peace wich you alone can restore to my tortured bosom and do My dear Col hamilton on my kneese Let me Intreate you to reade my Letter and Comply with my request tell the bearer of this or give her a line you need not be the least affraid let me not die with fear have pity on my my freend for I deserve it I would not solicit this favor but I am sure It cannot injure you and will be all the happiness I Ever Expect to have But oh I am distressed more than I can tell My heart Is ready to burst and my tears wich once could flow with Ease are now denied me"

Whereupon with a guilelessness that one might suppose he had outgrown while he was clerking for Cruger twenty years earlier, the wise and brilliant Secretary Hamilton came slinking through unfrequented streets to resume the old relation, with the added degradation that Reynolds was now pimping for his wife. And of course the demands for money grew, with thirty dollars here and fifty dollars there, and Betsey's thrifty Schuyler management was being dissipated in little loans on any or no pretext.

"The variety of shapes which this woman could assume were endless," Hamilton marveled, but the explanation of the infatuated man's colossal folly does not lie there alone.

For the infatuation, as is the nature of the thing, had deprived him of the ability to reason, and he was a credulous, often stupid fool where women were concerned. His keen, accurate analysis of character, inclining toward cynical harshness, was reserved for his own sex. And so with Maria appealing alternately to his chivalry and his lust, with Reynolds borrowing and threatening and whining at his heels—and, incidentally, with Betsey announcing the probable arrival of their fifth child in the summer—the Secretary of the Treasury faced the first formidable assault upon what he considered his administration.

It came from friends quite as much as from enemies. Friends had persistently ignored his warnings to beware the pitfalls of speculation. Now the bubble had been blown to really noble proportions. For a moment it hung glittering in the sight of men. Then, while the opposition press, directed by shrewd brains in Philadelphia, yelped and clamored, the beautiful illusion burst and vanished, leaving just a trace of dirty reputations to mark the spot.

It was an experience which constant, periodic repetition has failed even yet to deprive of its power to surprise. The first of United States panics was preceded by a wave of insane optimism which deluded normally sober business men into the belief that a mere offer of an inflated price made securities worth the bid. They carried fictitious value to such a high pitch that on February 6, 1792, a stock exchange was opened in New York at 22 Wall Street, advertising "a large convenient room for the accommodation of the dealers in stock." A month later the new institution experienced its first crash as the impossibly swollen prices, more than 200 for Bank of the United States stock, found their true level.

On March 9 Duer, the most irrepressible bull in the market, suspended payment. There was hope that Hamilton would save him, for the desperate fellow argued, as financiers are wont to argue when their affairs sour, that the government's public duty is to save the capitalist, since he may drag others to ruin with him. Hamilton went far to meet the views of such men, but not that far. He allowed his Comptroller, Wolcott, to press Duer for funds due the government, while he himself assured the luckless gambler that he shared his anguish, recommended that he "act with *forti-tude* and *honor*," and added:

"I will not now pain you with any wise remarks, though if you recover the present stroke, I shall take great liberties with you."

Duer did not recover. Debtors prison claimed him, while Hamilton's prophecy that he would receive blame was amply fulfilled in the cries of angry mobs in the street, and some few other speculators shared his fate. The Congressional gamblers, however, sold out in time.

Most of the directors of the Society for Establishing Useful Manufactures were in jail or in despair, but in the stress of saving the national credit from being involved in the private crash, Hamilton snatched time to serve as the active head of his infant enterprise. He scurried about raising funds for it, even guaranteeing the Bank of New York against loss on a modest advance. The bank must have taken this as an official Treasury pledge, for the Secretary's personal finances were so low he was quite unable to meet a demand by Reynolds for three hundred dollars. He put the fellow off with fifty dollars, and occupied himself with consulting Major L'Enfant about plans for the Paterson factory and hiring hands to man it.

The crash, luckily, was purely a paper panic, and within a few weeks business resumed its normal course. Politics, however, fed on the theme for months, and the published invective grew so scurrilous that prudent editors announced they would have to have genuine signatures to contributions involving personalities, since it was the custom for insulted gentlemen to call out the editor if the author remained hidden behind a pseudonym.

The tone of the press only echoed the tone of the Cabinet. Jefferson and Hamilton had as yet found no single issue of any consequence on which they could agree. Nor were their differences concerned with questions on which either in conscience could yield. "Cocks in a pit," Jefferson described their altercations. The least disputatious of men, he hated his situation, but the pugnacious Hamilton reveled in the fray. The smaller man, quick in debate and at his best when demolishing the arguments of an opponent, conceived in these sessions a good deal of contempt for his adversary.

Jefferson, fluent in friendly conversation, cut a sorry figure in verbal fencing, public or private, and knew it. His weapon was the pen, which he wielded as persuasively if less logically than Hamilton. He had written the Declaration of Independence, but left it to be defended by the eloquence of Adams. Because he was so poor an orator he was at a later period to introduce the practice of having inaugural messages read instead of delivered in person. Ill at ease in uncongenial company, shy and out of his element in acrimonious discussion, his very manner enraged when it did not disgust Hamilton. For the Secretary of State habitually glanced uneasily around a room, never meeting the eyes of those he addressed, so that even his friends thought his expression "shifty." Hamilton could have applied a stronger word. Nor did he take to Jefferson's careless way of flinging himself into a chair, sacrificing decorum to comfort in what Hamilton regarded as a very boorish style.

Washington was, if anything, more unhappy about these scenes than Jefferson. The President, who had learned to control his own temper so well, was saddened when his associates lost theirs. He valued dignity, and the ill-natured bickering that developed in his Cabinet was unseemly. He had imagined himself as elected to preside over a sort of Council of War, where rules of conduct are rigid, but he was learning that a ministry divided on basic principles is a hopeless instrument. His own ideals were Hamiltonian despite his impartiality of manner, and outside the Cabinet the weight of his prestige was thrown, sometimes more heavily than he intended, behind Federalist measures.

Even he could not bridge the division between his principal advisers. Jefferson based his political theories on the virtues of mankind and his practice on the ascendancy of the landowning classes. Hamilton's philosophy was founded on human villainy and directed to the domination of capital. The Virginian, believing a government was good in proportion as it was weak, kept the belief largely in the realm of theory when he had a government of his own. He had said a country's soul needed something like Shays' Rebellion every twenty years or so, a bloodthirsty notion which he never tried out. The Creole, on the other hand, thought a government without power no government at all. Even when he was a rebel, he had not ceased to entertain a reactionary fondness for public order.

That Washington supposed he could drive such a political team in double harness through the mazes of a presidential year was one of his few Utopian dreams. He had refused to accept Jefferson's resignation when the disputes began, and as they continued he found himself unable to prevent the quarrel from slopping over into the press.

Some months earlier Jefferson had brought Philip Freneau, "the poet of the Revolution," to Philadelphia to establish a Republican paper, the existing journals being all Federalist. As a literary man, the poet was the superior of any contemporary editor, and his *National Gazette* was soon dealing blows that rallied the party. By summer, it was apparent that he was receiving information from some more than usually reliable source, and Hamilton was sure that source was Jefferson. This was a natural inference, since Freneau had been subsidized with a post as French translator in the Department of State, just as his chief rival, Fenno, received the Congressional printing. Actually Jefferson refrained from writing a line for publication.

Hamilton was not so scrupulous. Soon all who cared to know learned that the Secretary of the Treasury was scribbling for the papers, exchanging journalistic pot shots with the delighted Freneau. Washington thought it undignified, and in August he made his last appeal for harmony. Both his lieutenants replied on September 9 with politely firm refusals.

Hamilton in a comparatively short letter insisted he had no choice save to answer attacks inspired by Jefferson on the policy of the administration. His suggested remedy was that Washington get rid of the whole Cabinet and start afresh, a solution he would have accepted cheerfully enough since his own constructive work was done.

Jefferson, more intemperate and long-winded, delivered himself of a bitter excoriation of "a man whose history, from the moment at which history can stoop to notice him, is a tissue of machinations against the liberty of the country which has not only received and given him bread, but heaped its honors on his head." He complained, with some justice, of Hamilton's interference with the State Department. Then, rather tactlessly, since Washington highly approved of the general policy of the Treasury, Jefferson charged that its program "flowed from principles adverse to liberty, and was calculated to undermine and demolish the Republic." He proceeded to accuse Hamilton of corrupting Congress, and concluded by denying any part in the press campaign, not failing to point out the impropriety of another Cabinet member exercising his pen in the common prints.

Not all his rival's energies at this time were directed against the sage of Monticello. In September, carefully preparing for the elections, Hamilton discovered what he thought were the traces of a far more dangerous foe. It was reported to him that Senator Burr had designs on the Vice Presidency, having recently come of the necessary age. If he should slip into that place as he had slipped into Schuyler's Senate seat, Burr would be Washington's heir apparent, the Vice Presidency in those early days being regarded as really the second office of government.

During his year and a half in the Senate, Burr had pursued his own shrewd, independent way. Neither party could claim him with confidence, but he was popular with both, moving through society with polished grace and involving himself with no Maria Reynoldses. His political conduct had been as irreproachable, but somehow he had aroused Hamilton's darkest suspicions, and that September the Federalist politicians were being warned against Burr with a violence such as Hamilton permitted himself to use toward no other man.

"I feel it to be a religious duty to oppose his career," he explained.

This sudden blast of alarm contrasted oddly with the mildness of his tone when declaring that the more eminent Jefferson, "whom I once *very much esteemed,* but who does not permit me to retain that sentiment for him, is certainly a man of sublimated and paradoxical imagination, entertaining and propagating opinions inconsistent with dignified and orderly government." Hamilton liked the phrase "sublimated and paradoxical imagination" and used it frequently to describe Jefferson at the same period that the unsuspecting Burr drew such shafts as:

"He is determined, as I conceive, to make his way to the head of the popular party, and to climb, *per fas aut nefas,* to the highest honors of the state, and as much higher as circumstances may permit. Embarrassed, as I understand, in his circumstances, with an extravagant family, bold, enterprising and intriguing, I am mistaken if it be not his object to play the game of confusion. . . . I pledge my character for discernment, that it is incumbent upon every good man to resist the present design."

The menace of dictatorship, so much harsher than the ascendancy of a class, which Hamilton sought, was very real to him, and he knew how such things come about.

"If I were disposed to promote monarchy and overthrow State governments," he declared in oblique answer to some of the charges against himself, "I would mount the hobby-horse of popularity; I would cry out 'usurpation,' 'danger to liberty,' etc., etc.; I would endeavor to prostrate the national government, raise a ferment, and then 'ride in the whirlwind and direct the storm.' That there are men acting with Jefferson and Madison who have this in view, I verily believe."

Burr, it seemed to him, was just such a man. It became the fashion at a later day to read into this bitter animosity varying degrees of personal feeling. It was to be argued that Burr had crossed Hamilton in love and vice versa, that Hamilton knew Burr for a traitor the moment he saw him, that the Secretary had proof of some flagrant dereliction on the part of the Senator.

The romantic theory of a woman in the case rests on nothing but the rather sloppy sentimentality of those who evolved it. Hamilton at this time was up to his ears in the Reynolds mess, and in later years would certainly have called that man blessed who stole the fair Maria from him. In any case, Burr, who never in all his life took a love affair as seriously as a misspelled word in one of Theodosia's childish letters, is usually supposed to have been the injured party.

As for specific information of an impeachable offense, Hamilton admitted he had none, for, suddenly cautious, he wrote to Representative John Steele:

"My opinion of Mr. Burr is yet to form. . . . Imputations, not favorable to his character as a man, rest upon him, but I do not vouch for their authenticity."

This was rather shabby gossip, as were the reflections on Burr's private life, and Hamilton knew it. The Senator's "extravagant" family consisted of an invalid wife and a nine-year-old daughter, Mrs. Burr's children by her earlier marriage being at this time grown and independent. Burr was no more reckless with money and no more in debt than his accuser. Of evidence that he sought to raise himself to dictatorial power there was none either then or later that could impose on any save the most gullible.

But Hamilton relied on his instinct, and it told him Burr was the greatest threat to his political system that America

could produce. And so, although the two still met ostensibly
as friends, the Secretary poured forth his fears to selected
correspondents. In 1792 at least his apprehensions were premature. Burr got just one electoral vote, and Adams was
victorious by a plurality of twenty-seven over Clinton.

If Hamilton had been interested in popular vindications,
he could have claimed one this November, but the approval
of the electorate left him cold. He turned back to the business of his department and found there a disturbing bit of
information. James Reynolds was in jail for attempting a
fraud on the Treasury.

Finding the Secretary poorer pickings than he had supposed, he had turned his talents to other fields and with one
Jacob Clingman had committed the indiscretion of suborn-
ing a witness to commit perjury for the purpose of obtaining
letters of administration to the estate of a man who had a
claim against the government. The forgers neglected to wait
until the creditor was dead, and Wolcott, under whose
immediate supervision the case came, had the pair arrested.
Even in prison, however, Reynolds was notably perky, assuring Clingman that they would soon be released because a
word from him could "hang the Secretary of the Treasury."
Hamilton, however, refused to be blackmailed in his official
capacity, and ordered Wolcott to proceed at his discretion.

Reynolds and Clingman agreed to make restitution and
turn state's evidence against the Treasury clerk who had
been their accomplice. On this understanding, and without
Hamilton knowing about it, they were released, but Clingman confided to Speaker F. A. Muhlenberg of the House,
for whom he had once worked, that the Secretary had used
Reynolds in secret speculations based on official information.
Clingman, who was to succeed Hamilton in Maria's affections if he had not already done so, produced some notes
that certainly seemed to indicate a monetary relationship.

Such charges could not be ignored. Muhlenberg consulted
Representative Abraham Venable and Senator James Mon-

roe, both of Virginia, and their first impulse was to go to Washington at once. On second thought, they determined to confront Hamilton himself, and on the morning of December 15, 1792, very solemn and judicial, the three proceeded to his office. There Muhlenberg opened the conversation by declaring bluntly that they "had discovered a very improper connection between me and a Mr. Reynolds." For a moment the accused statesman raged with a fury worthy of Washington himself, or as he put it:

"I arrested the progress of the discourse by giving way to very strong expressions of indignation."

Indignation, however, would not meet the situation. Recovering his self-command as they explained the nature of their evidence, he informed them that he was "ready to meet fair inquiry with frank communication." He suggested that same evening at his house for the purpose.

In the intervening hours, choking back helpless anger and nursing a sense of humiliation such as he had never before experienced, he prepared his defense, which was to be nothing less than the whole sorry truth. He confided in only one friend, Wolcott, whose devotion had become almost idolatrous and was proof against the discovery of feet of clay. The Comptroller was known as a merry fellow in the Bingham salon, but that evening he was unwontedly solemn as he stood beside his chief to greet with careful ceremony Speaker Muhlenberg and the two gentlemen from Virginia. These last were not to be outdone in courtesy, and the air was positively frosty with politeness as the Secretary plunged into his explanation.

Whatever moods of baffled fury, shame, disgust and hopelessness he may have passed through that day, no feeling at all was apparent in the evening. With greater detachment than he ever employed in discussing a Treasury estimate, he told the sordid story of his passions and his humiliation. Before him on the desk were the vulgar, greedy letters of his mistress and her husband. As he proceeded in his even, clipped tones, it was the listeners who showed signs of embarrassment, as at the revelation of a secret weakness of their own. Venable and Muhlenberg in particular "were struck with so much conviction, before I had gotten through the communication, that they delicately urged me to discontinue it as unnecessary. I insisted upon going through the whole, and did so."

It took time, but at the end "Mr. Muhlenberg and Mr. Venable, in particular, manifested a degree of sensibility on the occasion. Mr. Munroe was more cold but entirely explicit." In short, all three agreed that there was nothing further to investigate and that the whole miserable business should be buried in the oblivion of gentlemanly confidence.

The painful scene was over, and it had its compensations. Reynolds had absconded the moment he got out of jail, disappearing from Philadelphia and recorded history at the same time. Maria had moved under the protection of the scurvy Clingman, freeing her former lover at once from her charms and her importunities. And as he put the pitiful evidence back in his strong box, Hamilton could hope that now at last he really had heard the last of the affair Reynolds.

XVIII

MONOCRATS AND JACOBINS

The interview with the three republicans had been a private test preparatory to the public struggle over genuine issues. Jefferson had been so successful, particularly in rural constituencies, in recruiting an army to oppose the corrupt squadron that after the Congressional elections of 1792 the two parties in the House would be more evenly divided, in numbers at least.

Outside Congress, however, a greater storm than any that ever disturbed domestic politics was fanning popular opinion into emotional flames that Hamilton could regard only as one more proof of the unfitness of the masses to govern themselves. The French Revolution, sending its luminous but hollow slogan of liberty, equality and fraternity vaulting across three thousand miles of ocean, made a great commotion in the bosoms of thousands who yawned at mention of banks, manufacturing societies, funding systems. These thousands were equally indifferent to the shibboleths of the agrarians—the sanctity of states, the burden of taxation, the superior merit of farmers.

These suddenly frenzied multitudes were men without land and without stock certificates, and they were mad with a madness that had possessed few of them in their own Revolution. They were more excited by the French upheaval because it was at once further away and, as seen from across the sea, simpler in its motivation, a splendid if terrible revolt of a people against oppression, injustice and degradation.

The first orderly bourgeois French reforms of '89 had aroused only a pleased notice among Americans that their ally was regaining her ancient parliamentary institutions. News of the fall of the Bastille that year was welcomed by some who usually did not like mobs, but rejoiced that America's hero, the Marquis de Lafayette had emerged from the turmoil as commander of the National Guard. A splendid era of justice and good will was dawning, and all shades of opinion were represented among Americans who wished well to the French Constitution.

Even in 1789, Hamilton had struck a dissenting note. With the prescience that was one day to cause the astute Talleyrand to exclaim in wonder, "He divined Europe," the young American who had never visited that continent had a vision of the disasters those solemn deputies to the States General were loosing upon the world. To Lafayette he wrote a warning that the course on which France had embarked in the pursuit of democracy led to mob rule, anarchy, war and a dictatorship on the model of the Caesars.

As events moved in strict, uncannily accurate accordance with this program, it was hardly surprising that the prophet was unmoved by the waves of insane enthusiasm on which the new religion of freedom was being wafted over the sea. Sharing his immunity was a group whose prestige made up for lack of numbers. Washington, Adams, Jay, the Morrises, Rufus King and Cabot, all men who doubted the wisdom of the people and felt that their Revolution was the exception proving the rule of public order being the highest good, were less and less attracted by reports from France.

By the end of 1792 this little band stood almost alone in repelling assaults of what they regarded as a transplanted sanscullotism. The debt of gratitude to France suddenly became sacred to men who had recently resented Secretary Hamilton's insistence upon the sanctity of the debt of cash. Nor were the crowds more mindful of the fact that the moral obligation, such as it was, was really due to the noblemen whose heads were rolling into baskets or being stuck on pikes in the name of the brotherhood of man.

Mr. Jefferson was asserting that the legal obligation was due to the country, not the individuals who ruled it, but he fulminated charges of base ingratitude if the legal argument was carried to its logical conclusion. The Secretary of State, with the supple twist of phrase that maddened his rival, wished to apply the sketchy law of nations only as far as it supported his prejudices. France was entitled to a small annual payment in accordance with the debt settlement. Jefferson not only wanted to recognize that it should be paid to the revolutionary government, but wanted to pay it all in a lump, anticipating the installments of many years. He was impatient of legal quibbles when it was pointed out that this was hardly justice to American taxpayers. Under the circumstances, Hamilton thought the apostle of democracy an unsafe person to trust with foreign relations, and soon the Secretary of State complained that his colleague of the Treasury was taking it upon himself to confer with the French and British ministers.

As news of that year's glorious and shameful September came across the Atlantic, the howling populace was in no mood to listen to reason if it ever had been, which Hamilton doubted. He heard men exclaiming over the marvel of those tattered, half-armed, utterly unorganized soldiers rushing to defend their beloved frontiers and rolling back through Argonne Wood the finest troops in Europe, upsetting in one heroic surge of undisciplined power all the accumulated military science of two thousand years. Men fighting for their homes and their faith had risen superior to the mere human machines that filled the Austrian and German ranks, and this, their admirers said, was democracy.

But Hamilton looked at the event of September through another pair of spectacles. He saw innocent blood flowing in the Paris gutters, the dregs of the slums shrieking with coarse merriment as their betters died. He saw cruelty, ignorance and lust exalted into organs of government as the mob set up its rule of Terror. And this, he said, was democracy.

A PORTRAIT OF ALEXANDER HAMILTON BY
JOHN TRUMBULL

The same despatches that told of the Terror reported that the National Assembly had conferred upon him and Madison honorary French citizenship for their contributions to liberty, meaning *The Federalist,* which had been read but not digested by the constitution makers of Paris. Unfortunately, the New Yorker's certificate was made out to "Jean Hamilton."

"A curious example of French finesse," was the recipient's terse endorsement.

A cabinet minister of aristocratic principles who thus rejected the homage of France presented a broad target, especially welcome to those of his enemies who were regretting that the specter of speculation had lost much of its power to frighten the fickle people. The prices of farm produce had risen and foreign trade was brisk. Grateful merchants were passing resolutions ascribing their prosperity to the wonderful management of the Secretary of the Treasury. His portrait was hung with acclaim in New York's City Hall. The Federalist press could not find words to exalt his wisdom. But of course prosperity was not universal, nor were Republicans disposed to give Hamilton credit for it as long as Freneau could chant:

> Whales on our shores have run aground,
> Sturgeons are in our rivers found—
> Nay—ships have on the Delaware sailed,
> A sight most new.
> Wheat has been sown—
> Harvests have grown—
> On coaches now, gay coats of arms are borne
> By some who hardly had a cent before—
> Silk gowns, instead of homespun, now are seen,
> Instead of native straw, the Leghorn hat,
> And, Sir, 'tis true
> ('Twixt me and you)
> That some have grown prodigious fat,
> And some prodigious lean.

For all the adulation and studied newspaper flattery, Hamilton was not a popular figure. No crowds gathered to cheer him in the streets. But he still wielded power, and men who professed to think that the voice of the people is the mandate of a master were disturbed by the ascendancy of one on whom the people expended no breath. So at the short session of Congress, beginning in December, 1792, the Republicans set out to destroy him. Although there was not a man in the opposition who cared to argue a fiscal question with Hamilton—Albert Gallatin was this year only a member of the Pennsylvania legislature—they thought they saw a way to ruin him without the need of getting within range of his tongue or pen.

The strategy of the attack was shrewd. Whispers that the Secretary himself was growing rich were constantly in the air and the suspicious Maclay had always been certain that he was the "head of the speculators." Jefferson and Madison knew better, but they were willing to take advantage of the gossip to pave the way for a plan that might disgrace their opponent without the need of actually proving anything disgraceful. With Representative Giles and, probably, Senator Monroe, they worked out the details of a trap of beautiful simplicity.

When it should be too late to get an answer at the current session of Congress, the watch dogs of the people were to begin barking for a complete and detailed report on the operations of the Treasury to date. Since no such thing had ever been suggested before, they could count on catching Hamilton by surprise. Later a few condemnatory resolutions could be introduced and shelved with ostentatious magnanimity to await his explanation. Then, while he worked on his figures during the long recess, the breach of trust implied in the resolutions would be driven so firmly into the minds of the people that no mere facts backed by tables of statistics could ever drive it out. The authors of the plan were well aware how little impression dull statistics have on public opinion.

Until January 23, only a little more than five weeks before the expiration of the Second Congress, they held their fire. Then Giles made his demand for detailed reports. Although he was the orator of his party, looked to for inflammatory speeches when the reasonable tone of Madison was deemed inappropriate to the occasion, there was nothing fiery about him this day. The quarry was not to be alarmed quite yet. Mr. Giles merely offered the thought that it was time the House be informed on the state of finances, and without any debate or record vote the resolution was adopted.

Hamilton was not to be caught by such tricks, not by men, anyway. He saw at once the use to which a delay in reporting could be put. Contemptible as the collective brains of Congress might be in his sight, it was incumbent upon him to produce forthwith the complete details of three years' government finance.

It was well that Cruger's clerk had learned the value of keeping routine work up to date and that he had trained his staff to be as thorough as himself. At that Wolcott, the perfect accountant, doubted whether the task could be done in the time allowed, but the Treasury flung itself into the job, every man copying, adding and compiling tables until the figures danced meaninglessly in the candlelight. Then home for a few hours' sleep, to return in the late winter daylight to begin again. The Secretary, last to leave and first to arrive, seemed not to sleep at all. He was alert, however, every moment, for his mind never tired, although the rosy cheeks grew pale and the first signs of middle age became apparent as his face grew a little haggard under the strain. The need for haste was obvious soon, for the opposition came out into the open with purposely vague charges, and on February 8 Wolcott was writing to his father:

"I presume Giles' motion and speech have been seen by you, in which he has intimated that the Treasury department have cabbaged several millions of the public money, for which they cannot account."

Wolcott had no time to enter into a protracted defense to his father. He was too busy with digits to write many words, for the rumor that millions were missing took the matter into the realm of what was then regarded as almost astronomical figures. The entire annual expenses of the United States, including service of the national debt, totaled less than $6,000,000.

In twenty-four days from the time of Giles's first resolution, Hamilton sent down to the House four fat reports, packed with tables, charts, explanations and analyses of every cent of revenue and expenditure, where it came from and where it went and why. The magnitude of the achievement can be measured by the triumphant shouts of the Federalists and the dejection of their enemies. These last did mutter that there was trickery, that they could not understand quite what the figures meant. Fenno's *Gazette of the United States* gave that cavil all the attention it merited with the merry verse:

> In such a puzzling case as this
> What can a mortal do?
> 'Tis hard for ONE to find REPORTS
> And understanding too.

The plan to drive Hamilton from office failed, although Giles, persevering in the strategy of the attack, introduced formal resolutions of censure three days before the close of the session. There was a forlorn hope that they could not be reached on the crowded calendar in time for a vote, but the Federalists were in no mood for such tactics. They allowed only brief debate, in which Madison admitted there was no evidence of criminality. One by one the criticisms were voted down, and as the results were announced, the Secretary was compared by ecstatic commentators to pure gold, "the more it is rubbed, the more it will shine."

The struggle to preserve the nation's sanity from the infectious example of France was neither as short nor as easy. It was a fight that could not be won by cold facts and tables of figures. Receiving only the most fragmentary, inaccurate accounts of European events, weeks late, the people were carried from one extreme to the other by waves of emotionalism that took no heed of what the European conflagration might mean to them. Hamilton, who had never supposed the masses capable of consistency, was relieved, not satisfied, when news of King Louis's execution sent the unsteady pulse of popular opinion beating suddenly but strongly against the Revolution and all its works.

He knew that mood, too, could not last. The exaggerated sympathy for poor Louis was as unstable as the frenzied applause that broke out when the untrained rabble threw the mighty armies of the invader back from the French frontier. Nor was it soothing to his fears that the foreign relations of the United States were in the hands of a man who could pass off the Terror as a little necessary blood-letting to which the good sense of a free people would soon put an end.

The reaction Hamilton expected came when England joined the coalition, and the embers of the spirit of '76 flamed up in hatred. King Louis was forgotten, and crowds were gathering in the ale houses to scream for war—war in defense of a sister republic—war to humble the arrogant Briton—war to destroy the Kings of Europe—war to assert the rights of man in general—war for the fun of fighting—war, war, war.

A new minister was on his way from France, too, and could be counted on to add a more formal demand for hostilities in accordance with the terms of the treaty by which France had helped to win American independence. Obviously Jefferson was not the man to trust with this problem, and in April the Secretary of the Treasury was writing Washington of the peril they faced, urging him to hurry back from Mount Vernon to the turmoil of what might be a new fight for their country.

Later in the month five men sat around a table in the Morris mansion to settle American foreign policy in its first real test. They were debating specifically the reception of the new minister, the young Girondin, Edmond Charles Genêt. The loose-limbed Secretary of State could see no alternative than to accept his credentials and admit that the treaty—by which the United States opened their ports to French privateers, guaranteed the French West Indies and agreed to a general defensive alliance—was still binding. The stately Randolph was inclined to take the same view.

But Hamilton thought such a decision must lead to the war with England for which the mob was yelling. He emphasized the highly disagreeable results, the British fleet let loose upon American ships and western Indians let loose upon American farms. And all in a quarrel that was three thousand miles away, a struggle between autocracy and mobocracy, a conflict in which the United States might very well be crushed but could win nothing except the satisfaction of establishing the blood-smeared heroes of the Paris slums, the Jacobins of the Terror, in a dictatorship which, because it abolished titles, Thomas Jefferson thought was democracy. Genêt, said the Secretary of the Treasury, should be told at once that the question of the treaty's validity was still open and to be decided in accordance with America's true interests, even if that meant denouncing the alliance. Knox rumbled approval.

Washington was on the side of his former officers. His love of democracy as exemplified by the Paris faubourgs was small, and he was never carried away by abstract enthusiasms. He agreed that the treaty problem should be postponed, and that before the French Minister arrived, a presidential proclamation of neutrality should be issued to settle doubts as to the administration's stand.

The appearance of that cold, executive document turned the wrath of Republicans from Hamilton, who drafted it, to his chief. Washington, for a change, was accused of acting at the behest of gamblers in public securities. He was taunted with aping court manners, with ignoring common people, with monarchical designs. When émigrés arrived and the President received Vicomte de Noailles, once a fighter for American independence but now a refugee from the French Republic, suspicious letter writers said there must be some royalist conspiracy afoot.

Meanwhile, to show their contempt for their President and his proclamations, hysterical crowds, convinced that the salvation of the world was bound up in the fate of a revolution that had already branded their hero, Lafayette, as a reactionary, paid homage to Genêt. His Girondin friends were fighting their last despairing battle for moderate ideals and being marked for the guillotine while he spent a month on a triumphal tour from Charleston to Philadelphia. Americans were as unable as he to keep up with the swift, inexorable progress of the Terror, so they set the Minister up as a symbol of liberty and gladdened the heart of Jefferson with their shouts.

All along the route, Genêt was feasted and toasted and acclaimed. Every town put on its show of marching mobs streaming through the streets with torches flaming on the liberty caps worn rakishly over one ear and with lungs straining at the words if not the music of "Ça ira" and the "Marseillaise." Everywhere patriots called each other "Citizen" and in the enthusiasm wrought by speeches and songs and ale hugged and kissed in what was said to be the true Parisian style—the whole performance, Chauncey Goodrich reported, being part of a mad desire "to be all equal to French barbers."

However much Jefferson's philosophical soul might be enraptured by this popular outburst, Washington and Hamilton, as practical men, viewed Genêt's triumphal progress with deep concern. It was the Frenchman's job to drag the United States into the war, and the joyous, unthinking mobs were showing him how blindly ready they were to follow his lead.

But men who had fought the last war were not eager for another, and Citizen Genêt was due for a shock. When at last he took time from his public appearances to present his credentials to the President, he was received by a tall, aloof man of icy restraint standing before portraits of Louis and Marie Antoinette.

The Citizen could not take a hint. A young diplomat of surprising brilliance and no common sense whatever, he assumed an air that might have become a Roman Pro-Consul on some barbarian frontier. Merrily he prepared to ignore the neutrality proclamation and the President who had signed it. Democratic clubs were springing up to support him, and Hamilton was not the only man who noticed their resemblance to the French Jacobin Societies. In New York the Society of St. Tammany, recently reorganized by the half-mad William Mooney to give common soldiers, the old "Liberty Boys," a weapon against the aristocratical Cincinnati, were taking the lead in tavern outcry. And the English were helping by a tactless Order in Council that called for the capture of all ships with cargoes of food for France.

In this emergency, Hamilton stepped in on the unpopular side of sweet reasonableness with a series of articles designed to win support for neutrality. They were of such effect that Jefferson insisted that the reluctant Madison answer them himself, but neither series had anything like the influence of Genêt's actions. Beneath the clamor whenever he appeared was discernible a certain impatience at being treated as a French colony. When the Minister refused to dine at the same table as de Noailles, men remembered that the Vicomte may have been a horrid aristocrat in France but had fought for freedom in America.

Then, in the exaltation of too much flattery, Genêt managed to defeat his own purpose. In defiance of the American government, he fitted out a privateer and sent her to sea with the threat to appeal from the President to the people. With that stroke he accomplished his unique diplomatic achieve-

ment; he united Hamilton and Jefferson on a single policy.
Both insisted that the French Republic be told to recall him,
but by this time Genêt's friends at home were in hiding, in
jail or in tumbrils rattling to the guillotine, and he had no
desire to face the Jacobin Convention in Paris. Recovering
some measure of prudence, he retired to private life, married
an heiress and lived out the remaining forty years of his life
as a quiet American citizen.

The harmony he had brought to the Cabinet was short-
lived, although a unity of aim persisted. Both Hamilton and
Jefferson were sincere in desiring to keep out of war. The
Secretary of State was writing masterly protests against British depredations, unanswerable state papers, firm but not insulting. The only possible objection to them was that they had
no effect. His proposal for a next step was strong measures of
retaliation for commercial injuries which those who suffered
them were willing to ignore, and whether he saw it or not,
that way lay genuine hostilities. Twenty years later Madison
got a war in just that manner. In 1793 it would have been a
war over the rights of Frenchmen rather than the rights of
Americans, although the philosopher would have said it was
all one, covered by the phrase "the rights of man." Because
this was not so clear to his opponents, he stormed at them as
"monocrats" and "Anglomen" and aristocrats.

Hamilton, whose Anglophile tendencies consisted of a belief that British institutions would work better than those
of revolutionary France, was also interested in keeping the
peace with a nation whose trade was essential to American
prosperity. Only "Jacobins," anarchists and vulgar demagogues would quarrel with his pacifism, he thought, and he
went out of his way to show sympathy for the émigrés. It was
not hard, for he was really touched by the plight of these
once carefree nobles and gentlemen reduced to the charity
of strangers, and much more attractive in poverty than in
wealth.

"I wish I was a Croesus," he wrote to Angelica Church. "I

might then afford solid consolation to these children of adversity, and how delightful it would be to do so. But now sympathy, kind words, and occasionally a dinner are all I can contribute."

The summer wore on, insufferably hot and sticky, with charges and countercharges keeping pace with the weather, until in September a greater menace than the French or the English, monocrats or Jacobins, aristocrats or democrats, struck the city, pouncing impartially on the squalid hovels along Water Street and the neat brick mansions at the "court end of town." Yellow fever was paying one of its mysterious, periodic visits, and terror of the invisible Death drove out all bitterness of politics. Thousands fled from the gloomy, steaming city where almost the only sounds were the tolling of funeral bells and the rumble of carts collecting the bodies of the dead. Farmers refused to come in with produce, and food grew scarce. As the death list mounted from hundreds to thousands, whole streets of houses stood empty and forlorn. The physicians tried their little tricks, but bleedings and potions were useless, and the medical men sickened and died with their patients.

Hamilton, who had taken a house in the Hills, not far from Morris's elaborate country estate, packed Betsey and the children off to Albany and rode daily into the depressing, terror-stricken city where he and Wolcott were remembered as almost the only men who smiled. They kept each other's spirits up, writing gentlemanly lies to their wives, until one day Wolcott missed his chief. He rode out to the Hills and found Hamilton laid low with the disease, but not so low that he failed to give his physician instructions on how to treat him.

Neddy Stevens, formerly of St. Croix, now a physician of some note, was at his bedside and was lucky enough to save one patient at least, for his boyhood friend had studied yellow fever and reached the conclusion that a cold water cure was the only remedy, thereby anticipating the medical wisdom of future generations. At the time it was thought odd that he should survive the treatment, but he did, saying generously that it was because of "the skill and care of my friend Dr. Stevens." When winter came to drive the plague away as mysteriously as summer had brought it, Hamilton was strong enough to travel slowly north to recuperate in the bosom of his family at the Schuyler home.

Returning health found him in a pacific mood. His slowly mending energies were of a benevolent nature, but perhaps that was because Jefferson was retiring with the new year, leaving Hamilton supreme, undisputed in the Cabinet.

XIX

SECOND IN WAR, SECOND IN PEACE

WITH THE PHILOSOPHER OF VIRGINIA RETIRED TO HIS BELOVED Monticello, Hamilton became not so much Prime Minister as the entire ministry. The Treasury, needing only a little supervision, left him free to shake the State Department out of what he considered the pro-French course of Jefferson, and to put new life into the War Department.

Randolph, who had succeeded his fellow Virginian, was a formal man, bound by legal rules and precedents. If he was aware that the more important decisions of his office were made at the Treasury, he gave no indication of resenting it. That the British Minister preferred to deal with Hamilton had been one of Jefferson's complaints, but Randolph remained calm under the usurpation, actually accepting drafts by Hamilton of papers he was to sign officially.

Harry Knox was more than acquiescent. The huge artilleryman had been overcome with admiration for the way the one-time youngest of his officers took hold in civil life. His mind, although far from being as slow and lumbering as his body, could not keep up with that of his colleague, and for some time it had been rather painfully obvious that his bellowing voice, so loudly commanding on the Delaware in '76, was now no more than the echo of Hamilton's crisp pronouncements. William Bradford of Pennsylvania, the new Attorney General, dealt only with routine matters, and Hamilton did not think these needed his professional attention.

Philadelphia after the yellow fever was a city in which a statesman had to walk warily. The capital, crowded by refugees from all parts of Europe, was a more cosmopolitan place than any American city would be for another hundred years. The exiles brought their Old World prejudices with them, few being as adaptable as Vicomte de Noailles, who had turned trader with singular enthusiasm. He brought to the Philadelphia exchange not only his tall good looks, his exquisite manners and an incorrigible gaiety but also a less aristocratic talent, and was seen of all men, "the busiest of the busy, holding his bank-book in one hand and a broker or merchant by the button with the other, while he drove his bargains as earnestly as any regular-bred son of a counting-house."

Equally popular were the poverty-stricken Dukes of Orléans, Montpensier and Beaujolais, unfortunate sons of Philippe Égalité, safe neither in France nor in the countries of the coalition. Here too came a greater man, greater even than the young Duke who was one day to be King Louis Philippe, but Philadelphia did not recognize the future Prince of Benevento in the unfrocked Bishop of Autun, the dandified, cynical, shrewd and unscrupulous Charles Maurice de Talleyrand-Périgord, predecessor of Gouverneur Morris in the easy affections of Mme. de Flahaut. Hamilton, however, appreciated the brain behind the pert features of the French diplomat, and Talleyrand was one of those to whom he most gladly extended his modest charity of a dinner.

The delicacy of the task of establishing a new government's prosperity in the midst of passionate differences was familiar to the Frenchman. He watched the young American with an admiration which few mortals were able to extort from that cold intelligence. Later Talleyrand was to learn even more of the troubles that beset a chief minister, and looking back on a life that had run the whole cycle from monarchy through republicanism and Napoleonic dictatorship back to monarchy, a life that had thrown him into more or less intimate contact with the notables of three generations, he declared:

"I consider Napoleon, Fox and Hamilton as the three

greatest men of our time, and if I were to pronounce among the three, I would give without hesitation the first place to Hamilton."

Jefferson's retirement, as the émigré was shrewd enough to see, had removed friction from the Cabinet, but had not eased the fundamental task. As England closed in a death struggle with the French republic, the position of bystanders became intolerable. Jefferson had made his last official work a "Report on Commerce" in which he again recommended reprisals. His followers in Congress were pushing his policy, but when Hamilton spoke of an army and a navy to defend such bellicose measures, the Republicans screamed that he was preparing to build an engine of tyranny.

Washington and Hamilton remained just as much opposed to war as they had been a year before. They knew the belligerents were suffering more than the neutrals. The President, completely clamor-proof, was earning his title of "first in peace," although his opponents were not allowing him the honor while he remained in office, and Hamilton was right behind him. The Secretary was writing for the papers again in an attempt to have the question considered in the light of American interests rather than American passions. The owners of the ships and cargoes which were being seized by England were strong for peace. Only men who had no material stake in the issue were crying for reprisals and insisting that the British would not dare to fight. The eloquent plea for the sacredness of property rang out loudly if a little oddly from orators who usually assailed Hamilton as too tender of the commercial section of the community.

Washington determined to try by negotiation to win what probably could not be had by force and would not be worth a war if it could. Hamilton wanted to be the negotiator, and was the choice of his party, but the Republican outcry against the "Angloman" who had said a kind word for the House of Lords had taken such firm hold on popular imagination that, although he was admittedly best qualified for a special mission to London, it would not have been safe to name him. Monroe protested formally to Washington, and even Rufus King confessed that his friend did not possess "the general confidence of the country."

Shortly afterward, Hamilton repaid the Virginia Senator by supporting him for the post of Minister to France in succession to Gouverneur Morris, who had made himself as objectionable to the real Jacobins abroad as Genêt had been to their imitators here. Meanwhile Hamilton withdrew his name from consideration and urged the President to appoint Chief Justice Jay. The tall New Yorker was famous for his diplomatic talents. He had helped negotiate the original peace treaty with England, a document of such admirable qualities that Hamilton had written him:

"The New England people talk of making you an annual fish offering."

With such a record, the Chief Justice was named. Then, while the Senate raved behind closed doors as it debated confirmation and the press teemed with cries that the nominee was as bad as Hamilton, the Secretary of the Treasury was drafting the instructions by which Jay was to bring back peace with honor. The busy author was so far from being the tool of British policy—one of the common newspaper charges —that the Cabinet toned his draft down in favor of larger concessions to England, and with the acclamations of the Federalists and the hisses of Republicans in his ears, Jay sailed from New York in May.

Having done all he could for peace, Hamilton turned to considerations of war. It was to be civil war, for the farmers of western Pennsylvania had followed the example of Shays and their own Revolution. They were in arms against taxes. The excise law, a fundamental of Hamiltonian financing, was at stake as the feud between mountaineers and revenue agents got under way. Tax collectors were hustled and run out of their districts, barns of informers burned, owners of illicit stills released from jail by armed mobs. The whole country spent its time, according to reports reaching Philadelphia, in attending mass meetings and pledging forcible resistance in mighty shouts.

The men who launched the so-called Whiskey Insurrection were a tough breed, many of them living in the wilderness beyond the protecting arm of government. Whiskey, the only transportable form in which to ship the produce of their painfully cleared farms, was at once their medium of exchange and their staff of life. Money they seldom saw, but the revenue men had to be paid in cash. By the summer of 1794 they had made their rebellious intentions so apparent that Hamilton saw a chance to save his fiscal system and at the same time strike a blow to prove his theory that the Federal government was strong enough to govern. The tax might bear with peculiar and unjust harshness on these rough backwoodsmen, but they must not be allowed to set aside any law that displeased them. It was the first sharp nullification debate.

News of the rebellion was sufficiently alarming to convince Washington he ought to take the field himself at the head of 15,000 militia. Hamilton, as eager for a chance at martial glory as he had been a dozen years before on the redoubt at Yorktown, did not propose to be left behind. He had been doing the work of the Secretary of War for months while Knox was on leave. Now he argued that since the rebellion was ostensibly directed at his taxes, "it cannot but have a good effect for the person who is understood to be the adviser or proposer of a measure which involves danger to his fellow-citizens, to partake in that danger: while, not to do it, might have a bad effect."

A few days later he rode out of Philadelphia at Washington's side, in all but official rank second in command of the expedition to vindicate by force of arms the financial policy of Alexander Hamilton. But he was thoroughly military on the march, secretly hoping that the insurgents would not heed the proclamation he had written for Washington's sig-

FEDERAL HALL, WALL STREET, ABOUT 1798, AFTER A WATER COLOR
BY ROBERTSON

nature, warning against the "efforts of misguided or designing men to substitute their misrepresentations in the place of truth, and their discontents in the place of stable government."

When it came to the point, the Whiskey Boys were not prepared to fight an army. Some of the loudest ranters fled or surrendered, and the bewildered remainder allowed themselves to be guided by leaders like the Swiss Albert Gallatin, who argued that they might redeem their condition by votes instead of force. So, with resistance melting before him, Washington turned back, leaving Hamilton in virtual charge.

Alas for dreams of daring exploits and victories snatched brilliantly from the jaws of defeat! The only visible enemy was the weather, visible in the form of a steady chilling rain, for it was a wet autumn. Victory over such a foe held little glory and less satisfaction. The rough tracks through the dripping forests mired the wagons at every step. The commander, although mounted on a good horse, was wet and splashed with mud and suffering from some obscure ailment which he attributed to last year's yellow fever. At night, drying himself at the smoky fires of villainous inns, he penned concise little reports to Washington, and as he advanced into the heart of insurgent territory, he could find consolation for the lack of martial fame in the complete submission to the excise. There was no fighting at all, just a little looting, which Hamilton tried in vain to check, and a couple of hundred prisoners, "among whom there is a sufficient number of proper ones for examples, and with sufficient evidence." The courts disputed him on that, convicting only two, and they were pardoned by Washington.

It was really dull, routine work, and Pittsburgh was an uncomfortable, badly built place of 12,000 souls, few of whom appealed to the fastidious Hamilton. The only thoroughly cheerful note in his letters to Washington was in a postscript to the last, written on November 19, which announced happily:

"In five minutes I set out for Philadelphia."

The Whiskey Boys had failed to gratify his martial spirit, but on the return trip he devised another use for their little uprising. The Democratic Clubs, those nests of Jacobins and anarchists, had been loud in their denunciations of the excise. Members had refrained from open insurrection, had even denounced it and, in many instances, served in the militia, but the returned warrior was soon saying in salons and lobbies that the rebellion had been the result of their pernicious Jacobin doctrines. Washington concurred, and the Presidential message to Congress contained a flat attack on the societies.

The Republicans thundered and growled, Madison seeing in the message "the greatest error in his political career" and Jefferson bewailing it as another iniquity of "the faction of monocrats." But the people still looked with awe to the father of his country, and under the frown of Washington the Jacobin societies withered and died.

Of course they had lost their foreign inspiration, too. In France the Terror was over. Marat was dead at the hands of Charlotte Corday. Robespierre had sent Danton to his death and, in the summer of the Whiskey Insurrection, the terrible little fanatic followed his victims to the guillotine. Democracy had run its course in France, the course that Hamilton had predicted to Lafayette. It was now drifting toward the Directory, consulate and empire. The fervid eloquence about the rights of man no longer cascaded over the world to sweep logic and sound principles aside. A saner appreciation of the rights of man might follow. So the Democratic Clubs quietly took the line of the mother society and, for the most part, vanished into emptiness, the emptiness of talk.

Five years had brought Hamilton to this triumph over his enemies. He had taken the non-existent credit of the United States and placed it as high as that of any nation in the world. He had established the government on the firm basis of its most powerful economic class. He had certified the doctrine that the Constitution could be stretched to cover reasonable needs of state. He had repelled the subversive attacks of wild men, theorists and anarchists. He and Washington had kept the country out of war. They had asserted the new government's authority over dissenting minorities. In short, he had helped to found a sovereign republic and taken the lead in molding it into a shape which it would never altogether lose.

The satisfaction of achievement and the respect of moneyed men would have to be his reward. Of popularity outside the class he had placed in control of the government he had none. And of material recompense, there was so little that he was heard to admit:

"I am not worth exceeding $500 in the world."

As a matter of fact, with his usual carelessness as to his personal budget, he was unduly optimistic. The great financier, only to be compared with the younger Pitt in his own generation, was actually insolvent, owing several thousand dollars more than his meager assets.

XX

ELDER STATESMAN

"YOU SAY I AM A POLITICIAN AND GOOD FOR NOTHING," Hamilton wrote in December, 1794, to Angelica Church. "What will you say when you learn that after January next I shall cease to be a politician at all? Such is the fact. I have formally and definitely announced my intention to resign, and have ordered a house to be taken for me in New York."

The astute Mrs. Church might have replied that her "petit Fripon" could cease being Secretary of the Treasury but would hardly cease being a politician.

He gave Congress two months' notice so that any questions or investigations might be launched while he was still available as a target. The Republicans accepted the challenge, falling back defeated in a new attempt to prove that he had "cabbaged" public funds. The attack gave added point to the eulogies his own party was bestowing upon him, exaggerated fulsome praise that was perhaps a little sickening.

As he passed this thirty-eighth birthday, Hamilton was well enough content. He regretted only that it was now impossible to enjoy the company of such a man as Madison, whose table was even more attractive than in his bachelor days since he had married the vivacious Mrs. Dolly Todd a few months before. The collaborators of *The Federalist* had drifted so far apart that the usually tolerant Madison was sneering ill-naturedly because Hamilton "pompously announced in the newspapers that poverty drives him back to the Bar for a livelihood." The wealthy Virginia planter, whose rich acres and many slaves made it impossible for him ever to know the sensation of being short of money, seldom forgot himself as far as this, but political animosity is not good for the manners.

Hamilton had learned to ignore taunts. He was the more indifferent to them on his retirement because he was picturing himself as pursuing the life of an elder statesman, advising others from some peaceful vantage point, himself safe from the striving for office. If he ever dreamed of returning to the arena—he was the most likely beneficiary of the Constitutional clause making the foreign born who were citizens at the time of adoption eligible for the Presidency—he never suffered a hint to escape him. At thirty-eight he really intended to follow the advice of McHenry, who, congratulating his old comrade in arms on his resignation, urged him to add felicity to fame.

"I have built houses," the Irishman explained. "I have cultivated fields. I have planned gardens. I have planted trees. I have written little essays. I have made poetry once a year to please my wife; at times got children, and at all times thought myself happy. Why cannot you do the same?"

Why not, indeed? New York was a pleasant place, far more agreeable socially than Philadelphia where politics divided men so strictly that few could enjoy the company of those who differed from them. Hamilton, it was true, had been one of the few, for strongly as he maintained his opinions, he did not obtrude them upon a host or a guest. He could even drink a glass with Senator Burr, and if the violet eyes heartily damned the black ones, it was not apparent in the graceful bow and smile that accompanied the toast. In New York, too, he might try McHenry's horticultural recipe. Of course in an emergency, his country would not call in vain for his services.

The Republicans were almost as glad to get rid of "the King of the Feds" as he was to go. Not so glad, of course, that any of them were present at the farewell dinner in February, which was an exclusively Federalist affair, with merchants and judges and party men in and out of office shouting like schoolboys for Alexander Hamilton. Then he was off for the little house Betsey had taken in Pine Street, New York, carrying a better certificate than the acclaim of the coffee houses, a certificate that would disconcert if not silence his critics.

"After so long an experience of your public services," Washington had written in a letter intended for show, "I am naturally led, at this moment of your departure from office—which it has always been my wish to prevent—to review them.

"In every relation, which you have borne to me, I have found that my confidence in your talents, exertions and integrity, has been well placed.

"I the more freely render this testimony of my approbation because I speak from opportunities of information which cannot deceive me, and which furnish satisfactory proof of your title to public regard.

"My most earnest wishes for your happiness will attend you in your retirement, and you may assure yourself of the sincere esteem, regard and friendship of

> "Dear Sir,
> > "Your affectionate
> > > "G. WASHINGTON."

Few men could boast letters subscribed "Your Affectionate" by the aloof, ailing hero in the Morris mansion. But Washington really had a good deal of fondness for the man who was leaving him. Not gifted with small talk himself, he listened with pleasure to the sprightly chatter of his Secretary of the Treasury. Their views were fundamentally in harmony, and the President, a great breaker of horses in his day, liked the mettlesome spirit which on occasion had taken the form of some disrespect toward himself. His Excellency, however, was not demonstrative, showing his affection only in tactful little gestures such as never letting the youngster know that he did not think him a military genius.

Armed with the written attestation to his virtues, which led angry Jeffersonians to declare the President had joined a political party, Hamilton rode quickly over the frozen roads to New York to collect a year's retainer fees in advance from such clients as could afford them and to receive the homage of the Chamber of Commerce. This last, in the form of a banquet at the Tontine Coffee House on the corner of Wall and Water Streets, was not marred by politics, although some Jeffersonian stalwarts attended.

"Great decorum as well as conviviality marked the entertainment," Fenno's *Gazette* reported, and the set toasts indicated as much. In honor of Hamilton the assembled guests, who included state dignitaries as well as merchants, drank off bumpers to:

The President
The Vice President and Congress
The Governor
Agriculture
Commerce
Industry and Improvement
Liberty and Law
Social Order and Social Happiness
The People of the United States, Brothers of one Family
General Wayne and the Army
National Credit
Integrity and Knowledge
Patriotism and Honest Favor
The Esteem of Their Fellow Citizens, an Inestimable Reward
    to Those Who Have Deserved Well of Their Country

These, however, were only the preliminaries. Informal toasts followed in order, and the chairman invited the gathering to drink to "The immortal memory of Baron Steuben," recently dead. Then the guest of honor gracefully proposed "The Merchants of New York, may they never cease to have Honour for their commander, Skill for their Pilot and Success for their Port," a sentiment which elicited nine cheers instead of the usual three. Chancellor Livingston offered "May Love and Honour be the Reward of Virtue." Judge Lansing gave them "The Commerce of the City of New York" and Judge Benson with admirable brevity "The

Honest Merchant." Mr. Hamilton withdrew at this point to permit the assembly to drink his health with three times three. On his return there were more toasts, but the reporter, pardonably confused by this time, was unable to record them.

As the prelude to a life of retirement, the feast was perhaps a little too elaborate. But the fate of an elder statesman is not all harmony and dignified pronouncements to reverential groups of admirers. Younger politicians in active practice want to think for themselves, and exactly twenty days after his resignation took effect, Hamilton heard that one of his minor measures for disposing of a part of the unsubscribed public debt had been replaced by a slightly different scheme.

"Am I, then, more of an American than those who drew their first breath on American ground?" he demanded with furious irrelevance of Rufus King. "Am I a fool—a romantic Quixote—or is there a constitutional defect in the American mind? Were it not for yourself and a few others, I could adopt the reveries of De Paux as substantial truths, and could say with him that there is something in our climate which belittles every animal, human or brute."

If a trifling change in his policy could call forth such an outburst, there was little likelihood that a serious issue would find him content with the role of cool, aloof elder statesman. And, although he plunged at once into a busy, lucrative law practice, riding circuit all up and down the Hudson valley, he could not keep his mind off the state of the nation and his pen dripped pages of sage advice to the President, the Cabinet and leaders in Congress. He was almost as much a prime minister as when he had been Secretary of the Treasury. He carried so much weight with Washington that Adams wrote many years later:

"The truth is, Hamilton's influence over him was so well known, that no man fit for the office of State or War would accept either. He was driven to the necessity of appointing such as would accept."

The suspicious Adams mistook agreement for influence. Because Washington knew his former aide's views would conform to his, he never ceased to ask for drafts of official papers. But Hamilton's hand was seen at what Republicans thought its worst when Jay brought back a treaty that cost the President his remaining popularity with Jeffersonians. The tall Chief Justice had not repeated his diplomatic triumph of '83. He had accepted terms that waived almost all the demands he had been sent to enforce and left almost all the grievances unredressed. It was so disappointing that Jefferson and Hamilton selected the same adjective, "execrable," to describe it, and Hamilton added that it was "an old woman's treaty." For all that, he realized, neutrality in a world war is worth a high price. Interruption of commerce, relinquishment of claims, arbitration clauses obviously favorable to Britain, even failure to end impressment of American seamen seemed not too much to pay for peace.

Hamilton, therefore, urged ratification of all except an article forbidding United States ships to carry certain non-military supplies to Europe. His advice was taken, but the Senate regarded the "old woman's treaty" as too humiliating to be made public. Naturally an opposition Senator refused to be bound by the vote enjoining secrecy and carried a copy to the press.

The resulting storm rocked society to its foundations. Effigies of the Chief Justice went up in flames from Maine to Georgia. Hogsheads were emptied to the toast: "Clipped wings, lame legs, the pip and an empty crop to all Jays." A wave of patriotic hysteria swept the country, and the cry of hatred against England—politicians who preferred drivel to issues used the same slogan for generations after this time—united a good many Federalists to the Republican opposition. The only chance of defeating the treaty and plunging the country into war rested now with Washington. For weeks, gales of furious propaganda swept that impassive figure, which had been famous for imperturbability in the face of greater storms.

In New York, Hamilton observed the rising anger of the populace with concern. From such fits come outbursts inimical to public order. A judicious mixture of eloquence and reason, he thought, might soothe the passions of the multitude. For the purpose of administering the dose, he advertised an open air "town meeting" to discuss the treaty.

Between five and seven thousand rabid partisans jammed Broad Street when the slender figure of the organizer, dressed more carefully than usual, mounted a stoop to say his piece, a Federalist David flinging his little morsel of logic at the Goliath of mob hysteria. But this giant of the people refused to succumb to pebbles, however smooth and shining. As he began to speak, the crowd was seized with a sudden craving for parliamentary rules.

"A chairman!" they shouted, "let us have a chairman!"

That functionary was duly installed out of harm's way on a balcony of the old Federal Hall, but the taste for formalities vanished as abruptly as it came. When Peter Livingston, opponent of the treaty though he was, began to speak, the noise prevented those nearest him from hearing a word he said. He withdrew to the front of Trinity Church, where a couple of thousand followed to listen. The rest remained to boo and hiss so that even Hamilton's clear tones were drowned, and at last he gave it up, merely sending a resolution in support of the treaty to be read by the chairman. The mob listened to a few phrases, then the shouts and cat-calls redoubled.

Suddenly a shower of stones rained upon the little group on the steps, and not all of them came from what Hamilton liked to call the rabble. Among the marksmen was Peter Livingston's young cousin, Edward, a new member of Congress, a future Mayor, United States Attorney, law-giver of Louisiana, Secretary of State, Minister to France. Rich and tal-

ented, he was already regarded as one of the coming chiefs of
the popular party, and here he was throwing stones with all
the enthusiasm—but perhaps not the accuracy—of a butcher's
apprentice. In the end, it was David who was struck by a
pebble from Goliath, and as he wiped the blood from his
forehead with a dainty lace handkerchief, Hamilton cried
contemptuously:

"These are hard arguments!"

Neither sneers nor logic were an effective answer in this
hot July noon on Broad Street with the yelling mob swelter-
ing in its closely packed numbers, cursing Jay and England,
Hamilton and treaties. But the elder statesman was no more
silenced by the mob than it had been by him.

"It is long since I have learned to hold popular opinion of
no value," he wrote to Washington.

If the public would not hear him, he would appeal over
the heads of the public to intelligent men who might still be
reached by reason. In a few days the newspapers began a
series of "Letters from Camillus," written very much in the
vein of *The Federalist*. There was no attempt to uphold the
treaty as a great work unjustly maligned. Taking the tone
adopted when appealing for the Constitution, he argued that
ratification was the lesser of two evils. The answers to his arguments only proved the truth of Burr's remark:

"Anyone who puts himself on paper with Hamilton is
lost."

One, however, was rated as having a chance in such a contest. Madison was almost as powerful if not so fiery a pleader,
and as the "Letters from Camillus" gushed forth in relentless
logic, Jefferson realized that it was no answer for his own
papers to print little verses:

> Sure George the Third will find employ
> For one so wise and wary,
> He'll call "Camillus" home with joy
> And make him Secretary.

"Hamilton is really a colossus to the anti-republican party," the sage of Monticello wrote to his favorite lieutenant. "Without numbers, he is a host within himself. . . . When he comes forward there is no one but yourself who can meet him. For God's sake take up your pen and give a fundamental reply."

But Madison, whether because it was too hot or because he was on his extended honeymoon with Dolly or because he did not think that in cold logic there was a fundamental reply to *Camillus,* refused to enter the lists. Meanwhile Hamilton had been condensing and clarifying his papers on the subject, and sent the result, thirty pages of close reasoning, to Washington to help make up that inflexible mind. Whether the President needed the assistance or not, he signed at last, and words as sharp as the stone that had cut Hamilton's forehead were flung in a newspaper war which, if one believed newspapers, indicated that not a single honest man survived in the land.

"A Calm Observer" accused Washington of overdrawing his salary with the connivance of Hamilton and Wolcott. When the President rejected a muckraking demand of the House for all papers relating to the treaty, Benjamin Franklin Bache, the Doctor's grandson, cried out that Washington was under the thumb of Hamilton, and scoffed:

"Though he has apparently discharged the nurse, he is still in leading strings."

Even the mild Jefferson, who fully appreciated Washington's character, mourned:

"I wish that his honesty and his political errors may not furnish a second occasion to exclaim, 'curse on his virtues, they have undone his country.' "

Of course all the mud was not slung in one direction. While Washington was making up his mind about the treaty, the formal, uneasy Randolph was being disgraced with a providential timeliness (from the Federalist point of view) which lent some strength to his feeble vindication. The British had captured and now made public a bundle of despatches written by the new French Minister at the time of the Whiskey Rebellion. One read:

"Mr. Randolph came to see me with an air of great eagerness, and made to me the overtures of which I gave you an account in my No. 6. Thus with some thousands of dollars, the republic could have decided on civil war or peace! Thus the consciences of the pretended patriots of America already have their price."

The battle of words dragged on. Federalists were accused of the Jay treaty, treasonable submission to England and gross corruption. Republicans were held responsible for the Whiskey Rebellion, Randolph's supposed betrayal, treasonable connections with France and gross corruption. A Cabinet post was so exposed to sniping that this, more than Hamilton's influence, was to blame for the difficulty in getting Secretaries. By the end of October Washington was calling for Hamilton's help. Paterson of New Jersey, Johnson of Maryland, Pinckney of South Carolina and Patrick Henry of Virginia had refused Randolph's office, while Marshall had declined the Attorney Generalship relinquished by Bradford. In this crisis, the President wanted the Federalist chief to talk King into taking the State portfolio and to advise as to the usefulness of Samuel Chase for Attorney General, an appointment which Washington hesitated to make since there had once been talk of "some impurity in his conduct." But Hamilton could not persuade King, and he himself had been Chase's chief accuser during the Revolution. (A year later the Marylander was found to be pure enough for the Supreme Court.)

Correspondence between the party leader and his old commander, despite partisan turmoil, was chiefly concerned at this time with a refugee youth named George Washington Lafayette, whose father was in an Austrian dungeon. For him, Hamilton stretched the "occasional dinner" into a home for the boy and his tutor, since in the excited state of factional feeling the gratitude due a Lafayette would be forgotten by self-styled patriots if the Marquis's old General offered the hospitality of the executive mansion to the Marquis's son.

For some months Hamilton strove harder to cheer the wretched, bewildered little émigré than to find a Secretary of State. He was deriving some pleasure from his house full of children—he was frequently absent from it for professional reasons—and he became almost as interested in pedagogy as was Burr. His eldest, Philip, was already showing an aptitude for study, and Angelica was quite wonderful, her father thought, as she performed on the piano her Aunt Angelica Church had sent from London. The proud parent decided there was something to be said for McHenry's advice. He began to consider building a house and certainly, as the first year of his career as elder statesman slipped by and he reached the ripe age of thirty-nine, he thought himself happy.

XXI

PARTY LEADER

HAMILTON WAS NOT THE ONLY ELDER STATESMAN IN THE country. On his hill at Monticello, Jefferson had been animating the forces of democracy, organizing, writing, demanding contributions to party papers, and realizing the joys of retirement recommended by McHenry. The former Secretary of State was full of a thousand varied questions on subjects ranging from crops to cosmic philosophy, from the health of his slaves to the larger freedom of mankind. But, no more than the former Secretary of the Treasury, had he relinquished his party leadership. So, in the presidential year of 1796, the opposing forces were led by two of the most active self-styled recluses the world has ever seen, each pursuing two or three careers any one of which would have wearied the energies of normal men.

Jefferson, in spite of his plantation, his scientific notes, his books, his little inventions and his enormous correspondence, found time to rally the army of the discontented, and added to it the agrarians who had been learning discipline these four years. Federalists turned to Hamilton for advice, since Washington had refused to stand for a third term. The elder statesman was writing almost as much as Jefferson, instructing the members of the Cabinet in their tasks as if he were Pooh Bah himself, and slaving away far into the night on behalf of his clients until Talleyrand, returning past the lawyer's house very late and seeing him through the window still bent over his papers, exclaimed in wonderment:

"I have seen a man who made the fortune of a nation laboring all night to support his family."

The forbearance indicated in this relative poverty of a man who had once handled millions was incomprehensible to the ci-devant Bishop of Autun. But Hamilton had no avarice, and the practice of the law was a sort of game of wits which he found a positive relaxation from the grimmer battle of statesmanship. In this last the stability of his system seemed to be at stake, and he explained:

"It is far less important who of so many men that may be named shall be the person, than that it shall not be Jefferson."

Meanwhile his spare moments were devoted to a state paper which even more than *The Federalist* has been quoted by statesmen of five generations, never without reverent admiration. Washington was preparing his Farewell Address, regretting that he had not made it sooner, and as usual he was relying on Hamilton for the writing. In the spring of 1796 while the lawyer was in Philadelphia earning five hundred dollars for a fortnight's work in arguing an elaborate case involving constitutional interpretation, the two had discussed what the President ought to say and leave unsaid. For example, there would be no need to put in what he gave as one strong reason for retiring, "a disinclination to be longer buffeted in the public prints by a set of infamous scribblers."

The substance, as was usual in these collaborations, consisted of the plain, strong thoughts of Washington. The order, the telling emphasis, the clear expression were Hamilton's. In his New York study he wrote, pondered and revised, pacing the floor as he tried to clothe the President's earnestness in a fittingly eloquent dress. Then he called for Betsey so that he could read to her aloud, hearing for himself how the phrases sounded, and years afterward she could still remember his fond smile and tender tone as he said:

"My dear Eliza, you must be to me what Molière's old nurse was to him."

The admirable Betsey was willing to be even that, and there was no doubt in her mind as to the perfection of the lines declaimed by those firm, beloved lips. Curiously enough, generations of political experts who would have been insulted at being compared in intellect to Mrs. Hamilton accepted the address with exactly the same unthinking rapture.

Neither her husband nor Washington had counted on that. They had hoped for a reasoned consideration of the solemn warnings in the light of what the country had been experiencing. The powerful plea to avoid partisan animosities was as seriously meant as the more generally quoted passage against entangling foreign alliances. Washington thought his administration had suffered from both. He sincerely hoped his successors would not be plagued by rivalry of faction or the desire of Americans to save Europe from itself by armed intervention.

Actually the Farewell Address was composed and delivered in the midst of an almost universal disregard of its tenets. Party feeling ran higher and dirtier than ever. Even when the President was holding his last levee and all the world knew his political career was over, the bitterness engendered by his past support of the Federalists broke out in *The Aurora's* considered opinion that "if ever a nation was debauched by a man, the American nation has been debauched by Washington; if ever a nation was deceived by a man, the American nation has been deceived by Washington." This was mild compared to Tom Paine's open letter:

"As to you, sir, treacherous in private friendship, and a hypocrite in public life, the world will be puzzled to decide whether you are an apostate or an impostor, whether you have abandoned good principles, or whether you ever had any."

Such a response to the plea for composing party differences augured ill for the warning against entangling alliances. The only thing that kept the nation neutral was a fairly even division between those who wished to fight France and those who aimed at England. And it was in this atmosphere that the presidential campaign was fought.

The futility of Washington's appeal to sink party squabbles might have been predicted long before the Farewell Address was delivered when the Republicans discovered a new proof of oligarchy in the fact that Hamilton and a few of his friends in private talks had decided on Adams and Thomas Pinckney of South Carolina for their candidates. Federalists in turn hooted at the democratic pretensions of their enemies, pointing out that a little group of Republican leaders with equal privacy had decided that Jefferson and Burr should constitute the hope of honest men.

Hamilton, penning noble sentiments on the evils of faction and practical letters on strict party organization, saw that the close co-operation of influential men working through Chambers of Commerce and the Cincinnati was still more than a match for agrarian numbers. The Jeffersonians had not carried their enthusiasm on behalf of democracy to the point of enfranchising propertyless men in Republican states, and in most of them presidential electors were still chosen by the legislatures.

In the confusion of issues and methods of election, Hamilton saw a chance to achieve the disciplined party that was his ideal. That was a machine obedient to his commands and with operators who would take their line unquestioningly from him. In such an organization there could be no place for John Adams, who had a policy of his own, very much a will of his own and a philosophy which, while fundamentally similar to Hamilton's, was founded on the domination of the Adamses rather than the Hamiltons of this world. However, the Boston patriot was the only Federalist left with any general popularity, and even in the then state of the ballot a candidate had to have some appeal.

Hamilton proposed to use that popularity to win the election, but thought there was a way of shoving the Duke of Braintree into the background. Each elector voted for two

men without stipulating which he favored for President and
which for Vice President. Some of the Southerners would
never vote for a Massachusetts man, and in some places
Pinckney might be coupled with Jefferson. The ostensible
Vice Presidential candidate might thus pile up a bigger total
than his nominal chief. This, of course, was as clear to Adams
as to Hamilton, and his friends withdrew so many northern
votes from Pinckney that, in spite of South Carolina, which
cast its ballots for Jefferson and the favorite son, Pinckney
was defeated for the Vice Presidency, Jefferson coming in
only three votes from the top of the list. The same maneuvering had been going on in the other camp, with the result that
Burr polled less than half the true Republican strength, the
electoral vote being: Adams, 71; Jefferson, 68; Pinckney, 59;
Burr, 30, and the rest scattering.

The winner, his vanity outraged by the contrast to Washington's victories, quite naturally suspected the good faith of
a party leader who allowed the prime enemy to slip into second place. It would not have occurred to him that Hamilton
regarded the new President as a figurehead, and was preparing to carry on as if Adams really had been defeated. Washington's Cabinet would naturally remain to serve his successor, and three of its four members were almost blind followers of Hamilton. Wolcott at the Treasury would take no
step without consulting his predecessor. McHenry, who had
ignored his own advice in order to become Secretary of War,
had learned on Washington's staff to accept the lead of his
friend. The years since then had only served to heighten his
respect and devotion. He knew he owed his place to Hamilton; he did not know the recommendation read:

"He would give no strength to the Administration, but he
would not disgrace the office."

The almost despairing search for a Secretary of State had
ended in the almost despairing choice of Timothy Pickering,
an old-fashioned New England Puritan who had been occu-
pying the office of Postmaster General, not yet of Cabinet

rank, when the retirement of Knox and the disinclination of better men sent him to the War Department. His promotion to first place in the Cabinet had gone to his head, never very strong, although he knew how many others had been asked ahead of him. But Pickering, unconscious of his own short-comings, was the sort of man who waved his arms violently to emphasize the cry: "I abhor gesticulation."

On the chief issue confronting the new administration, Hamilton was more in accord with Adams than with any of his three henchmen, if he had only known it. For the great problem was how to keep out of war with France. Hardly had peace with England been secured than the storm blew hard the other way, and before long the chant of "war! war! war!" was rising against the sister republic. The heedless invective which accompanied the cry was as distasteful as ever to Hamilton, who wrote somewhat magisterially to Wolcott:

"Hard words are very rarely useful in public proceedings. *Real firmness* is good for everything. *Strut* is good for nothing."

The strut of which he complained was a cheerful readiness to fight the whole world. Monroe, popular in Paris but considered too pro-French by both Washington and Hamilton, had been recalled. French anger at the Jay treaty was so strong that the Paris government refused to receive Monroe's successor, Charles Cotesworth Pinckney, brother of the candidate. Immediately those Federalists who were as pro-English, anti-French as Hamilton was supposed to be wished to avenge the insult in blood. Pickering, Wolcott and McHenry all belonged to this group. They would not have understood their party leader's sane remarks to Rufus King this winter:

"We are laboring hard to establish in this country principles more and more *national* and free from all foreign ingredients, so that we may be neither 'Greeks nor Trojans' but truly Americans."

Even before Adams took office the elder statesman in New York had been proposing the sort of extraordinary mission that had kept peace with England, and Adams too had this in mind. Both, remembering Jay, thought the embassy should consist of three men, two Federalists and a Republican to keep the opposition quiet. It was characteristic of Hamilton that, having seen the main outline of his policy adopted, he should have taken the stand that ruin was inevitable because some of the details were changed. Everyone agreed Pinckney should be one of the envoys. Hamilton wanted George Cabot or Rufus King for the other Federalist and Jefferson or Madison for the Republican. Adams chose Marshall, a Federalist of his own stamp rather than Hamilton's, and Elbridge Gerry, a personal friend although a Republican.

Hamilton was gloomy about all this, for he knew the man with whom the mission must deal. Talleyrand was in office again, and there was more to fear from his unscrupulous cleverness than from the politics of the ambassadors. He could be counted upon to excel in trickery the three Americans put together.

The task of party leader, to a man who believed leadership meant giving orders, was rendered more thankless by the manner in which Adams received a draft of an administration program for domestic and foreign policies. Hamilton had written it out carefully in a long letter to be shown to the President, who remarked:

"I really thought the man was in a delirium."

Thus rebuffed, Hamilton was moved to display disgust for his position, a passing mood, but which while it lasted drew from him this analysis of public life in the United States:

"The opportunity of doing good, from the jealousy of power and the spirit of faction, is too small in any station, to warrant a long continuance of private sacrifice."

The occasion for this low estimate was a happier one than the tone implies. The fame of the "man who made the fortune of a nation" had spread outside his own country and reached even to the corner of Ayrshire where the Hamiltons of the Grange had their respectable being. And, apparently for the first time in forty years, they remembered that their black sheep brother had gone out to the West Indies and begot himself this precocious offspring. Although illegitimate, he might be useful to another young Hamilton setting forth to conquer the New World, and so a friendly letter, requesting good offices, went across the Atlantic. The recipient was enormously gratified, and in honor of this recognition by his father's relatives essayed his only adventure in autobiography, a brief, carefully edited account of his career. Of his father, to whom he had been forwarding small but not very conveniently spared sums for years, he wrote:

"I have strongly pressed the old gentleman to come and reside with me, which would afford him every enjoyment of which his advanced age is capable, but he has declined it on the ground that the advice of his physicians leads him to fear, that the change of climate would be fatal to him."

Perhaps the son was not sorry, for the perennial failure could hardly have fitted very well into a life which, in spite of the inconsiderate independence of Adams and the ingratitude of republics, was very pleasing to Hamilton. At forty the rosiness of his cheeks had departed, his features had sharpened somewhat and, as he wrote to Washington, "I seem now to have regularly a period of ill health every summer," attributed alternately to yellow fever and the delayed effects of war privations. His dress was less colorful, too, but this was one of the French Revolution's victories. He yielded to the fashions if not to the politics inspired by that leveling movement, and although the lace ruffles on his chest continued to be of the finest quality, his shoes were without buckles and his coats of sober shades.

The settled family man, rejoicing in the notice of Scottish Hamiltons, noted that he was prospering in his profession, that his friends were amiable and witty, that his children "yield me much satisfaction." He had moved to a more comfortable house in Partition (later Fulton) Street, and "it is impossible to be happier than I am in a wife." They were going to have still another child, and the fees were rolling in so fast that he and Betsey were thinking of building a place in the country, when of a sudden the shadow of James and Maria Reynolds fell across their contentment.

After that painful December evening in Philadelphia nearly five years before, the frigid Monroe had become custodian of the documents which had first aroused suspicion. He had also enjoyed a further interview with Clingman and Mrs. Reynolds, who hinted that Hamilton's story was a fabrication against her virtue in order to conceal the truth. Monroe had filed a memorandum of this conversation with the other papers "in the hands of a respectable character in Virginia."

By the summer of 1797, the ex-diplomat's temper was on edge. He had been for some months the target of anti-French attacks in the usual billingsgate style of the day, and the sting was made greater by the fact that some of the charges, particularly his acquiescence in an anti-American diatribe by a French official in Paris, were true.

Only through his malice or carelessness could the Reynolds papers see the light, and just when Monroe was at his sorest, a Republican hack of no conscience, James Callender, came out with a thickish pamphlet which he grandiosely called "The History of the United States for the Year 1796." Here appeared those old fragments of letters to Reynolds, the story of Clingman and the flat charge that Alexander Hamilton as Secretary of the Treasury had been the partner in speculation of a sharper and a cheat.

Although a singularly shabby trick, it was clever. The authors obviously thought Hamilton dared not avow publicly the explanation that had satisfied his enemies in private. If he did not, he was ruined surely; if he did, his reputation, they believed, could scarcely be less damaged. Monroe could hardly have desired a neater revenge.

Hamilton wished to meet the charge with a blanket asser-
tion by the three inquisitors of that December day that they
knew the facts and knew Callender lied. Such a statement
could be published as a vindication without going into the
actual facts. He got from Venable a denial of issuing the
papers and the cautious admission that Hamilton's explanation had been "satisfactory." Monroe and Muhlenberg declared that "we had no agency in or knowledge of the publication of these papers till they appeared." This letter,
signed jointly, added that the originals were still with the
"respectable character," but they were never produced, nor
was the holder more closely identified.

Hamilton, certain that Monroe was lying, spent several
miserable weeks trying to pin him down. The realization
that the Virginian had been prowling about in search of
further dirt after Hamilton's humiliating explanation was
intolerable. And his record of these unsavory researches
hinted at some belief in the charges. The recalled envoy, not
displeased to see his enemy squirm, refused to repudiate the
intimations in so many words. Rather than do so, he was
ready to offer that other form of satisfaction "which I am
ever ready to meet."

"I have authorized Major Jackson to communicate with
you and to settle time and place," Hamilton replied on
August 4. It was the day Betsey was giving birth to their
fifth son.

"If you meant this last letter as a challenge to me," Monroe retorted, "I have then to request that you will say so,
and in which case, have to inform you that my friend, Col.
Burr, who will present you this, and who will communicate
with you on the subject, is authorized to give my answer to
it, and to make such other arrangements as may be suitable
in such an event."

These polite approaches to pistols for two were as close
as Hamilton came to satisfaction. Burr, finding that his colleague at the bar was under the impression of being the

challenged party, thought honor could be appeased without a duel. He drew up the memorandum which avoided it, and in which Monroe again disavowed giving out the papers.

If the danger of a personal meeting with Monroe had been ended, the menace of the Callender pamphlet remained. In the privacy of his study, Hamilton was coming to the conclusion that he would have to sacrifice his private reputation to his public justification, and in October the opposition press was able to howl with delight because the Federalist leader "published a book to prove he was an adulterer."

Once having decided on his course, the author went at his task with a coolness through which the hot anger of a man betrayed bursts forth only occasionally, and then with consummate art. If, as *The Aurora* chuckled, it was necessary to bring out "an attestation of his having cuckolded James Reynolds," he had at least done it in a style worthy of *The Federalist* and the Farewell Address. There was a long preamble on the sin of evil speaking and the contemptible practice of the "Jacobins" for resorting to calumny to discredit men they could not reach by truth. Cunningly he pointed out that the revered Washington was not immune to slander either.

"The charge against me," he wrote, coming at last to the point, "is a connection with one James Reynolds for purposes of improper pecuniary speculation. My real crime is an amorous connection with his wife for a considerable time, with his privity and connivance, if not originally brought on by a combination between the husband and wife with the design to extort money from me.

"This confession is not made without a blush. I cannot be the apologist of any vice because the ardor of passion may have made it mine. I can never cease to condemn myself for the pang which it may inflict in a bosom eminently entitled to all my gratitude, fidelity, and love. But that bosom will approve, that, even at so great an expense, I should effectually wipe away a more serious stain from a name which it cherished with no less elevation than tenderness."

Then, for the benefit of a public which went quite hysterical with glee over the exposure of a great man's amours, he revealed the whole miserable story, analyzed it without self-pity or excuse, documented it with the full correspondence, affidavits and receipts.

The sensation was enormous. The press teemed with ribald comment, and society was no more charitable. Witticisms and jests flew about with the rapidity of bad news, and in due course some of them reached Mount Vernon. The master of the estate, a man of austerity in such matters, could nevertheless feel for his old protégé. In retirement he had recovered his prestige and with infinite, kindly tact he threw it to the support of the harried author in New York, writing:

"Not for any intrinsic value the thing possesses, but as a token of my sincere regard and friendship for you, and as a remembrance of me, I pray you to accept a wine cooler for four bottles. It is one of four which I imported in the early part of my late administration of the government."

For once Hamilton appreciated to the full the largeness of that nature which could be so delicate in attentions to one pursued by the derision of the world. For once he responded with something approaching the gratitude the occasion merited, replying on receipt of the gift:

"The token of your regard which it announces, is very precious to me, and will always be remembered as it ought to be."

Where Washington condoned, it was not for mere mortals of that age to condemn, and his support brought Hamilton through the public storm. As for the domestic aspects of the case, he was equally lucky. Betsey went beyond mere forgiveness to a passionate championship of her husband that took the form of commiseration for one cruelly wronged. Her pain was not that of the deceived wife. Hamilton, not she, had been betrayed, and her fury against the villains who had put him on the rack never waned. More than thirty years later, when both she and Monroe had passed their seventieth birthdays, the card of the ex-President, last of the great Virginia dynasty, was brought to her as she sat in her New York garden.

"What has that man come to see me for!" she muttered.

"Why, Aunt Hamilton," said a young nephew who was with her and supposed that age had affected her memory, "don't you know, it's Mr. Monroe, and he's been President, and he is visiting here now in the neighborhood, and has been very much made of, and invited everywhere, and so— and so I suppose he has come to call and pay his respects to you."

The youth might have imagined she was deaf as well as forgetful for all the attention she paid his explanation. She hesitated a moment, then, erect and slim, she walked rapidly back to the house. Monroe rose to meet her in a parlor sacred to the memory of the man she was so sure he had hounded with bitter malice, and she did not ask him to sit down again. Facing him, she listened to a conciliatory little speech from the lion of the hour, who thought that after all these years, when both were nearing the grave, they might forgive and forget old differences.

"Mr. Monroe," Betsey told him, "if you have come to tell me that you repent, that you are sorry, very sorry for the misrepresentations and slanders and the stories that you circulated against my dear husband—if you have come to say this, I understand it. But otherwise no lapse of time, no nearness to the grave makes any difference."

"She stopped speaking," the nephew remembered. "Monroe turned, took up his hat and left the room."

XXII

GENERAL WITHOUT AN ARMY

THE WORLD'S MEMORY WAS NOT AS LONG AS BETSEY'S. IN TIME
the savor departs from the juiciest scandal, and within a
matter of months the affair Reynolds was so far forgotten
that it was mentioned only in the course of newer attacks on
the Federalist chief. There were other men, more up-to-date
scandals, to invite the attention of the press and the drawing
room.

At no time was the central figure's public position affected.
Even while the story was fresh in every mouth, the Cabinet
was taking its politics from the former lover of Maria Reynolds. When Adams asked for advice on a message to Congress that was to meet in December, 1797, he got it only
from Hamilton, although he did not know it. Pickering,
Wolcott and McHenry turned to New York for their inspiration, and McHenry hardly bothered to rephrase the
paper furnished him by the party leader.

The country, said Hamilton, should be prepared for a
failure of the special mission to France with an army, a navy,
an understanding if not an alliance with England, a loan and
some new taxes. Even if war could be avoided, there might
be a use for the troops, and the funds, although this he did
not say yet. In his mind, as in many minds, was the idea that
Americans rather than Spaniards should exploit Louisiana
and the Floridas. To all sorts of people interested in land
and expansion, it was evident that the country west of the
Mississippi and south of Georgia was by "manifest destiny"
a part of the United States. Hamilton wished Spain to cede
these territories peacefully, by purchase if need be, but the

252

existence of strong armed forces would help negotiations. And in case of war, Spain was France's ally and might be despoiled.

It was not so easy to push his measures through a Congress which still hoped for peace and did not like the idea of standing armies. What was needed was a clarion cry that would rally all patriots, one of those exhilirating phrases that overpowers caution and good sense, the compelling but not necessarily accurate slogan without which a war can hardly be fought. Pinckney, the haughty South Carolinian, provided it when he flung proudly into the faces of avaricious Frenchmen the stirring defiance:

"Millions for defense, but not one cent for tribute!"

The occasion for this eloquence was an attempted hold-up, or shake-down, by three extra-official gentlemen acting ostensibly on behalf of Talleyrand. No one who had known the French Foreign Minister as an émigré in America could consider the story implausible. When the report was sent to Congress in the early spring of '98 and published to the country with the three blackmailers appearing in the discreet anonymity of X, Y and Z, the United States had a battle cry and a *casus belli*. Inevitably the documents became known as the XYZ papers, and with Mr. Pinckney's "Millions for defense" flying over the land, the most ardent Jeffersonians feared the people could not be kept from fighting France because Talleyrand was a crook.

Wars in better causes than that need continuingly favorable publicity if the people are to be kept at battle pitch, and in the long delays to which communications were subject, the friends of France saw some chance for calmer consideration. Meanwhile they had to acquiesce in the enlistment of an army, the creation of a Navy Department with a Secretary in the Cabinet, abrogation of the treaties with France, a loan and one of Hamilton's favorite taxes—a levy on buildings ranging up to a dollar a room for houses of seven rooms or more. This extremely unpopular measure was estimated by its author to be worth $1,000,000 a year, if it could be collected, so rapidly was the country being built up.

So far the program was just what Hamilton ordered, but the Federalists in Congress went beyond his recommendations and incurred his dignified censure. There had been nothing dignified about them, however, and the personal abuse reached a climax when the sharp-tongued Matthew Lyon, a Vermont Irishman dubbed "Hibernian Mat" in the Federalist press, resented a slur upon his courage by spitting in the face of Representative Roger Griswold of Connecticut. Since most of Lyon's compatriots were Republicans, there was a strong anti-foreign bias among the Federalists, reflected in a letter from the aristocratic Jonathan Mason, Jr., of Boston, who declaimed:

"I feel grieved that the saliva of an Irishman should be left upon the face of an American & He a New Englandman. My good Father Powell says, that if Griswold had been in the presence of God himself, he ought to have taken his revenge upon the spot, & beat his brains out."

A few days later Griswold tried to follow the good Father Powell's advice, coming to the House armed with a club for the purpose. Lyon defended himself with the Congressional fire tongs, and in a moment two Representatives of the sovereign people were rolling on the floor, locked in combat like dogs. And, like dogs, they were finally pulled apart by the hind legs.

Into that legislative assembly were introduced the measures known as the Alien and Sedition Acts. With rumors of an imminent French invasion repeated everywhere, and even believed, the hysteria mounted until horrid visions of slave insurrections and sansculotte terror were seen in the most unlikely places. William Cobbett, who was to close his career as an English radical of dread redness, was at this date still a tory, battling, he liked to think, for his King in foreign lands. Hamilton had enlisted his *Porcupine's Gazette* in the cause of Federalism. Cobbett, whose quills stung and festered as he lashed out at his enemies, had a gift for satire unsurpassed in his generation, and he was not concerned with truth if he could get the United States into the war on his country's side. So he was repeating and embellishing the most alarmist tales of French descents on the coast, throwing peaceful, gullible citizens into conniptions of fear.

Congressmen may not have believed, but they seized the opportunity to pass bills extending the naturalization period to nineteen years, suppressing "alien enemies" and making it a crime to say anything about the President or Congress "to bring them . . . into contempt or disrepute, or to excite against them . . . the hatred of the good people of the United States."

A party leader who does not share the madness of his followers has small chance of controlling them. Hamilton, eminently sane except in an occasional rare crisis that left his followers cool and unperturbed while he raged in solitary anguish, was scornful of the wild invasion talk. He saw, too, the full peril of the Alien and Sedition Acts, and cracked the whip over Cabinet members and Congressional spokesmen alike.

"Let us not be cruel or violent," he advised.

"Let us not establish a tyranny," he commanded again. "Energy is a very different thing from violence."

His party would not heed. For the first time the well-drilled "corrupt squadron" mutinied and its former commander, helpless, watched it riding off on a reckless looting expedition which he could not prevent and for which he knew he would be blamed. The sponsors of the bills, indeed, thought they had been very clever, ending the Jacobin menace forever, and they pointed with pride to approving newspaper doggerel:

> Each factious alien shrinks with dread
> And hides his hemp-devoted head;

While Slander's foul seditious crew
With gnashing teeth retires from view.

Hamilton knew that was a foolishly optimistic sentiment. Slander's foul seditious crew would not retire before any mere legislative enactments, and he could see that an attempt to enforce them must react violently upon a party that defied the thoroughly human desire to call one's enemy names. But the mischief had been done, and soon he had more important things to think about, for on July 28, 1798, two weeks after the Sedition Bill passed, he was agreeing to take the post of Inspector General of the new army with the rank of major general.

"At a crisis like the present," he wrote McHenry, "I esteem it my duty to obey the call of the government."

As a matter of fact he had worked hard to get the call issued. Two days later he was urging McHenry to summon him into active service at once, but there was a slight hitch. Hamilton, who had never doubted, and never proved, his talents for high military tasks, took it for granted that he outranked anyone else in the army except Washington, who had accepted the command in chief on the express understanding that he would not be active until troops actually took the field. However, there were two other major generals being commissioned, C. C. Pinckney and Harry Knox, both of whom had outranked a brevet lieutenant colonel in the Revolution.

Adams, who resented the deference his Cabinet paid to the "bastard brat of a Scots pedlar," thought he could place the three in any order he liked, although Hamilton's name was first on a list submitted by Washington. He had been put there, wrote the unenthusiastic commander, "with some fears, I confess, of the consequences, although I must acknowledge at the same time, that I know not where a more competent choice could be made." On that lukewarm basis he gave his support to Hamilton's pretensions, although he

could not see why his old aide should object to being Pinckney's junior. The Federalist chief, however, had his party
sufficiently in line to be able to insist that he was "called by
the voice of the country" and to speak of being "degraded
beneath my just claims in public opinion."

No one but himself heard that voice or was able to find
military ground for his claims, but there were plenty of
political reasons, which are often more effective in obtaining
military advancement. After nearly three months of bickering, Washington was persuaded to declare he would not keep
his post unless Hamilton was second in command. Adams
yielded, of course, but he never forgave the man who had
triumphed over him. Neither did Knox, whose deference to
Hamilton extended only to civil life, and he refused to serve.

Knox might sulk and Adams fulminate against "the most
restless, impatient, artful, indefatigable, and unprincipled
intriguer in the United States," but Hamilton was certain
that at last he had found his real mission in life. Convinced
that he had military genius of a transcendental kind, he gave
up his clients and fees with such joyful alacrity that before
he had received his commission, Robert Troup wrote sadly:

"The law has abandoned him, or rather he has forsaken
it."

The capacious mind that had retained all the details of
Treasury routine reveled in the complexities of army organization. Hamilton drew up plans for fortifying New York
harbor and saw them carried out under his own eyes. He
drafted pages upon pages of rules on discipline and tactics.
He concerned himself at length with problems of pay, allowances and servants for officers. He devised a program for garrisoning troops when they should have been raised and drew
up a curriculum for a military academy. He sketched uniforms for the various corps, complained that cocked hats
furnished by the War Department were humiliatingly ridiculous because they could be cocked only on one side instead
of three—"nothing is more necessary than to stimulate the

vanity of soldiers"—and wrote exhaustive reports on rations, distribution of supplies, the exact personnel of regiments, the need for doctors and engineers. He conducted scientific experiments to determine the proper length of a step on the march, and reached the revolutionary conclusion that at the double men should be permitted to take a full stride, not the mincing run then current in well-trained armies. In between he lectured McHenry like a schoolboy, for the Secretary of War fell lamentably short of Hamilton's vigorous notions of the military executive.

"Pray, take a resolution adequate to the emergency, and rescue the credit of your department," he urged, and to Washington he admitted:

"The administration of the War Department cannot prosper in the present *very well disposed* but very *unqualified* hands."

Displaying superior talents for the paper work of high command, Hamilton should have but did not thank his lucky stars for keeping him from risking his reputation in actual battle. Even his capacity for handling large bodies of troops in peace maneuvers was not put to the test, for the popularity of war faded among the masses who were supposed to furnish the raw material. The "millions for defense" slogan, unsupported by French invasions, was losing its potency. Moneyed men, first to cool and last to warm to such enthusiasms, had bargained for eight per cent. on the war loan Wolcott was floating, and common men saw little difference between tribute to Talleyrand and tribute to bankers.

Recruiting, therefore, was slow and disappointing, no more than 3,000 having volunteered for the ranks. Desertions, on the other hand, were so frequent that a good deal of Hamilton's military correspondence was taken up with this evil. McHenry could only suggest a few disciplinary executions, but Hamilton was "on the side of forbearance."

"The temper of our country is not a little opposed to the

frequency of capital punishment," he explained. "Public opinion, in this respect, though it must not have too much influence, is not wholly to be disregarded. There must be some caution not to render our military system odious by giving it the appearance of being sanguinary."

The common man's desire for war may have weakened, but his self-styled betters were in spirited mood. Fifteen thousand of them applied for commissions, five officers for each private, and the wire-pulling for place kept the politicians busy. Adams was getting so thoroughly sick of the expensive and humiliating business that he cried:

"This damned army will be the ruin of the country."

And then he saw a chance to get rid of it. He heard on what he considered good authority that France really did not want to fight. Vain as he was, John Adams was honest enough to be willing to sacrifice his popularity for peace and be proud of the chance. His information came in part from Gerry, who had stayed in Europe, and Adams was one of the few Federalists who could take a Republican's word seriously.

Hamilton, indulging in a thoroughly military style of thought, had convinced himself that war was inevitable. He also reached the conclusion that it was desirable, for he had a shrewd suspicion that Spain was preparing to cede Louisiana to France—which happened soon—and he knew the danger of allowing westward expansion to be blocked by a really powerful, ambitious nation.

"We ought certainly to look to the possession of the Floridas and Louisiana, and we ought to squint at South America," he told McHenry.

Squinting in another direction, he made one of his rare diplomatic mistakes, whether because the overweening confidence of a major general had undermined his judgment or because he had known Talleyrand too well to be unbiased. At any rate, he was sure the Frenchman was up to some trick, whereas the forthright Adams was willing to take at face value assurances that new envoys would be received fittingly. So while Adams was growing more attached to peace, the virtual head of the army was working out a scheme of attack that included joint operations with Great Britain.

"This man is stark mad, or I am," Adams exclaimed when he saw the plan. "He knows nothing of the character, the principles, the feelings, the opinions and prejudices of this nation. If Congress should adopt this system, it would produce an insurrection of the whole nation from Georgia to New Hampshire."

Actually Hamilton was not as crazy as the angry President supposed. While he was proposing to co-operate with England, he was not blind to the usual fate of England's allies.

"I am against going immediately into an alliance with Great Britain," he wrote the headstrong, Anglophile Pickering. "It is my opinion that her interests will insure us her cooperation to the extent of her power and that a treaty will not secure us further. On the other hand a treaty might entangle us. Public opinion is not prepared for it."

Holding these sane views himself, Hamilton would have said it was Adams who was the madman, and he did hint at it. The head of the party was very angry because the Chief Executive, having learned at last that when he asked for the views of his Cabinet he got the views of Hamilton, ceased asking. This was without precedent and, Hamilton told his henchmen, disloyal of the President. That Pickering, Wolcott and McHenry owed their loyalty to Adams was never mentioned. They saved what they had of that uncertain commodity for Hamilton.

In the leisurely state of diplomacy, the odd state of neither war nor peace dragged on for months, a delay lengthened by the minor revolution which turned the French Directory into a triumvirate. Adams's plan for a new mission was first mentioned in October, 1798. The envoys actually sailed in October, 1799.

The manner in which peace was assured—the President acted without the benefit of Hamilton's advice—angered the Major General almost as much as his rank in the army had enraged Adams. But the year's delay gave Hamilton time to see that at bottom Adams was right and war could be avoided. All the same, he was furious with the man who avoided it. Despising each other with the heartiness that was characteristic of both, the President and the General prepared in an oddly aloof co-operation to save their country and ruin their party.

Hamilton's influence was needed. The war fever had given the Federalists a fine Congressional majority in the election of '98, and it was a majority Adams could not control in spite of the fact that the ablest man of his faction, John Marshall, had won a seat in the House. Hamilton, however, had renewed his grip on the Congressmen who had bolted over the Sedition Act. Even Harrison Gray Otis, brilliant young Representative from Boston, took dictation humbly. Otis was a proud man, proud of his good looks, his clothes, his clever conversation, his family, his connections, his position and his talents. But when he addressed the leader of his party he was obsequious beyond the normal politeness of the day in begging "the indulgence of an interview" in which Hamilton might condescend to "devote an hour to my instruction."

Using his influence over such men, Hamilton assisted Adams to call off the dogs of war, but in doing it he showed so plainly who, in his estimation, was master that the breach between them grew too wide ever to bridge. Hamilton saw the President now only as a vain, pompous ass, and was regarded in turn as a sly, greedy, conscienceless adventurer. Perhaps if he could have seen the Duke of Braintree allowing "His Rotundity" to be harnessed to a chair and dragging his grandson around the parlor to the detriment of Abigail's carpets, he might have been more lenient. If Adams could have seen his "unprincipled intriguer" mapping moral and healthful studies for his children, teasing his wife and spoiling his daughter, he might have been less harsh. But they no longer saw each other as men as they faced the battle for control, each armored in his good intentions and confronting only the forbidding steel of the other's lowered visor.

XXIII

THE FILIBUSTER

DREAMS OF MARTIAL GLORY REMAINED AFTER VISIONS OF triumphing over the invincible hordes of revolutionary France had faded. Even as he reluctantly dismissed from his mind all hope of humbling the victor of Lodi, Hamilton turned with fresh enthusiasm to other ideas of conquest. As his hand penned precise, clerkly reports on food and clothing, supplies and munitions, his thoughts wandered thousands of miles away, southward and westward, ranging restlessly over a whole hemisphere. By an unhappy chance the equally restless thoughts of Aaron Burr would be directed that way, too, but Hamilton's was the grander scheme. It was nothing less than the "liberation" of Spanish America from California to Cape Horn. The fee for this service to the colonies of King Carlos IV, for which they had not as yet shown any passionate desire, was to be Louisiana and Florida.

"I have long been in the habit of considering the acquisition of those countries as essential to the permanency of the Union," he explained.

General Hamilton, therefore, was in a mood to share ambitions dancing in the brain of a fiery little Venezuelan, Francisco Antonio Gabriel de Miranda, who burned with a premature fervor to free his countrymen from what it was not yet bromidic to call the intolerable yoke of Spain. Miranda, looking for help, turned up in New York, where his imagination met its equal in the virtual commander of the United States Army.

Hamilton was eager to fling himself into the glorious adventure, but he had more substantial reasons than the pursuit of honor and glory. He was sufficiently a child of the Western Hemisphere to wish European, at least continental European, authority to be kept out of it. He wanted not only to weaken an ally of France but to strike down the whole system of American dependence on the Old World. However, that did not mean he envisaged a family of democratic republics.

"A government must be fitted to a nation," he wrote at this time, "as much as a coat to the individual; and, consequently what may be good at Philadelphia, may be bad at Paris and ridiculous at Petersburgh."

His pattern for South America was cut to a republican fashion, but the "liberated" states were to be under the protection of the liberator. They were to be permitted to evolve for themselves any "moderate government" that would assure the protector certain commercial privileges. With this crusade in mind, he accustomed himself to think of the army that grew so slowly as destined for a glorious filibustering expedition. Between organizational details and impatient complaints that "my friend McHenry is wholly insufficient for his place," he conferred with Miranda in a haze of golden dreams and wrote more practical letters to Rufus King.

These last were designed to enlist the help of the former Senator, now Minister to Great Britain. No one was mad enough to suppose that the army Hamilton desired to lead through the Americas could travel by land. The only navy capable of such an enterprise was British. So, since complete exclusion of European powers from the western world was as yet not practicable, Hamilton was willing to allow London to share equally in the commercial privileges and assume joint guardianship of the new states in return for the use of a fleet. As for his own part:

"I should be glad that the principal agency was in the United States, they to furnish the whole land force if necessary. The command in this case would very naturally fall upon me; and I hope I should disappoint no favorable anticipations."

His plan was based on a disregard for or misunderstanding of popular feeling of which at twenty he would have been incapable. The idea that the English would give the chief command to an American was to be compared in its fantastic optimism only to the notion that Americans would co-operate in a filibustering expedition with the English. However, as a captain of artillery, Hamilton had not hated the English, even while he fought them. As a Major General he saw no reason for hating them now. Confident that he could convert the necessary numbers to his own sensible point of view, he raised Miranda's hopes to delirious heights, promising:

"I shall be happy in my official station, to be an instrument in so good a work."

Hamilton's judgment may have been weakening, but not to the point of embarking on his adventure until it should be, as he put it, "patronized by the government of the country." Certainly without such patronage there was no hope of leading these brave new regiments against Spain. Hamilton was no Marlborough to steal an army, march it halfway across a continent and come back in triumph with a Blenheim embroidered on his banners. However, as long as there was a threat of war with France—and American ships were already battling French vessels on the high seas—he nursed his hopes, although when the filibustering idea was hinted to Adams, he remarked curtly:

"We are not at war with Spain."

Nor with France, since General Bonaparte, a practical, hard-headed man, saw nothing to be gained by war with the United States, and France was learning to enjoy taking his orders. The incomparable warrior's sudden pacifism was a long time filtering across the Atlantic and meanwhile the American army drilled in dusty fields or deserted through the woods, worried about the narrowness of its hat brims and grumbled about the irregularity of its pay.

Its Inspector General had not yet confided his scheme to the real Commander-in-Chief, but he had a notion that Washington could be won over at the proper time, for the farmer of Mount Vernon understood the value of western lands, in which he had proved his interest through a period of forty-five years. It never occurred to anyone to doubt the availability of Washington in an emergency. Already his contemporaries had endowed him with the cold attributes of a public monument, but the heroic figure had been ailing for years. He clung doggedly to duty, and on December 12, 1799, he was writing Hamilton a letter on the subject of the proposed military academy. Two days later he was dead, and his former aide, in Philadelphia on army business, was realizing that in "the long-tried patron—the kind and unchanging friend," he had lost the chief prop of his policy. Although the event "filled my heart with bitterness," it was on public rather than private grounds.

"Perhaps no man in this community has equal cause with myself to deplore the loss," he informed Tobias Lear, Washington's secretary. "I have been much indebted to the kindness of the General, and he was an *Aegis very essential to me*. But regrets are unavailing. For great misfortunes it is the business of reason to seek consolation. The friends of General Washington have very noble ones. If virtue can secure happiness in another world, he is happy. In this, the seal is now put upon *his* glory. It is no longer in jeopardy from the fickleness of fortune.

"P.S. In whose hands are his papers gone? Our very confidential situation will not permit this to be a point of indifference to me."

Slightly relieved to hear that Judge Bushrod Washington was the custodian of all his uncle's records, he nevertheless wrote to Pinckney:

"Perhaps no friend of his has more cause to lament on personal account than myself. The public misfortune is one which all the friends of our government will view in the same light. I will not dwell on the subject. My imagination is gloomy—my heart is sad."

There was good reason for gloom. He had succeeded to the real command of the army, but even as he issued orders for appropriate ceremonies at all garrisons, he knew that the bulky figure of John Adams stood between him and the realization of his dreams. The funeral guns were booming at their prescribed half-hourly intervals for the only man who could have moved the President out of the way. Of course another President might be easier to handle, and as the nineteenth century opened in the midst of mourning— but also, for the United States, in the midst of peace—the Federalist elder statesman of not quite forty-three, the eager filibustering colleague of Miranda, Major General Alexander Hamilton was working out the details of a scheme for depriving Adams of the reward of his labors.

Jefferson was engaged, of course, on the same task. The Vice President, quiet and avoiding all society where political discussions might wax warm—almost all Philadelphia society, therefore—had perfected his organization for the coming struggle. He was making the most of the unpopular Alien and Sedition laws, the unpopular expense of the army, the unpopular personalities in the government. These last did not include Adams, for the irascible patriot still had his following in the country, particularly among the many thousands who could not be affected by the Sedition Act but were grateful for peace. Because of his popularity it would be impossible to nominate anyone else, but not impossible, perhaps, to manipulate the election against him.

Hamilton's strategy was, broadly, the same as in '96. One of the variants was that he proposed to have his army colleague, C. C. Pinckney, instead of brother Thomas, slip into first place. The General was well liked, particularly in the South, presentable, affable, able. The plot was possible because in eleven of the sixteen states presidential electors were chosen by the legislatures rather than by popular ballot. It was always easier to manipulate the machinery of legislative appointments than to twist the democratic process into defeating the will of the people.

It was likely that New York, which was one of the eleven, would decide the issue with her twelve electoral votes. Hamilton, returning from Philadelphia, found that his grip on the State had weakened noticeably since Burr had been retired from the Senate. Jay had been elected Governor, it was true, but he was not nearly so clever a wielder of the patronage club as Clinton had been. Even the monopoly of the Bank of New York, potent political weapon, had been broken, and by Burr, too.

The ex-Senator's institution, a triumph of politics, law and finance, was the by-product of another yellow fever epidemic. More than 1,500 New Yorkers had died of it, and as the pestilence raged through a hot summer, the city became acutely conscious of its inadequate water supply. The Collect Pond was still the source, and most houses were supplied from hogsheads mounted on carts. As the plague subsided, this primitive system was denounced as uncivilized, and in April, 1799, the Legislature passed without much debate Colonel Burr's draft of "An Act for Supplying the City of New York with Pure and Wholesome Water."

There was a good deal of elaborate phraseology about the proposed Manhattan Company's rights and privileges and duties, and there was a rather simple sentence permitting any surplus funds to be used for "operations not inconsistent with the laws and constitution of the State of New York." Under that clause the Bank of the Manhattan Company was organized at once, in time to rescue good Republicans who needed loans from the Federalist pressure of the Bank of New York. The water, not very pure at that, began to be furnished about a year later.

Others than bankers exerted pressure on the defenseless voter of those days, for there was no such thing as a secret ballot. Troup, Hamilton's friend, colleague at the bar and blind follower, had explained quite frankly one of the factors in the Federalist success at the polls in '99.

"We have at last," he exulted, "prevailed upon the merchants to exert themselves. In the last election they were essentially useful. They told the cartmen that such of them as supported the democratic ticket would be dismissed from their employ. The consequence was we had a strong support from the cartmen. . . . Mr. John Murray spent one whole day at the poll of the Seventh Ward, sometimes called the cartmen's ward or Livingston's stronghold—and his presence operated like a charm."

Against this influence, Burr rallied an organization which for more than an hundred years after his time was capable of holding its own—and a little more—against almost any combination of merchants the city could pit against it. The genial Colonel found the Society of St. Tammany indulging in its purposeless, boisterous festivities in a Wigwam which the fastidious called "the Pig Pen." Rescuing it from its meaningless round of beer parties, parades in Indian feathers and interminable war reminiscences, Burr launched the association of toughened veterans into politics, an effective reply to Hamilton's Cincinnati.

While the ex-officers were electing the Federalist chief to succeed Washington as President General, the Colonel exercised his persuasive charm on all sorts of lowly fellows. Hamilton was campaigning among the Cincinnati against Adams, to the rage of the President when he heard of it, and Burr was campaigning against both. But Hamilton did not confine himself to the Cincinnati. He was at least as active as Burr and much more conspicuous.

"Mr. Hamilton is very busy, more so than usual," Burr's friend, Matthew L. Davis, noted, "and no exertions will be wanting on his part."

He would be driven into an error before long, however, and the first boss of Tammany Hall waited for it. Burr had divined the plan to supersede Adams, and he knew that

Hamilton would need a legislature of complacent tools ready to name electors who could be relied upon to cast their ballots exactly as the leader ordered. When the list of Federalist candidates was completed, it contained not a single person of real prominence, and as Burr scanned a copy, he exclaimed in quiet satisfaction:

"Now I have him hollow!"

It was the opening he had expected, and he hurried to take advantage of it. Against Hamilton's slate of nonentities, he would throw the most notable leaders of the Republican party, the most distinguished set of Assemblymen in history. The venerable Clinton headed the list. There followed, in addition to the compiler himself, Horatio Gates, still the hero of Saratoga; Brockholst Livingston, Hamilton's old schoolfellow, a leader of his clan and a future ornament of the Supreme Court; Samuel Osgood, Washington's first Postmaster General, and a careful cross-section of the city's great.

Anybody could nominate such men; the trick was to make them accept, and Burr's talents were equal even to that. Cajolery, flattery, pleas on the score of personal friendship and public duty reconciled the ancient feuds that had existed between the factions represented on the ticket, and in the end every man of them consented to make the race.

Reading over the names, Hamilton saw at once that more than his filibustering expedition was at stake. Federalist supremacy and his own position as party leader would be decided at the end of April, 1800, by that fraction of New York's sovereign people who possessed the franchise. The issues were now clearly drawn, the lists measured for the tournament, the trumpets lifted to sound the charge. But before the rival champions could meet on the political field, there was a little matter of private business that required their close co-operation. What time they could spare from raising factions against each other, they spent in intimate, amicable discussion on points of evidence in criminal law.

They had been retained, together with Brockholst Living-

ston, to defend a young man accused of killing his girl, and
while the case was coming on for trial, the leaders of the
disputing political parties laid aside their weapons to see
what could be done for a client. The whole town was raging
unreasonably against the fellow, although there was doubt
that any murder had been committed. However, to such
experienced campaigners as Hamilton and Burr, it was plain
that the popular prejudice was as dangerous as evidence.

About all the prosecution had to show was that on December 22, Guilielma Sands, an attractive but not too circum-
spect young woman, fell, jumped or was pushed down a well
which the Manhattan Company was digging at the corner of
Prince and Barclay Streets. The body bore no more bruises
than the fall justified, but the theory of accident was unlikely and the idea of suicide peculiarly repugnant to the
girl's relatives. Her uncle and aunt, the Elias Rings who kept
a boarding house in Greenwich Street, were Quakers and
could not believe that one with the light of their faith
within her could commit the horrid sin of self-destruction.
They preferred to bring a charge of murder against one of
their lodgers, Levi Weeks, brother of the builder of City
Hall. Half their friends—and soon all the town—knew that
Guilielma had been his mistress, and he was the last person
known to have seen her alive.

The trial began in the old Federal Hall on March 31, a
Tuesday, and lasted all the rest of the week. Burr made the
opening address for the defense, the summation being reserved for his colleague, for he "accorded the palm of eloquence to General Hamilton." From then on, the dark head
and the fair one bent close together as the two dapper little
lawyers exercised the ingenuity which was being used elsewhere for each other's political destruction to save a life
here.

It was Hamilton who conducted the cross examination
which finally broke down the chief prosecution witness. As
the man stammered and mumbled, Hamilton pushed the

candles close to his face and called on the jury to rule that those were the features of a liar and a villain—and indeed, the fellow was hanged in England years afterward. The examination was a theatrical performance which left a deep impression on those who saw it, not least on Colonel Burr, who was also able to appreciate the gentle skill with which Hamilton then drew out the evidence to show that Weeks had not been the girl's only lover, a circumstance that for some reason cooled public resentment.

The strategy employed had been devised by the two attorneys in concert, and as the judge charged the jury, virtually directing an acquittal, both lawyers were well pleased with themselves and each other—as lawyers. But each was more than ever convinced that the other was a little too slippery to be trusted. And no doubt it was because Hamilton had taken the lead in court that it was to him the enraged Mrs. Ring turned when the verdict was announced. Shaking her fist under his nose while he stepped back with gentlemanly distaste for the scene, she cried venomously:

"If thee dies a natural death I shall think there is no justice in heaven!"

XXIV

REARGUARD ACTION

THE VICTORIOUS ATTORNEYS EMERGED FROM FEDERAL HALL into the midst of a campaign which has never been equaled for scurrility. The abuse was proportioned to the issues, and these were serious indeed. The agrarians believed they or the commercial and moneyed interests must perish. So did the merchants. The question of which class should rule the country seemed to the contestants to be well worth hating and lying and fighting for. Nor were many of them particular about weapons.

Families and friends were divided in bitter feuds which time itself would hardly heal. Unrestrained language was reinforced with pistols and knives and fists. It was at this time that children in Federalist households learned to believe that Republicans were fearsome fellows who ate little boys for breakfast and gnawed at the bulwarks of civilization for lunch. During many years no professing democrat dined with Chief Justice Theophilus Parsons of Massachusetts, and the presence in their home of the first one, a kinsman from Maine, was awaited with eager interest by the Parsons offspring. To their surprise he seemed a very ordinary individual, but they watched him narrowly and in silence until at the end of the meal the Chief Justice lifted his glass courteously to his guest. Then the youngsters knew that the whole thing must be some sort of elaborate adult hoax.

"Why, he's not a Jacobin after all!" exclaimed Theophilus, Jr., then about fifteen.

"Did you think I was?" asked the amused visitor.

"Yes, sir, but I see you are not, for I have heard father say, again and again, that nothing on earth would make him drink wine with a Jacobin."

Theophilus, Jr., one learns, was invited pressingly to leave the table. He had all too accurately reflected what had been his parent's sentiments in 1800, sentiments that were shared by thousands. Society was divided on politics, and only a few rarely logical souls stepped across the barrier of partisan animosity. Hamilton was among the few. He drank quite cheerfully even with such a dangerous Jacobin as Colonel Burr, if the wine was good enough.

Neither of them had as much time as their constituents for drinking. All through that April, liquor flowed freely to every voter. Speeches and pamphlets and newspaper articles railed and threatened as if there had never been a law of libel, let alone of sedition. A grimmer tone than usual was noticeable behind Hamilton's dinner table banter, but as he urged upon moneyed men the necessity for extra exertions to check the rise of mob spirit he wrote to Henry Lee that "I feel no despondency of any sort," for he was confident the country "is too young and vigorous to be quacked out of its political health." In even more cheerful mood a few days later he explained:

"You see I am in a humor to laugh. What can we do better in *this best of all possible worlds?* Should you even be shut up in the seven towers, or get the plague, if you are a true philosopher you will consider this only as laughing matter."

He himself, however, was not a true philosopher, and as Burr's inroads on Federalist strength became more obvious, merriment departed from the Hamilton house at 26 Broadway. With enormous energy and infectious gaiety—only it did not infect Hamilton—Burr was showing the country how politics can be transformed from a class struggle into the national sport, a game for the disfranchised as well as for the voter. He had his men stressing the iniquity of the Sedition Act, the standing army, the high taxes, the tremendous bor-

rowing at high interest. But he knew these issues roused enthusiasm only in the minority immediately affected. A more
primitive appeal was devised for those New Yorkers to whom
the usual Jeffersonian agrarianism seemed a trifle insipid.

Bands of marching, singing men roared happily through
the streets working up a tremendous thirst. The rough Sons
of St. Tammany were put up to entertain with coarse wit
the crowds that cared little for Hamilton's reasoned eloquence. There was a good deal of fun, too, in playing pranks
at the enemy's meetings and outwitting the law by qualifying
whole gangs of leather-breeched, leather-lunged artisans by
deeding a house lot of sufficient value to associations of them.
By making politics a game at which even the apathetic many
could play, Burr roused in them a demand for universal
suffrage, which owed more to this than to any amount of
philosophic disquisition on the injustice of allowing only
one man in fifteen to vote.

Meanwhile the many could show their appreciation of
Colonel Burr's friendliness by yelling and drinking and singing. He egged them on, and at the same time proceeded
along more methodical lines. He card-indexed every voter
in the city, noting preferences, weaknesses, prejudices. He
assessed his party members for money and work, shrewdly
calling on lazy men for funds and stingy men for services.
He appealed to every disgruntled element, and as April 29
approached, the day for opening the polls, his army had been
drilled to meet the slashing attack of the "corrupt squadron."
He was wary but confident, writing:

"Hamilton works day and night with the most intemperate and outrageous zeal, but I think wholly without effect."

Voting lasted for three days, so that the rivals had plenty
of time to work on each individual as he came up to cast his
ballot. On the little group of voters the eloquence, charm,
liquor and lies of some of the most brilliant men in the
country were lavished without stint. From early morning
until dark, Hamilton was never still. On a white horse of

notable endurance he galloped from one polling place to another, haranguing, cajoling, jesting. Handbills fluttered in his wake like leaves in autumn and words poured from his lips like rain in spring. Burr was just as active, and when their paths crossed they bowed with courtesy or perhaps engaged in impromptu debate. The Republicans had their handbills, liquor dispensers and liars well trained, and Burr himself spent a solid ten hours in the Seventh Ward watching out for the cartmen who had been intimidated before. Under his eye they voted their choice.

At sunset of the third day it was all over, and a few hours later the city was turning itself inside out over the news that the Republicans had captured the Assembly. It was a narrow squeak—a shift of 250 votes would have won for Hamilton—but it was enough. On joint ballot of the two houses there would be a majority of twenty-two for Jefferson.

The beating knocked Hamilton's judgment groggy. Before the week was out he was writing Jay an angry, wild plan for defeating the result of the election. He proposed to call the old Legislature into special session to pass a law for choosing presidential electors by popular vote in districts, which would give the Federalists some at least of New York's twelve votes.

"It is easy to sacrifice the substantial interest of society to a strict adherence to ordinary rules," he argued. "In observing this, I shall not be supposed to mean, that any thing ought to be done which integrity will forbid, but merely that the scruples of delicacy and propriety, as relative to a common course of things, ought to yield to the extraordinary nature of the crisis. They ought not to hinder the taking of a *legal* and *constitutional* step to prevent an atheist in religion and a fanatic in politics, from getting possession of the helm of state."

For once Hamilton was more fanatic than the man he stigmatized, and much more so than the run of his party. The cool, precise Jay was not one to be swept off his feet, nor to believe that his own were the only good principles known to man. The crisis did not seem to him to be as critical as all that. He filed his friend's madness away in the archives with only the endorsement:

"Proposing a measure for party purposes which it would not become me to adopt."

For a time Hamilton was sure the entire system of public credit which he had so painfully built up, the sanctity of property, the domination of the capitalist were destined for destruction. He saw visions of the United States reduced again to the hopeless, helpless discord of the Confederation, and before he had time to recover from one shock another blow descended upon him. Adams, who shared a popular belief that Hamilton was invincible when he set his mind and heart to a task, thought the man Jefferson was to label "your arch-friend of New York" had deliberately betrayed him.

Suddenly the President's outraged vanity and the long-nursed resentment of Hamilton boiled over in a burst of wrath that left the appalled McHenry, first to be exposed to it, under the impression that his chief had taken leave of his senses. The Secretary of War promptly resigned, and the sputtering Adams turned on Pickering, who was invited by letter to retire. He refused, and was promptly dismissed, to be replaced by Marshall. Only Wolcott, whose mild, smiling manner failed to rouse the President's suspicion, remained to represent Hamilton.

In New York that gentleman was as furious with Adams as with Burr. He really believed the Duke of Braintree had showed disloyalty in kicking out his spies. And, although the campaign was still going on, Burr's victory and this new insult had so warped his reason that he was tempted for a time to bring a slander suit against some of those who were accusing him of pro-British treason.

"You see I am in a very belligerent humor," he told Wolcott.

In that humor he undertook to fight Adams and the conquering Republicans at the same time. The loss of New York, serious as it was, might have been repaired by gains elsewhere through close Federalist co-operation and a union of forces behind Adams. There was only a slim chance that even such united efforts could win, but it was the only hope, and with a passionate petulance engendered by his misfortunes, Hamilton threw it away. His character was being spoiled by adversity. Instead of trying to save what he could, he only redoubled his efforts to run Pinckney ahead of Adams. In a thoroughly rule or ruin mood, he wrote after hearing of McHenry's resignation:

"For my individual part, my mind is made up. I will never more be responsible for him by my direct support, even though the consequence should be the election of *Jefferson*.

"If we must have an enemy at the head of the government, let it be one whom we can oppose, and for whom we are not responsible, who will not involve our party in the disgrace of his foolish and bad measures."

In reality Adams's foolish and bad measures were those of his party, and even the worst and most foolish, the Sedition Act, now had Hamilton's approval. In these months of his lapse from good sense he said the oppressive law was necessary to meet a horrid emergency, and he looked on approvingly as Federalist judges and prosecutors were let loose upon the Jeffersonians. But the Federalists were poorly trained in tyranny. They made enough examples to enrage the people, not enough to cow them. And while the roar of anger was rising from common men—many of them with votes—Hamilton was wasting the best brains in his party on a crusade against its most popular figure, honest "bonny Johnny" Adams.

So thoroughly was his temper spoiled that he was ready to make a rather sneaking use of confidential state papers which in his days of power he had consistently declined to publish. He told McHenry and Pickering that before they quit office they should copy "all such documents as will enable you to explain both Jefferson and Adams." Pickering had already offered to undertake "a bold and frank exposure of Adams," but Hamilton entered eagerly into the treacherous combination, even took the lead in it, demanding of Wolcott further evidence "and much in detail" to reveal to the party "the facts which denote unfitness in Mr. Adams."

One of these facts was an uncompromising aversion to standing armies, and in the summer of 1800 Major General Hamilton was disbanding the regiments he had dreamed of leading through peril and tropical jungles to the heights of glory. He made the painful task an excuse for a personal tour of New England to agitate against Adams, while the unfortunate Miranda, with the true filibustering optimism, went off to England to excite the imagination of Castlereagh and permit Sir Arthur Wellesley to stop off to see what might be done in Spain on the way to Venezuela.

Hamilton came back from his tour convinced that there was work to be done which only his pen could do. His chief correspondents, the Cabots and Kings, Tracys and Sedgwicks, needed no stimulus to abandon Adams, but local leaders of lesser understanding clung to the aging patriot. To show them the error of their ways, the retired General sat in his study preparing a slender volume entitled "The Public Conduct and Character of John Adams, Esq., President of the United States."

Unfortunately Hamilton had not lost his literary ability along with his political judgment. His pamphlet was a more damaging document than anything the hottest Jeffersonian produced. With clear, vigorous strokes the Federalist leader limned an ugly caricature of the Federalist candidate to show he had "great and intrinsic defects in his character which unfit him for the office of chief magistrate." With a rage that only Burr of all his other enemies was able to arouse, he tore, as he thought, the veil from "the disgusting egotism, the distempered jealousy, and the ungovernable indiscretions of

Mr. Adams's temper." He attacked the President's policies, philosophy and sincerity and expressed fear that the government must collapse under another term for the creature of "an imagination sublimated and eccentric." Then, after unleashing the full fury of his gift of philippics, he reached the surprising conclusion:

"Yet with this opinion of Mr. Adams, I have finally resolved not to advise the withholding from him a single vote. The body of federalists, for want of sufficient knowledge of facts, are not convinced of the expediency of relinquishing him. It is even apparent, that a large proportion still retain the attachment which was once a common sentiment."

And yet in his madness he printed it. He meant it for very private circulation among those minor party chieftains who were still loyal to Adams. The idea was to take advantage of the President's popularity in the election, wherever there still was one, but to arrange for the electors to veer to Pinckney. Cooler heads argued in vain that the pamphlet was folly, dangerous and futile, but the author was not to be dissuaded.

Burr justified their fears. His excellent espionage system brought him one of the first copies, and if he had not been such a dignified little man he must have gone dancing down the streets for joy. Seldom is it given to a politician to expose so powerfully the dissension in the enemy camp or to quote one of his rivals fatally against the other. Hamilton's confidential composition soon was running in all the Republican papers, reinforced with stinging comments. Jeffersonians whooped with glee, and the Federalists were so demoralized that the usually optimistic McHenry foresaw doom, and was thoroughly disgusted with the conduct of his colleagues, scoffing:

"They write private letters. To whom? To each other. But they do nothing to give a proper direction to the public mind."

So in the greatest possible confusion the elections ended.

Both Adams and Pinckney were snowed under. The "atheists" and "anarchists" were in control and the careful structure of a capitalist government seemed doomed. In the eyes of the vanquished, a new revolution threatened. Some of them dreamed of the Paris Terror. Others were boldly ready to attempt a coup d'état to circumvent the will of the people. Still others muttered darkly of secession. And Hamilton was actually thinking of publishing a sequel to "The Public Conduct and Character of John Adams."

"In this case I shall reinforce my charges by new anecdotes," he wrote Pickering. "My friends will, no doubt, be disposed to aid me. You probably possess some which are unknown to me. Pray let me have them without delay."

Suddenly, as though the whole horrid campaign had been prepared by a jealous Providence solely to test their constancy, the "corrupt squadron" saw a chance to snatch at victory. The Republicans had been so intent on getting every possible vote that it was probable Jefferson and Burr would come to the electoral college with exactly equal numbers. The choice must then be thrown into the lame duck session of the House, which was comfortably Federalist. Here was a God-given opportunity for throwing an apple of discord into Republican ranks. The Federalists could elect Burr, detach him from Jefferson and, even if they did not gain him for themselves, they would split the victors into forever irreconcilable fragments.

Recovering from the debacle of the campaign, Hamilton was jolted back to political sanity by this mad scheme, he being immune to the madness of others. It had been more than eight years since he conceived it a religious duty to oppose Burr. Now his own followers were proposing to elevate the "embryo Caesar" into Washington's chair! Undeterred by his experience with Adams, he reached for his pen, and as the statesmen gathered in a muddy, half-built village on the Potomac to inaugurate the new capital, page after page of fine thin writing went out from 26 Broadway to the men who had once obeyed its tenant.

He had led them these last months on the principle that the end justifies the means, and now that he had reached the limit of that philosophy, they rushed on ahead into a region of political suicide. Some were talking of preventing an election altogether, so that the country might be induced to accept as its chief magistrate a Federalist president pro tem of the Senate, and they did not care if this meant civil war. But most were bent on electing Burr, who was after all a gentleman, they said, of sound New England stock. Hamilton had long ago taught them to believe his colleague at the bar to be unprincipled and ambitious, a combination they thought would make him susceptible to Federalist temptation.

However plausible the argument, Hamilton knew it was fallacious. Burr was not a weaker man than Jefferson, nor less able, and he was infinitely bolder. The Virginian at least based his philosophy on property, even if by that he did mean land. But Burr thought people much more important; the fellow liked people, individually and in the mass, and was quite capable of attempting to set up a system under which the rights of property would yield to the rights of man. That smacked to Hamilton of the French Revolution, and he doubted not that Burr had cast himself for the role of Bonaparte.

"If there is a man in the world I ought to hate, it is Jefferson," the elder statesman told Gouverneur Morris, now a Senator. "With Burr I have always been personally well. But the public good must be paramount to every private consideration."

The bitterness which followed showed Hamilton up to his old trick of confusing his beliefs with facts, his preferences with abstract justice. While it may have been true that he ought to hate Jefferson, it was obvious he did hate Burr. Nor was this feeling diminished by realization that his views had lost their potency with the party. Cabot was sure the New

Yorker was more pliable than Jefferson. Bayard of Delaware thought he could be bought. John Rutledge predicted his election would "disjoint" his party. *The Centinel* of Boston published the horticultural information "that a good tree cannot bring forth bad fruit, nor vice versa," and pointed out that the grandson of Jonathan Edwards was "a practical gentleman who will have judgment, taste and genius enough to appreciate the usefulness of our federal fabric, and nerve enough to preserve its integrity."

All this was just so much more proof to Hamilton that Burr had a dangerous talent for blinding gullible men to his real aims. Feverishly he set forth this view, and the post was enriched with bulky specimens of the finest Hamiltonian invective.

"His private character is not defended by his most partial friends . . . as unprincipled and dangerous a man as any country can boast—as true a Catiline as ever met in midnight conclave . . . will use the worst part of the community as a ladder to climb to permanent power . . . bankrupt beyond redemption, except by the resources that grow out of war and disorder . . . sanguine enough to hope every thing, daring enough to attempt every thing, wicked enough to scruple nothing . . . more *cunning* than *wise*—far more *dexterous* than *able* . . . a man who, on all hands, is acknowledged to be a complete Catiline."

In the midst of these letters he broke off to go out to dine, and the recipients of his further confidences were edified to discover that he had been the guest of Colonel Burr. It had been a gay meal, too, with the beautiful Theodosia, soon to be married, presiding and the gallant General Hamilton, apparently full of nothing but good nature and compliments, playing the spy upon his rival. Then he was back in his study, explaining to his correspondents with that certain elevation of language which was the sign he was conscious of committing a baseness:

"The peculiarity of the occasion will excuse my mentioning in confidence the occurrences of a private table."

Burr would not have excused it, although the damning bit of evidence broadcast by his observant guest was the host's offering toasts to the French republic, the men who had negotiated the peace, General Bonaparte and the Marquis de Lafayette. Lest Federalist leaders doubt this was sufficient grounds for excluding a man from the Presidency, the tale bearer dipped his pen in gall and wrote on and on:

"Corrupt expedients will be to him a *necessary* resource . . . no principle, public or private; could be bound by no agreement . . . almost certain he will attempt usurpation . . . never appeared solicitous for fame, and great ambition, unchecked by principle, or the love of glory, is an unruly tyrant . . . has talked pure *Godwinism* . . . *selfish* to a degree which excludes all social affections . . . decidedly profligate . . . no means too atrocious to be employed by him . . . all the habits of excessive expense . . . Will any prudent man offer such a President to the temptations of foreign gold?"

A good deal of this was false; most of it was wild exaggeration; all of it was futile. Federalists in Congress remained overwhelmingly for Burr, and some of Hamilton's bitterest strictures strengthened their advocacy. For if the New Yorker could be reached by money, that was just what the "corrupt squadron" wanted. Hamilton had taught them to fight for an administration that would give them economic privileges for nothing. Failing in battle, they were eager to buy in a not too open market, and they thought Burr just the man for them.

If they or Hamilton had been right, they could have had him. But Burr, extravagant as Hamilton and as much in debt, was as incorruptible. In Albany arranging for his adored Theodosia's marriage—a more important event than any presidential election—his literary efforts were in admirable contrast to Hamilton's. He wrote only one letter, to General Samuel Smith of Baltimore, and it read:

"It is highly improbable that I shall have an equal number of votes with Mr. Jefferson; but, if such should be the result, every man who knows me ought to know that I would utterly disclaim all competition. Be assured that the federal party can entertain no wish for such an exchange. As to my friends, they would dishonour my views and insult my feelings by a suspicion that I would submit to be instrumental in counteracting the wishes and expectations of the United States, and I now constitute you my proxy to declare these sentiments if the occasion should require."

Duly published by Smith, this letter had as much effect as if it had never been written. No one believed Burr really meant he would not stoop for the Presidency. Sure the disclaimer was merest talk, the Federalists schemed to get the suddenly sphinx-like Burr to commit himself.

Then it was February, cold and snowy and gray, and the elder statesman in New York was almost as silent as the candidate in Albany. The House was ready to vote; he had sent off the last letter that could reach any member in time. Bitterly he waited for news to be brought by messengers toiling through the snow from Washington, and the best he could hope for was that Thomas Jefferson was President. Decidedly a tasteless prospect, and one day diners at the Tontine Coffee House heard the clear voice of General Hamilton calling the health:

"May our government never fall a prey to the dreams of a Condorcet nor the vices of a Catiline."

One or the other seemed inevitable, and at last riders from the new capital were struggling northward. The House began its task on February 11, and for six days of roll calls not a man changed. A majority of each state's delegation determined its vote; a majority of the states was necessary to a choice. Jefferson had eight, Burr six with two deadlocked by ties. Of the individual Representatives, Burr had a lead of

55, every one a Federalist, to 51. Hamilton's writings had had so little effect that the normally devoted Bayard, who had received the bulkiest of the arguments, cast the vote of Delaware thirty-five times for Aaron Burr.

Slowly it dawned on the Federalists that they were working for a man who did not thank them for their pains, and on the thirty-sixth ballot they gave way. Bayard had understood Jefferson to promise that Federalist officeholders would be secure in their jobs and that public credit would be maintained. No one could get anything out of Burr. So at last the Federalist Representatives of Vermont and Maryland, the two deadlocked states, refrained from voting, allowing the Republicans to add those two to Jefferson, and Bayard, casting a blank ballot, wrote disgustedly to Hamilton:

"The means existed of electing Burr, but this required his cooperation. By deceiving one man (a great blockhead), and tempting two (not incorruptible) he might have secured a majority of the States. He will never have another chance of being President of the United States, and the little use he has made of the one which has occurred, gives me but an humble opinion of the talents of an unprincipled man."

"Had Burr done anything for himself," agreed J. Fenimore Cooper's father, "he would long ere this have been President."

In New York there was modified rejoicing in a house on Broadway. The year of his great bitterness was ended, and Hamilton was in truly humble frame of mind, perhaps the most genuine humility of his life. It was a mood induced by the knowledge that he was sunk so low he could regard it as a victory to see the fanatic Jefferson, "a mischievous enemy" and "a contemptible hypocrite," mount to power on the ruins of his own political career.

XXV

THE SQUIRE OF HARLEM HEIGHTS

MELANCHOLY SATISFACTION WAS THE KEYNOTE OF HAMIL-ton's public correspondence as from his distance he watched the new administration settle itself most uncomfortably in Washington. Jefferson was preserving federal authority, in a weak, philosophical manner to be sure, but still preserving it. The methodical Swiss genius of Albert Gallatin had been introduced to the Treasury, operating in general on lines his predecessor approved and discovering a truth he was generous enough in later years to proclaim.

"All Secretaries of the Treasury of the United States since the first," he learned, "enjoyed a sinecure, the genius and labors of Hamilton having created and arranged everything that was requisite and necessary for the successful operation of the department."

Once convinced that "Mad Tom" did not intend to pull down upon his head the pillars of national credit, Hamilton found plenty to complain about in details of government. Soon the papers were running critical articles signed *Lucius Crassus,* a pseudonym that did not hide from the discerning the style of the Federalist elder statesman.

No tinge of melancholy, however, marred for the moment his satisfaction with the joys of private life. He thrived on Betsey's devotion, and his children were almost as dear to him as was Theodosia to Burr. The oldest girl, Angelica, was his favorite, a slim, lovely child with a musical talent beyond the ordinary and a quick, nervous mind which gave as yet no indications of the insanity which was soon to overtake it. Another girl, Eliza, had been added to the stock. Their older brother, a chip of the old block with improvements, his father thought, was graduated with high honors from Columbia and wished to follow the paternal footsteps. Highly gratified, Hamilton drew up a careful schedule for the lad's guidance, the thought showing perhaps more affection than the language. Headed "Rules for Mr. Philip Hamilton," it ran:

"From the first of April to the first of October he is to rise not later than six o'clock; the rest of the year not later than seven. If earlier, he will deserve commendation. Ten will be his hour for going to bed throughout the year.

"From the time he is dressed in the morning till nine o'clock (the time for breakfast excepted), he is to read law. At nine he goes to the office, and continues there till dinner-time. He will be occupied partly in writing and partly in reading law.

"After dinner he reads law at home till five o'clock. From this time till seven he disposes of his time as he pleases. From seven to ten he reads and studies whatever he pleases.

"From twelve on Saturday he is at liberty to amuse himself.

"On Sunday he will attend the morning church. The rest of the day may be applied to innocent recreations.

"He must not depart from any of these rules without my permission."

Somewhere in this rigorous course of training, Philip found sufficient leisure to become one of the better behaved young blades of town, to indulge in mild revels at the coffee houses and to talk politics with his comrades, settling the affairs of the nation with a lordly certainty that his father and Jefferson might by this time have envied. The scurrilous habits of speech developed in 1800 still lingered in 1801, and in his wanderings Philip met one of the lesser adepts at slander, a fellow named George Eacker. The political quarrel led to personal remarks which it became a youth of spirit to resent, and on a November afternoon the student put away his law books, slipped out of the house without permission and walked down to the river. A boat and a couple of friends were waiting for him on the Manhattan shore; Eacker and pistols for two were to be confronted at Weehawken, New York's favorite dueling ground.

They brought the boy back dying, and for the first time in his life Hamilton knew what real mourning was. His friends worried about him, for he seemed to take it as hard as Betsey, who grieved without restraint so that it was some days before Angelica Church could report "my sister is a little composed." The father's nerve held—"his conduct was extraordinary during this trial," his sister-in-law noted—and he answered letters of condolence with a steady hand.

"The brightest as well as the eldest hope of my family has been taken from me," he wrote, and it was only when he tried to console himself with thoughts of religion and the evils that his son had escaped that he broke out:

"He is now out of reach of the seductions and calamities of a world full of folly, full of vice, full of danger, of least value in proportion as it is best known."

No need to examine too closely the cry of a heart in anguish, but this was sincere enough to induce a great disgust for the politics which had cost Philip his life. Even the delinquencies of Jefferson went unnoticed at this time, while into Hamilton's letters crept a note of philosophical speculation hitherto as foreign to his correspondence as to his conversation. Perhaps he was feeling his age—he passed his forty-fifth birthday that winter. In any case he viewed the past, the present and the future with what he thought was critical detachment, and wrote to Morris:

"Mine is an odd destiny. Perhaps no man in the United States has sacrificed or done more for the present Constitution than myself; and contrary to all my anticipations of its fate, as you know from the very beginning, I am still laboring to prop the frail and worthless fabric. Yet I have the murmurs of its friends no less than the curses of its foes for my reward. Every day proves to me more and more, that this American world was not made for me."

Even the appearance of Burr at a Federalist banquet, where he actually proposed a toast to "The union of all honest men," failed to draw more than a sneer at this "phantom." Hamilton did throw out a half-hearted warning against taking the man as a standard bearer of Federalism, but it was more by way of habit than anything else. He was much more concerned about Betsey, who bore him another child in June. They named him Philip for his dead brother, and a few months later Hamilton was writing to Pinckney:

"A garden, you know, is a very good refuge of a disappointed politician. Accordingly I have purchased a few acres about nine miles from town, have built a house and am cultivating a garden."

He was enjoying it, too. Men who have known all other successes and wearied of them, turn with delight to the conquest of a lawn and a few trees. The Hamiltons had spent several summers on rather high ground far up on the island where once young Major Burr had guided a demoralized brigade of rebels to safety. Hamilton liked the spot and at a point not far from the Albany road, where 142d Street would one day be cut through, he built a handsome square house at rather greater cost than he could afford. He borrowed heavily, furnished the place lavishly and never tired of plotting and replotting the gardens, devising new embellishments, picking up new plants.

Driving up from his office or the courts in a light two-wheeled carriage, he generally took what they called the Middle Road, later as Fifth Avenue to become more populous. It was a little out of the way, but he liked to stop and talk flowers and shrubs with Dr. David Hosack, whose gardens and greenhouses adorned a peacefully rural site which was not to know much of horticulture again until a terrace garden bloomed at Rockefeller Center. Dr. Hosack supplied a good deal of advice and some cuttings for his friend's estate.

HAMILTON GRANGE

General Schuyler provided timber for the house from his upstate woods. The master of the place gave it a name, the Grange, after that dwelling from which James Hamilton had set out nearly fifty years before to conquer the world.

The Grange in Manhattan was more imposing than the one in Ayrshire, for its owner felt he could splurge. His practice brought in as much as $14,000 a year, his share in some western land ventures might be expected to yield large returns in the dim future, and clients came faster than he could handle them. He spent a good deal of time away from home, jolting over the rutted roads to Albany in the stage that took three days for the journey or pacing the decks of the uncertain Hudson River sloops as they tacked lazily against wind and tide. He kept a house in town, from which he and Betsey could sally forth on their frequent visits to the theater or the sessions of the Philharmonic Society at Snow's Hotel.

His practice and his family and his social engagements had never filled Hamilton's time, and now the leisure that had once been turned to government and diplomacy and the mazes of partisan strategy were spent by the squire of the Grange in fishing for the rare striped bass of the Hudson off his estate or roaming the woods of Harlem Heights with a single-barreled shotgun in search of woodcock and grouse. He still read avidly, going through a mass of assorted books and periodicals from all over the world; he began to collect works of art within the range of his purse; he sketched designs for new gardens.

He was almost reconciled to the course of politics, particularly when Jefferson threw his principles overboard and bought Louisiana. He thought he was insuring thereby the perpetual domination of the agrarians. Hamilton, who had seen that moneyed men still found it worth their while to unite their interest to that of the government, was not deceived. He knew now that as long as the machinery he had set up remained undisturbed, the growth of capitalism would proceed inexorably, regardless of how many farmers might settle beyond the Mississippi. A thorough-going democracy, he thought, would be a real threat to his system, but he was persuaded that the Jefferson who wrote an abolition clause into the Ordinance of the Northwest Territory and himself kept 154 slaves in Virginia would not prove too revolutionary in bestowing power upon the unthinking masses. Hamilton had maintained when urging that Jefferson be chosen over Burr that the philosopher never meant to weaken an executive authority which he might one day wield.

"Nor is it true," this unfriendly analyst of the President's character had continued, "that Jefferson is zealot enough to do anything in pursuance of his principles which will contravene his popularity or his interest. He is as likely as any man I know, to temporize; to calculate what will be likely to promote his own reputation and advantage, and the probable result of such a temper is the preservation of systems, though originally opposed, which being once established could not be overturned without danger to the person who did it. To my mind, a true estimate of Mr. Jefferson's character warrants the expectation of a temporizing, rather than a violent system."

This unfriendly portrait was hardly just, but Hamilton was not notable for scrupulous fairness to an opponent. The very fact that Jefferson was shrewd enough to proceed no faster than public opinion could keep up with him was in itself a fault to the impatient New Yorker, who gladly left public opinion behind as a useless encumbrance. But the Virginian's willingness to compromise with the literal meaning of his principles soothed his adversary's fears, and the rigid integrity of Gallatin at the Treasury was an even more welcome sign of reasonableness in a Republican administration.

Hamilton's thrusts at the dominant party were, therefore, far milder than some launched by his erstwhile colleagues in the bitterness of their defeat. He had his own newspaper now, for he had founded *The Evening Post* with William

Coleman as editor, just in time to report in one of its earliest issues the painful details of Philip's death. The bereaved father, born journalist that he was, could not keep out of print for long. He wrote and advised, and it was largely owing to his counsel and contributions that the sheet took first rank in the city. Perhaps the comparative calm of its tone helped, for the citizenry could not be expected to maintain the frenzied pitch of 1800 and were wearying of unadulterated invective.

The Federalist die-hards could not understand this. In New England they fretted and fumed and fulminated gusty protests until with the purchase of Louisiana they worked themselves again into a secessionist frame of mind. Pickering and Cabot and Roger Griswold believed with Jefferson that the vast new territory assured an agrarian ascendancy forever. The prosperity of their businesses should have shown them how wrong they were. Nevertheless they proposed to cut loose from the unwieldy bulk of an enormously swollen country. Secession was not a new idea. There had been talk of it among Westerners ever since '84 when they began to feel themselves neglected, among the Connecticut and Massachusetts leaders in '94 and '96 when they feared a Jeffersonian victory, among Southerners in '98 when war with France threatened. In 1803 the New England movement assumed serious proportions, and Hamilton in his best elder statesman vein admonished its proponents with mild rebuke and reasoned words.

In this mellow mood, he found himself plunged into a new fight with the usual roles oddly reversed. Hamilton, the "monocrat," was defending the liberties of the people against an oppressive tyranny of Jeffersonians. The Sedition Act was dead, but the party in power found a convenient substitute in the law of criminal libel. By applying English precedents, the courts had succeeded in making an example of Henry Croswell, a Federalist editor, whose *Wasp*, published in the town of Hudson, lived up to its name.

Accused of repeating a charge that Jefferson had paid Callender for "grossly slandering" good men, Croswell offered to prove his words. The Jeffersonian court applied the old English maxim of "the greater the truth the greater the libel." The editor was duly convicted, the jury being permitted to decide only on the fact of publication, not of truth or intent.

Hamilton entered the case on appeal, and for six hours he held the attention of a bench of four judges in what Chancellor Kent, a keen critic, considered his finest achievement as a lawyer. He carried the question above the mere point of whether Croswell could have proved his case, although he could have shown that Jefferson helped subsidize Callender. The problem, as the pleader saw it, was whether men should be jailed for telling the truth about their so-called servants, and the whole argument was summed up in the first paragraph of his brief.

"The liberty of the press," he said, "consists in the right to publish with impunity Truth with good motives for justifiable ends though reflecting on Gov't, Magistracy or Individuals."

The court divided evenly, so the appeal was lost, but Hamilton had exposed the absurdity of the doctrine that papers dare not print the truth about politicians. The Legislature wrote Hamilton's argument into a law which was copied by most of the states and still offers belligerent publishers their chief protection against the anger of officialdom.

Secession and freedom of the press brought Hamilton a little way out of his retirement. Aaron Burr brought him all the way out, and fighting, too. Many men supposed that the election of Jefferson by the House had ended Burr's political career, but the Vice President was not of their number. True, his party leaders gazed on him with dark suspicion, excluded him with studied care from their councils and made no secret of their determination not to renominate him. The Virginia dynasty did not propose to let him upset the rule of planters as he had upset the rule of merchants, and the incipient tradition that a Vice President should succeed his chief was not to be followed again. Clinton, now sixty-five and once more Governor of New York, was slated for the post. In 1808 he would be too old to dispute the succession.

Burr was no passive instrument in this program. He decided that since Clinton was to succeed him, he would succeed Clinton and as Governor of New York build up a machine that could meet the Virginians on their own ground. The Federalists who had sought him out in 1800 might be rallied now, and many of them were willing. Hamilton's denunciations had convinced them Burr would fall in with their secession scheme and pull New York after him. The Vice President's idea was that he would use the secessionists and thereafter avoid any excuse for secession.

His candidacy brought Hamilton raging out of the Grange. Woodcock and striped bass were forgotten, the joys of horticulture abandoned, the leisurely life of theaters, concerts and family dinners thrown into the discard. The enemy was knocking at the gates of constitutional stability, and for the last time the lover of order, of guarantees for property and of conservatism flung himself into the fight. The old eloquence, the old invective, the old energy were displayed once more to the New York electorate, but the necessity was so distasteful that it wrung from him the cry:

"I say nothing on politics, with the course of which I am too much disgusted to give myself any future concern about them."

The present, of course, was different, and the day he wrote those words he was stumping the city in the name of law and order. As the April voting ended, Hamilton, "King of the Feds," had elected another Republican, Morgan Lewis. But Burr had gone down to defeat by the comfortable margin of 10,000 votes. His conqueror, relieved, could return to the peaceful pleasures of his spring garden.

XXVI

THE DUEL

"Is THE VICE-PRESIDENT SUNK SO LOW AS TO SUBMIT TO BE IN-sulted by General Hamilton?"

The sneer, directed at both men with impartial venom, came from the scabrous James Cheetham, a Jeffersonian newspaper hack who had learned the art of political journalism from Cobbett. But Cheetham relied upon the bludgeon rather than the lash, a typical example of his reportorial style being his charge, during the campaign, that the brothels of New York were filled with the unhappy victims of that wholesale seducer, Aaron Burr.

A gentleman of Burr's quality could not with propriety notice officially what such trash might say. Nevertheless, as the Vice President contemplated his political future in the early summer of 1804, he was as cast down as was possible for that gay and sanguine temperament. The hatred of Jeffersonians and Hamiltonians pursued him with a violence that was in some respects flattering, but just at this time, defeated and a little sore, he was in no humor to appreciate the subtle compliment.

He was accustomed to the vigorous blows exchanged in the political arena, but since he himself did not indulge in personal abuse, he did not tolerate it in his equals. He had known well enough for years who his real enemy was in New York; he had heard hints without being able to put a finger on anything definite of how that enemy habitually reviled him. And at last he fell across a statement, not very precise but still something in black and white that warranted a de-

296

mand for explanations. On June 18, therefore, Hamilton in the quiet of his retirement, received this curt note:

"Sir: I send you for your perusal a letter signed by Charles D. Cooper, which, though apparently published some time ago, has but very recently come to my knowledge. Mr. Van Ness, who does me the honor to deliver this, will point out to you that clause of the letter to which I particularly request your attention. You must perceive, sir, the necessity of a prompt, unqualified acknowledgement or denial of the use of any expressions which would warrant the assertions of Dr. Cooper."

With such sharp courtesy did duels begin, and as Hamilton read the lines under the solemn stare of Lawyer William Van Ness, Burr's devoted friend, he could not miss their import. He managed to preserve the glacial calm proper under the circumstances, even as he read on in the Doctor's letter the paragraph to which Van Ness now sternly pointed:

"General Hamilton and Judge Kent have declared in substance that they looked upon Mr. Burr to be a dangerous man, and one who ought not to be trusted with the reins of government. I could detail to you a still more despicable opinion which General Hamilton has expressed of Mr. Burr."

Two days went into the composition of a reply, more time than had been lavished on many numbers of *The Federalist,* but this was a delicate task. The dilemma was inescapable. Behind the comparatively mild words of Dr. Cooper lay the complex difficulties of the Code of Honor. If Burr really meant to press the issue, there was no alternative between the duel and ignominy in the eyes of gentlemen. It would be easy enough to repudiate Dr. Cooper, but that would hardly satisfy the conventions of the code. Burr would undoubtedly demand some comprehensive and public statement repudiating also any personal remarks on which Cooper's opinion could have been founded. Recalling the highly insulting phrases of some of his letters, Hamilton knew he could never give his opponent an honest and satisfactory an swer. A lie, even if he had been willing to manufacture it, would only make him ridiculous and infamous among those who had received his confidences.

All the same, Hamilton did not want to fight. His aversion to dueling, which had kept him from calling out Monroe, had become a passionate distaste since poor Philip had fallen. But between refusing to send a challenge and refusing to ac cept one was a gulf which his pride would not permit him to bridge. All he could do was attempt by his pen to avert the penalties of the sword—or rather of pistols.

The careful circumlocutions of his reply to Burr were in odd contrast to that gentleman's plain language. With con siderable skill, Hamilton played with the meaning of "des picable" and "more despicable" as applied to unspecified opinions. He hoped that Burr would agree with him after mature reflection. He went over the difficulties of deciding just what he was supposed to disavow, adding:

"I deem it inadmissible, on principle, to consent to be in terrogated as to the justness of inferences which may be drawn by others from what I may have said of a political op ponent in the course of fifteen years' competition."

This was highly reasonable. The only trouble with it was that it missed the point, as Burr did not fail to see at once. The Vice President did not care about Hamilton's views on the justness of other men's inferences. He wanted a dis claimer of what Hamilton himself would consider "despi cable" references. If none had ever been meant or uttered, it was easy—and no more than fair—to say so. On this point they haggled painfully, stilted expressions of their antipathy passing between them in the hands of solemn, formal, meticu lously garbed and meticulously spoken friends who bowed low, said little and never smiled. Pertinacious as a skillful cross examiner must be, Burr pressed for a direct answer. Had General Hamilton impugned his honor or not? Des perately the squire of the Grange juggled and parried, but there was no escaping that remorseless question, and he had no intention of making a flat statement.

Within a week the business had passed into a still more formal phase. Van Ness had assumed the burden of Burr's correspondence. Major Nathaniel Pendleton, a trusty ally, wrote for Hamilton. The emissaries were no more successful in reaching an agreement than their principals, and on June 27 Van Ness ended the unsatisfactory fencing with a direct challenge.

"I shall want a little time to make some arrangements respecting my own affairs," Hamilton said in accepting, and the day was set for July 11.

For the first time in his life, the veteran of the raid on Trenton and the storming of a Yorktown redoubt had an opportunity to display his physical courage to the full. In the Revolution he had looked gaily at danger, for that was the price of fame. There had been, too, the odd exaltation that comes upon many men when facing peril with their fellows. This meeting with Burr was altogether different, thoroughly distasteful, unaccompanied by the hope of glory or the inspiration of idealism. He must go forth toward a death that would prove nothing, benefit no one and add no luster to the name of Hamilton.

He met the test. With complete calm he went about his business, played with the children, bantered Betsey about her domestic preoccupations, jested with his friends. Son James, wrestling with the problem of a speech he was to deliver at Columbia, appealed for help, and one morning his father, as willing a ghost writer for his children as for Washington, left him a draft with this note:

"I have prepared for you a Thesis on Discretion. *You may need it*. God bless you."

He himself needed fortitude as well as discretion for display in public. The day after the duel was definitely arranged, he presided over the Cincinnati's Fourth of July celebration at Ross's Hotel, where, the minutes relate, "a number of appropriate toasts were drunk and the evening spent in that harmony and social glee, which has ever distinguished the Society on that auspicious day."

As the wine flowed and conversation rang through the hall, smoke rising in clouds and laughter punctuating with festive hilarity some rather feeble jokes, the President General was the merriest in a merry throng. His effervescent spirits were commented upon, and the former officers agreed that political reverses had not soured his temper. They called on him for song, and as he rose, flushed and smiling, the still reddish hair brushed back from the still youthful face, they broke into cheers. Then the pleasant tenor, wandering off key at intervals, rose above the smoke and chatter:

"We're going to war, and when we die
We'll want a man of God nearby."

The singer's head was thrown back, his lips twisted in a faint grin even as he sang, the slender hands waved graceful accompaniment. A few feet away only one of his old comrades in arms was grave, expressionless among those smiling listeners. Elbow on table, cheek on hand, Colonel Aaron Burr stared solemnly at the life of the party. The black eyes never winked, the normally cheerful countenance was almost glum. Even after the song ended, his neighbors noticed that their usually garrulous fellow was rather silent. They forgot about him for a while, and when they looked for him again, he was not there. Colonel Burr, wonderful to relate, had gone home early.

Hamilton stayed to the end, but his next week was not filled with fun. He was extremely busy putting his clients' business in order, getting papers together, preparing cases to be tried by others, writing notes. As for his own affairs, he could only shake his head over them. He had supposed himself, what with his western lands and the Grange, to be worth the tidy sum of $10,000. But as he sat writing in the privacy of his study after Betsey and the children had gone to

bed, he totted up the various sums he owed and "am pained
to be obliged to entertain doubts, whether, if . . . the sale
of my property should come to be forced, it would even be
sufficient to pay my debts."

The short July nights hardly gave him time for all he had
to write. There were letters to clients, letters to creditors, letters to friends, and one painful letter to Betsey, who would
never understand why he had to go out and get himself
killed just like Philip in a senseless quarrel of men. Often
he rose from the desk to pace the floor, muttering to himself
as once he had muttered under the trees on Batteau Street
thirty summers ago. The man's problems gave more cause
for muttering than the boy's had ever done. For he hated to
leave his children, and for once tenderness and affection
broke through the bonds he had imposed upon himself, and
the pen that was more at home in the hot strife of politics
or the cool mazes of finance traced for Betsey gentle, simple
words of love from the man who appreciated her qualities if
he could not match her devotion.

He had public duties, too. There must be left behind a
reasoned statement of the motives that impelled him to accept a challenge in spite of religious, moral, personal, private
and public reasons for declining. He numbered them, and
went into some detail to refute them. His future usefulness
"whether in resisting mischief or effecting good . . . would
probably be inseparable from a conformity with public prejudice in this particular." To emphasize his disinclination, he
left on record the statement that he intended to throw away
his first fire to give "opportunity to Col. Burr to pause and
reflect."

There were other letters on his financial condition and
apologies for extravagance at the Grange—"To men who
have been so much harassed in the base world as myself it is
natural to look forward to a comfortable retirement." There
were letters on public affairs and in the last of all, a note to

Theodore Sedgwick on July 10, he made his final assault upon the spirit of secession and the spirit of democracy.

"I will here express but one sentiment," he wrote, "which is, that dismemberment of our empire will be a clear sacrifice of great positive advantages without any counterbalancing good, administering no relief to our real disease, which is *democracy*, the poison of which, by a subdivision, will only be the more concentrated in each part, and consequently the more virulent."

That was his political testament. His personal testament, leaving what he had to leave along with good advice and the hope that his debts would be paid by his wife and children, was drafted more easily. (Not far away Burr was making the same sort of will, for he too had debts to bequeath and the urgent hope that Theodosia would display "a little more perseverance, determination and industry in the cultivation of her mind.") Hamilton, at least, could mention his wife's prospects as a daughter of Philip Schuyler—an allusion "that venerable father, I am sure, will pardon. He knows well the nicety of my past conduct." On that note the busy pen became still—its work when published read "like the confessions of a penitent monk" to Burr—and for a few hours the writer slept.

The dawn was misty, the sun a red blur low over Brooklyn when Hamilton passed toward the river through the quiet city, cool in the early summer morning. Pendleton and the botanical Dr. Hosack were with him on the trip by barge to Weehawken, where Philip had fallen, and as they approached the rocky shore, covered with trees and shrubs, they could see Burr and his second were before them. The sun had risen clear of the haze now, and the air was warmer as the little party—leaving the doctor in the boat, for he must know nothing officially of the illegal enterprise on which they were bound—climbed slowly to a broad shelf in the steep slope. Only a few yards long and less than half as wide, the ledge presented a level stretch of grass overhung with rocks and trees.

The preliminaries were soon arranged. The ground was measured, the pistols loaded, the seconds conferred briefly. Pendleton won the choice of position, and Hamilton found himself standing at the northern end of the confined space, back to a huge boulder, weapon in hand, gazing out across the river where little waves danced in the sun. He could see for miles, beyond where the masts of a dozen ships swayed at anchor in the harbor, beyond the sloping lawns and gardens, beyond the tiny houses of the city to the misty outline of Staten Island, a purplish blotch of color swelling up from the lower bay. It was his city, his home, and between him and the glorious panorama of the summer landscape stood the dark, menacing form of Aaron Burr. A voice was saying something about making ready, a slow firm voice it was, and two motionless, slim, black figures confronted each other across twenty feet of dew-freshened grass.

"Present," said the voice.

Burr's arm rose with slow deliberation, it seemed to the watchers. The man was calm as on the day when he had carried Montgomery's body through the British fire at Quebec. Then in the silence the shot roared harshly on that rocky slope. A second roar, prompt as an echo, replied as the other pistol spoke sharply, and Hamilton, drawing himself up on tiptoe, crashed forward on his face. His arm, too, must have been raised, perhaps involuntarily, for Van Ness saw a leaf, severed from the top of a tree by the bullet, fluttering to the ground.

For a split fraction of a second, that falling leaf was the only movement on the ledge. Then three men burst into rapid action. Burr moved impulsively toward his fallen adversary. Van Ness leaped to intervene, while Pendleton ran to kneel beside his friend. Dr. Hosack and the bargemen were scrambling up the rocks, and Burr's second, screening his principal with an umbrella from identification, led him away into obloquy and ostracism to embark on strange adventures, suffer tormenting tragedies and close thirty years of wandering in a shabby old age.

There was still life in the quiet figure on the turf. With infinite care they carried him to the boat, laid him tenderly on cloaks spread in the bottom and pulled like mad for the New York shore. Before they reached it, Hamilton was conscious, and that he really had fired involuntarily through a merely convulsive movement was evidenced by his remark on the trip across the river.

"Take care of that pistol," he murmured. "It is undischarged and still cocked; it may go off and do harm."

He had already assured Dr. Hosack in his confident way but in a weak voice that the wound was mortal, and as they neared the Manhattan shore he whispered:

"Let Mrs. Hamilton be immediately sent for—let the event be gradually broken to her, but give her hopes."

They bore him to William Bayard's house in Jane Street, and sent for Betsey and more doctors. But there was nothing anyone could do. A little laudanum scarcely eased the intense agony of thirty hours broken only by brief intervals of merciful unconsciousness. The bullet had broken a rib, passed through the liver and was resting against the spine. He lay there in the big square room on the second floor, quiet and uncomplaining, and never saw the red sun of his morning go down in festal glory behind the green of Castle Point. But he breathed and suffered through the night, surrounded by a wife and friends so distracted they forgot to treasure for posterity the few broken words he could still utter.

The sun came up again to find him living yet, and in torment. It was July 12, 1804, and as the room grew hot with the glare of summer and the faint scent of Bayard's flowers wafted in at the open windows, the painful twitchings of the man on the bed relaxed, the low moans of agony ceased. Betsey sobbed among her weeping children, spent with grief, while the callous Gouverneur Morris, cynic and roué in whom some doubted the existence of a heart, went groping down the stairs, reeling, blinded by his tears. Alexander Hamilton, who had closed his career at thirty-eight, was dead at forty-seven.

XXVII

ESSAY ON IMMORTALITY

FAME WAS THE GOAL THE BOY FROM THE WEST INDIES HAD SET for himself when he came north on the wings of the great hurricane. Fame he had, secure and only a very little tarnished, long before the pistols cracked at Weehawken. Now popularity, which he had never sought, was added. The mob, which he had despised for its lack of logic, worked itself into a frenzy of unreasoning enthusiasm for the man who had steadily refused to court it. They had stoned him in Broad Street in '95; they wept for him in 1804, stirred by the pathetic spectacle of a family left destitute and a genius fallen martyr to the custom of dueling, which was not so highly approved as its victim had supposed.

"His most determined enemies did not like to get rid of him in that way," explained the unforgiving Adams, but it was not only that.

The intelligence of the masses may have been no greater than Hamilton maintained, but their instinct was sound. Among the handy fellows who cleared the wilderness, grubbed in the fields, sailed the ships and pounded out the tools of civilization there was small understanding of the intricacies of finance or the interplay of social forces. (Was there more among their so-called superiors, the merchants and speculators of Mrs. Bingham's salon?) But just because it reasoned so badly, the crowd's feeling was true, and it felt this summer that it had lost a hero. For it nursed no grudges and was content to remember only the services of a man who had done much for his country.

"Our most unprincipled Jacobins," sneered Burr, "are the

loudest in their lamentations for the death of General Hamilton, whom, for many years, they have uniformly represented as the most detestable and unprincipled of men."

So New York mourned and the guns thudded dismally and the bells tolled sonorously for Cruger's clerk, for Washington's military secretary, for the savior of public credit, while Gouverneur Morris, his tears dried, sat at home and puzzled over a speech. As the dead man's friend, he was to deliver the funeral eulogy, but Hamilton was unfortunate in his friends. Mr. Morris was a prig as well as a cynic. A stricken family and a city's startling dejection had left him "wholly unmanned," but he regained possession of himself so speedily that the words he was writing had the cold, hard polish he had given to the Constitution. He found it a difficult task, confiding to his diary:

"The first point of his biography is that he was a stranger of illegitimate birth; some mode must be contrived to pass over this handsomely. He was indiscreet, vain, and opinionated; these things must be told, or the character will be incomplete. . . . His share in framing our Constitution must be mentioned, and his unfavorable opinion cannot therefore be concealed. . . . I can neither commit myself to a full and pointed approbation, nor is it prudent to censure others. All this must, somehow or other, be reconciled."

Next day, while actually walking in the funeral procession, the puzzled statesman mused:

"I must not, either, dwell on his domestic life; he has long since foolishly published the avowal of conjugal infidelity."

The huge crowd passed, with only the mutter of its marching feet to break the silence, through streets whose every shop was closed. The workmen in their leather breeches, the farmers in their homespun, were as solemn and reverent as the silk-clad gentlemen who paraded under the banner of the Chamber of Commerce. The very pigs and dogs were hushed, but the throng was so great that Morris could make himself heard to no more than a small fraction. He had reconciled his dilemmas with frigid ornateness, flattering himself that it was a good job, and he was disappointed to be obliged to record:

"I find that what I have said does not answer the general expectation."

Yet who could have done more? For it was not to his own generation that Hamilton could look for the full glory he had earned. Sufficient to that day that they gave him the honors of a Major General in the Army. It would have been enough for him. He would have been content to leave it for his descendants to see, as they did see, that even the triumphs of Jefferson were achieved on Hamiltonian principles—the purchase of Louisiana, the growth of national solidarity, the very governmental authority which enabled the sage of Monticello to hand the scepter on to his disciples.

For Hamilton had grounded the government of the United States on the solid basis of modern capitalism, and sixty years of agrarian political ascendancy could not check the progress he had initiated. Of course even without this system, the greater economic strength of capitalism must have triumphed over the looser cohorts of the agrarians, but it need not have been so swift, so complete, so sure. It is easy to say with Jefferson that it need not have been so corrupt either. But Hamilton did not make the corruption; he used it, turning the baseness of his fellows, their greed, their selfishness, the ugly pride of caste, into elements of strength for his country.

The big business he served so well and so directly never withheld from him that meed of praise which was his due. Agrarians and proletarians, much as they may dislike his principles, could do worse than honor his memory. He gave the farmers a government which for one hundred and fifty years, despite their wailings, served them better than they could have served themselves. And even Marx admitted that his dreams could come true only if capitalism paves the way. The plantation economy so beloved of the Virginia dynasty could hardly have created the industrial and financial machine which carried national expansion to the Pacific. Under the conditions of the nineteenth century, that could have been done only by moneyed men uniting their interests with those of the state. However upleasant that truth may be in retrospect, it was what Hamilton saw and Jefferson never dreamed of.

"A government is organized once and for all," said Gallatin after full experience of what his predecessor had wrought, "and until that of the United States fairly goes to pieces, no man can do more than alter the work accomplished by Hamilton."

The work, so carelessly taken for granted by later generations, was nothing less than the practical economic basis of a true national government. Others improved upon or weakened it, but the little Creole with his ruffles, satin smallclothes and powdered hair, his brilliant pen, his wit, his prejudices and his faults, conquered local apprehensions, mass ignorance and the class selfishness or the most obviously powerful group in the country, the big planters, to make the United States a thoroughly rounded, self-contained empire, strong alike in industry, commerce and agriculture.

Jefferson, it is true, triumphed as a politician, and lived to see the day when his party was the only one in the country, when the name of Federalist was a term of reproach. But he lived, too, to see that party of his carrying out proudly the policies of Hamilton.

They had reviled the Federalist for creating a central bank; in less than thirty years they copied him, adding a few features that were more objectionable and corrupt than his. They had reviled him for making the national government supreme in taxation; in power, they copied his excises. They had reviled him for wishing to suppress states' rights; they nearly ruined the country by insisting on them. They beat him at every point save in ideas, and only after he was dead did they realize—some few of them—that Hamilton had scored a posthumous triumph. His work lived in the practical, everyday affairs of men. His opponents survived only in their words, in the yeasty froth the drinker blows aside to get at the beer. The gentry of empty phrases have never forgiven him for it.

"It was even feared that his faith in democracy was imperfect, that he did not trust the people. Why should he? . . . Crowds had no sanctity for him—he had seen far too many— and the purely arithmetical basis of democracy failed to impress."

That is Philip Guedalla speaking of the Duke of Wellington. He might just as well have applied the paragraph to Hamilton, for how indeed could the apostle of order, expansion and progress trust the 3,000,000 Americans of his day, unlettered and completely out of touch with the world? They lived in a narrow circle of local preoccupations, knowing nothing and caring hardly more about what happened outside their villages. But he was building a nation for them all, and for their children's children, too. Far loftier minds than theirs had failed to understand his intentions and his achievements.

No, he could not trust them, for it is not in brain power that the people excel, and he could work only with reason. This was his mistake, but if, with all the rest, he had realized that it is in the instinct of the masses, not their intellect, that statesmen can confide, what would have been left for Jefferson?

BIBLIOGRAPHY

MANUSCRIPTS

The chief source of this book is the collection of Hamilton papers—109 volumes and several hundred miscellaneous pieces— in the Library of Congress. The devotion of Elizabeth Hamilton in the fifty years of her widowhood and the somewhat less ardent efforts of her sons in gathering and arranging these papers before they were turned over to the government have left us an unusually complete record. Other collections are those of the New York Public Library, the New York Historical Society, and the New York Society Library. Further Hamiltoniana are to be found in the Knox, Pickering, Jay, Pinckney and other papers.

NEWSPAPERS

The Argus *The National Gazette*
The Aurora *The New York Daily Advertiser*
The Columbian Centinel *The New York Evening Post*
Gazette of the United States *Porcupine's Gazette*

BOOKS AND ARTICLES

ADAMS, ABIGAIL, *Letters.*
ADAMS, JOHN, *Works.*
ALEXANDER, EDWARD P., *A Revolutionary Conservative, James Duane of New York.*
ATHERTON, GERTRUDE, *A Few of Hamilton's Letters.*
—— *The Hunt for Hamilton's Mother* (*North American Review,* July, 1902).
BAILEY, RALPH EDWARD, *An American Colossus.*
BANCROFT, G., *The Relations Between Hamilton and Washington.*
BEARD, CHARLES A., *An Economic Interpretation of the Constitution of the United States.*
—— *Economic Origins of Jeffersonian Democracy.*

BEARD, CHARLES A. and MARY R., *The Rise of American Civilization*.

BEVERIDGE, ALBERT J., *The Life of John Marshall*.

BROOKS, NOAH, *Henry Knox*.

BOWERS, CLAUDE G., *Jefferson and Hamilton*.

—— *Jefferson in Power*.

CARRINGTON, E. F., *Battles of the American Revolutionary War*.

CHASTELLUX, MARQUIS DE, *Travels in North America*.

COLEMAN, WILLIAM, *A Collection of the Facts and Documents Relating to the Death of Major General Alexander Hamilton*.

DAVIS, MATTHEW L., *Memoirs of Aaron Burr*.

Dictionary of American Biography.

DRAKE, FRANCIS S., *Life and Correspondence of Henry Knox*.

DUNBAR, SEYMOUR, *History of Travel in America*.

ESTABROOK, HENRY D., *The Lawyer, Hamilton* (*American Law Review*, 1901).

FERRAND, MAX, *The Records of the Federal Convention*.

FORD, HENRY JAMES, *Alexander Hamilton*.

FRANKLIN, BENJAMIN, *Writings*.

GALLATIN, ALBERT, *Writings*.

GAY, SIDNEY HOWARD, *James Madison*.

GIBBS, GEORGE, *Memoirs of the Administrations of Washington and John Adams, Edited From the Papers of Oliver Wolcott*.

GRAYDON, ALEXANDER, *Memoirs of His Own Time*.

GRISWOLD, RUFUS WILMOT, *The Republican Court*.

HAMILTON, ALEXANDER, *Works* (Edited by Henry Cabot Lodge).

HAMILTON, ALEXANDER, JAMES MADISON and JOHN JAY, *The Federalist*.

HAMILTON, ALLAN MCLANE, *The Intimate Life of Alexander Hamilton*.

HAMILTON, JAMES A., *Reminiscences*.

HAMILTON, JOHN CHURCH, *History of the Republic as Traced in the Writings of Alexander Hamilton and His Contemporaries*.

—— *The Life of Alexander Hamilton*.

HILL, FREDERICK TREVOR, *The Story of a Street*.

HUDSON, FREDERIC, *Journalism in the United States*.

HUGHES, RUPERT, *George Washington*.

JAY, JOHN, *Correspondence and Public Papers*.

JEFFERSON, THOMAS, *Writings.*

Journals of the Continental Congress.

KERKHOFF, JOHNSTON D., *Aaron Burr.*

KING, CHARLES R., *Life and Correspondence of Rufus King.*

LIANCOURT, DUC DE LA ROCHEFOUCAULD, *Travels Through the United States of North America.*

LIVINGSTON, EDWIN B., *The Livingstons of Livingston Manor.*

LODGE, HENRY CABOT, *Alexander Hamilton.*

—— *Life and Letters of George Cabot.*

LOSSING, BENSON J., *The Life and Times of Philip Schuyler.*

MACLAY, WILLIAM, *Journal.*

MADISON, JAMES, *Writings.*

MCCALL, SAMUEL W., *Alexander Hamilton—the Lawyer as a Constructive Statesman.*

MINER, CLARENCE EUGENE, *The Ratification of the Federal Constitution by the State of New York.*

MORISON, SAMUEL ELIOT, *The Life and Letters of Harrison Gray Otis, Federalist.*

MORRIS, GOUVERNEUR, *Diary and Letters.*

MORSE, JOHN T., JR., *The Life of Alexander Hamilton.*

—— *Thomas Jefferson.*

NEW YORK, STATE OF, *The Debates and Proceedings of the Convention* (Poughkeepsie, 1788).

OLIVER, FREDERICK SCOTT, *Alexander Hamilton—An Essay on American Union.*

PARTON, JAMES, *The Life and Times of Aaron Burr.*

—— *Life of Thomas Jefferson.*

PAYNE, GEORGE HENRY, *History of Journalism in the United States.*

PELLEW, GEORGE, *John Jay.*

PICKERING, OCTAVIUS, and C. W. UPHAM, *Life of Timothy Pickering.*

RIETHMULLER, C. J., *Alexander Hamilton and His Contemporaries.*

ROBERTS, JAMES A., *New York in the Revolution.*

SCHACHNER, NATHAN, *Aaron Burr.*

SCHMUCKER, S. M., *The Life and Times of Alexander Hamilton*

SCHUYLER, JOHN, *Institution of the Society of the Cincinnati.*

SHEA, GEORGE, *Life and Epoch of Alexander Hamilton.*

SHRINER, CHARLES A., *Alexander Hamilton as a Promoter.*

SMERTENKO, JOHAN J., *Alexander Hamilton.*

SMITH, THOMAS E. V., *The City of New York in the Year of Washington's Inauguration.*

STEINER, BERNARD C., *Life and Correspondence of James Mc-Henry.*

STEVENS, JOHN A., *Albert Gallatin.*

STRYKER, WILLIAM S., *The Battles of Trenton and Princeton.*

SUMNER, WILLIAM GRAHAM, *Alexander Hamilton.*

—— *The Financier and the Finances of the American Revolution.*

TORREY, RAYMOND H., *Hamilton Grange (Scenic and Historic America,* 1934).

VANDENBERG, ARTHUR H., *The Greatest American, Alexander Hamilton.*

WARSHOW, ROBERT IRVING, *Alexander Hamilton, First American Business Man.*

WARVILLE, J. P. BRISSOT, *New Travels in the United States of America.*

WASHINGTON, GEORGE, *Writings.*

WHARTON, ANNE HOLLINGSWORTH, *Salons Colonial and Republican.*

WHARTON, FRANCIS, *State Trials of the United States During the Administrations of Washington and Adams.*

WILDES, HARRY EMERSON, *Valley Forge.*

WILLIAMS, JOHN, *The Life of Alexander Hamilton.*

WILSON, JAMES GRANT, *The Memorial History of the City of New York.*

WOODWARD, W. E., *George Washington, The Image and the Man.*

THE ILLUSTRATIONS

The two views of Wall Street reproduced in this volume are taken from the original water colors in the New York Historical Society's collection. The Trumbull portrait of Hamilton hangs in the New York City Hall.

INDEX

Adams, Abigail, 183, 261
Adams, John, on Hamilton's ancestry, 16; on rebellion, 49-50, 51; elected President, 243; works for peace, 244-5, 259-62; relations with Cabinet, 252; quarrel with Hamilton, 255, 265; object of Hamilton's conspiracy, 267 seq.; dismisses Cabinet, 277; attacked by Hamilton, 278-80; defeated, 281; 80, 116, 152, 164, 166, 169, 181, 187, 191, 198, 203, 207, 232-3, 242, 246, 306
Adams, Samuel, 45, 48
Alexander, Lady Kitty, 36, 37, 88, 151
Alexander, Lady Mary, 36, 37
Alexander, William (see Stirling, Earl of)
Alien and Sedition Acts, 254, 255-6, 261, 267, 274, 278, 293
Ambler, Mary, 111
Ames, Fisher, 152
André, John, 95, 98-9
Arnold, Benedict, 56, 76, 94-7
Arnold, Peggy, 94-8, 190
Asia, warship, 53
Assumption Bill, 173-8
Aurora, The, 241, 249

Bache, Benjamin Franklin, 236
Bank of Manhattan Company, 268
Bank of New York, 124, 197, 268
Bank of United States, 180-2, 186-7, 196
Barber, Dr. Francis, 34, 36, 38
Bard, Dr. John, 41, 44
Bauman, Col., 148
Bayard, James A., 283, 286
Bayard, William, 304
Beaujolais, Duke of, 221
Benson, Judge, 231

Bingham, Anne, 183-4, 185, 191, 306
Bingham, William, 183
Bonaparte, Napoleon, 19, 221, 263, 265, 282, 284
Boudinot, Elias, 35, 36, 38, 175
Boudinot, Susan, 86
Bradford, William, 220, 237
Brandywine, Battle of, 76
Burgoyne, John, 75, 76, 95
Burr, Rev. Aaron, 19, 110
Burr, Aaron, education, 39; saves Hamilton, 60-1; friendship with Hamilton, 109-10; appearance, 110; as lawyer, 123, 271-2; elected Senator, 186; attacked by Hamilton, 200, 202, 281-4, 294-5; defeated for Vice President, 203, 243; second for Monroe, 248-9; organizes 1800 campaign, 268 seq.; presidential contest, 281-5; duel with Hamilton, 296 seq.; 56, 69, 83, 98, 111, 141, 151, 159, 189, 229, 238, 242, 263, 290, 292, 306-7
Burr, Mrs. Aaron, 186, 202 (see also Prevost)
Burr, Theodosia, 186, 202, 283, 284, 287, 302

Cabot, George, 207, 245, 282, 293
Callender, James, 16, 247, 248, 249, 294
Camillus, Hamilton pseudonym, 235, 236
Carroll, Charles, 45, 135
Castlereagh, Viscount, 279
Centinel, The, 283
Chase, Samuel, 91, 99, 237
Chastellux, Vicomte de, 86, 92
Cheetham, James, 296
Church, Angelica, 150, 156, 185, 217,

315

Date Due